T0330078

General Equilibrium Analysis
and the Theory of Markets

A José Luís, Maria Clara e Rui

General Equilibrium Analysis and the Theory of Markets

Manuel Luís Costa

Professor of Economics, University of Porto, Portugal

Edward Elgar
Cheltenham, UK • Northampton, MA, USA

Published by
Edward Elgar Publishing Limited
Glensanda House
Montpellier Parade
Cheltenham
Glos GL50 1UA
UK

Edward Elgar Publishing, Inc.
6 Market Street
Northampton
Massachusetts 01060
USA

A catalogue record for this book
is available from the British Library

Library of Congress Cataloguing in Publication Data
Costa, Manuel Luís, 1957–
General equilibrium analysis and the theory of markets / Manuel
Luís Costa.
Includes bibliographical references and index.
1. Equilibrium (Economics)   2. Markets.   I. Title.
HB145.C673   1999
339.5—dc21   98–29697
                                                                     CIP

ISBN 1 85898 958 2

Printed and bound in Great Britain by MPG Books Ltd, Bodmin, Cornwall

Contents

Acknowledgements

I am deeply grateful to Robert W. Clower for his patient guidance and stimulating criticisms. In fact, the dissertation from which this text originated would not have been possible without the inspiration from him and his work. Apart from the dissertation work, I benefited from reading more recent work by Donald A. Walker as well as from encouraging comments by him and Peter W. Howitt (especially regarding Chapter 2 and Appendix E, respectively). Also, I thank Ronald Wilder and Bill Kiker for their continued support. I would also like to acknowledge all my other professors at the Department of Economics at the University of South Carolina for their teachings, especially John Chilton.

Thanks are extended to my colleagues at the University of South Carolina for their help and support, especially Paulo Guimarães, Pedro Portugal, Álvaro Aguiar and Vitor Mendes dos Santos. At the Faculdade de Economia da Universidade do Porto, I extend special thanks to António Almodovar for inspiring conversations, and to my colleagues in the Macroeconomics and Economic Policy courses for their support and the extra workload derived from this project.

Special thanks to my dear friend Guida for being present from the start with love, understanding and encouragement. Also, I would like to thank my friends Barney, Anupam, Lígia and Anabela for easing my work, and Amândio for his support. Finally, I dedicate my work to my beloved family, especially my parents, my brother and my uncle Armando, as well as to the memory of my grandparents.

I acknowledge the financial support of the Universidade do Porto, the Luso-American Foundation for Development, the Junta Nacional de Investigação Científica e Tecnológica, and the Centro de Estudos Macroeconómicos e de Previsão, financed by the Fundação de Ciência e Tecnologia. I am grateful to many colleagues and friends at the Faculdade de Economia do Porto, Escola de Economia e Gestão da Universidade do Minho, Banco Português do Atlântico and Espaço Atlântico who encouraged and enabled my studies, especially António Vale e Vasconcellos, Carlos Costa, Fernando Freire de Sousa, Fernando Teixeira dos Santos, António Abílio Brandão, José Costa and Rui Alves. I owe a special acknowledgement to Edições Afrontamento, for the preparation of the camera-ready proof, especially to José Miguel Reis and Ana Maria Santos. Moreover, I owe very special thanks to the editorial staff at Edward Elgar, especially Dymphna Evans, Julie Leppard and Fiona Peacock, whose help, understanding and support greatly eased my final revisions and the editing of the text.

Finally, I acknowledge permission of the History of Economics Society to include in Chapter 2 an only slightly revised version of the article 'Walras and the NeoWalrasian Diversion', originally published in the *Journal of the History of Economic Thought*, vol. 20, no. 1, Spring 1998, pp. 51–69.

1. Introduction

This is an exercise in criticism and it should be made clear at the outset that no more than that is intended. That something is wrong with the neowalrasian[1] general equilibrium approach as an explanation of the working of markets, and as a basis for applied economics, is common knowledge in the profession. But to assess what and how it came to be so, it has been necessary to conduct a careful review of the literature to uncover anomalies and gaps that previous writers may have overlooked or ignored.

My main result is simple. Progress in the theory of exchange has been conceived as a refinement of equilibrium dispositions, and it became concerned with little else than the virtual (never actual) consistency of trading plans (mental states) of hypothesized 'transactors'. Along the way, formal theory has been emptied of potentially observable activities of transactors; and theoretical accounts of markets and exchange arrangements have been emptied of empirical content.

None of this is new; as Hahn observed more than a quarter of a century ago:

> The achievements of economic theory in the last two decades are both impressive and in many ways beautiful. But it cannot be denied that there is something scandalous in the spectacle of so many people refining the analyses of economic states which they give no reason to suppose will ever, or have ever, come about. (Hahn 1970, p. 1).

This refinement has as one of its salient manifestations the so-called 'problem of existence of a competitive equilibrium', an empirically inconsequential exercise since its methods of proof bear no interpretation as any economic mechanism. Other intellectual puzzles created by the existence problem vastly outweigh the purely mathematical problem that was its source. Specifically, the existence problem has diverted attention away from such crucial economic issues as stability of real-time adjustment processes and real-time logistics of exchange. In effect, the existence of equilibrium as a set of prices at which purely notional trading plans are consistent, has been confused with the different question of how plans based on notionally predetermined equilibrium prices can actually be carried out.

The problem is not that the generality of the economics profession is only subsidiarily interested in the question of how equilibrium might come about, but that many authors are wrong in their implicit belief that the stories entertained to sustain such mechanisms are reasonable foundations of the

1

final equilibrium states (a central goal in this book is to appraise and relate assorted instances of such inadequacies). Therefore, the interest that many authors show in these stories and the importance they assign to the implications of such mechanisms for the configuration of the final equilibrium states, may possibly just lie in the vague uneasiness about the understanding of the mechanisms that are involved in the exercises these authors refer to, and about the analytical practices that underlie the applications they perform. As for the majority of the profession, it seems they have carried on accepting the surmised stories that underlie these exercises and practices, captive as they may have become of such habits of thought.

It is, in this respect, revealing that the most telling critical reflections on the state of the general equilibrium approach as a basis of standard microeconomic analysis are expressed by those authors that most contributed to its creation, like Arrow and Hahn, who have often shown discomfort about the paths their foundation led to. These authors have a clearer view of the robustness of the analytical exercises they have attempted to tackle, having labored nevertheless under the unwarranted belief that the formalization of their models conformed to realistic mechanisms.

The accomplishments of the general equilibrium analysis by Arrow, Debreu and others, have played an invaluable role in providing a framework of thought capable of dealing with problems of empirical relevance, even though the implications are more straightforward in a negative mode (cf. Hahn 1973a; see Chapter 2 on 'The neowalrasians', below) than in constructive pursuits, that is, with respect to descriptions of real world phenomena. The problem I raise is, however, that after this framework of thought was provided by the proofs of existence of equilibrium for a 'private ownership economy', a concentration of efforts on the completion of this exercise set by logical problems inherent in the methods of proof, led the theory to pursue abstract constructions in frictionless mathematical worlds, which eventually became all that mattered. The neowalrasian general equilibrium approach has become the cornerstone of microanalysis.

That is the primary motivation for our inquiry, to look at the present state of general equilibrium analysis in the light of the proposals that originated it and to assess its developments as to their empirical relevance. At this point, I cannot resist quoting extensively from Peter Howitt on '[e]xplanation and the neowalrasian code':

> In many ways, modern economic theory has gone the way of geometry, although without having accomplished what geometry did. That is, it has ceased to be a theory designed to make sense of the real world (measuring distances and angles, or accounting for the determination of prices and quantities transacted) and has become instead a purely logical discipline in which the objective is to follow a set of a priori rules with no connection to the external world. Economic theorists are meanwhile suffering from a similar kind of confusion to that which afflicted

mathematicians when they had not yet realised that what they were doing had no connection with any concrete interpretation, and that because of this, any one set of axioms was as justifiable as any other as long as it was logically coherent. Economists building 'rational models' to account for things not found in conventional theory think of themselves as seeking explanation in the usual sense, whereas in fact they are just addressing purely semantic question that do not even arise once one ventures out of the neowalrasian cloister. Only by the rarest fluke could someone working under such delusions come up with a convincing scientific explanation of anything. (Howitt 1996, p. 76).

The general equilibrium approach is an endless pursuit since the solution to logical, formal problems has no intrinsic bar. The reality, having become just a mirage to contemplate and not the origin of the problems to explain and solve, offers no discipline in that research agenda. The relationship of theory to reality was inverted in formal general equilibrium exercises as far as the common practices of research for empirical disciplines are concerned. If we grant that the proofs of existence of general equilibrium would serve as a basic theoretical framework, we might equally grant (on the grounds of accepted 'normal' methodology) that the next step to further analytical exercises would be to drop the postulated abstractions and consider the several frictions, if the exercises so require. Referring to the 'remarkable ability' that the neowalrasian code has shown in 'absorbing attack on the foundations of conventional theory', Peter Howitt describes the way in which 'real world "frictions" ' that are difficult to assimilate in the neowalrasian analysis, have been digested, concluding with the following sentence:

But accounting for some phenomenon in a discipline dominated by an elaborate code consists not of telling stories designed to convince others that this is why the phenomenon exists, or why it appears the way it does, but of telling stories, no matter how *ad hoc,* that incorporate some aspect of the phenomenon, no matter how trivial, without violating the code. (Howitt 1996, p. 75).

In the general equilibrium approach this has been the case, not only in the early developments, but also to this day. First, most stability analyses became clogged with the mathematical results of the existence problem, instead of looking for the implications of convergence processes; namely, that prices, equilibrium or otherwise, are determined in abstraction of bargaining and independently of the opportunities to execute trading, and that, even in the cases where bargaining is formalized, these prices, once determined, are supposedly disseminated and freely known to individuals. Second, only marginal attention was directed to the feasibility of execution of transactions, and when this was dealt with, the two exercises, the mathematical determination of equilibrium prices and the proofs of stability of this equilibrium position, were presumed to be accomplished independently of the formalization of the trading mechanism.

At the origin of this methodological handicap seems to lie a misconception as to the analytical parity of a 'theory of price determination' and a 'theory of how equilibrium is achieved' in competitive exchange, even in the particular case that only the characterization of equilibrium states has been at issue. This problem was at the root of Walras's two exercises, which he defined as the theoretical (mathematical) solution, and the solution attained in exchange through tatonnement.[2] The prefiguration of this misconception may be traced to the historical role that Walras's theory of tatonnement played in the construction of his theory of general exchange. Although Walras saw the two exercises as separable, the need to show their compatibility was the driving procedure in Walras's exposition of the theory of general exchange, in his words 'the essential point': the attempt to demonstrate that the mathematical problem (the solution of a system of equations of exchange) is the same 'problem that is in practice solved on the market by the mechanism of free competition' (Jaffé, ed. 1954, pp. 162–3).

With the neowalrasians, the concern with 'the essential point' faded, and eventually the concentration on the exercise of the determination of equilibrium prices, Walras's first problem, led to a reversal of the theoretical perspective, after which no recognition was apparent of Walras's second problem of explaining convergence to equilibrium through the mechanisms of free competition.

After the Arrow–Debreu models became the norm, the concern with resolving the link between the outcome of market interaction and the mathematical solution was apparently neglected. The reasons for this detour may be of several orders. First, the Nash (1950) equilibrium solution to '*N*-person games' may here have played a role, which stems from the belief that Nash equilibria are a proper representation of the termination of some implicit process, either that some means of communication and virtual pre-play has taken place, or that it is the end result of the convergence of game iterations – where the definition of rules and procedures of such pre-play or iterative process might be presumed of no consequence to the end result (cf. Arrow 1994, pp. 4–5; Kreps 1990, Chapters 3, 5, 6, esp. pp. 32 ff., 123, 140 ff.; Rubinstein 1995, esp. p. 11). An unwarranted interpretation is that there must perforce exist an algorithm capable of replicating the exchange mechanisms in markets, and that, given enough ingenuity, time (number of iterations) and computation capacity, the equilibrium result would be attained. Nevertheless, I gather that a more immediate reason for the neglect of the link between the mathematical and the market solutions lies in the problem of formal tractability, as is implicitly assumed by the authors who worked on the analyses of stability, and who not seldom explicitly avowed the analytical difficulties of such proofs unless under limited specific assumptions (cf. Arrow and Hahn 1971; see Chapter 2, below). However, Debreu stands apart since he was concerned solely with the logical consistency of the axiomatic world he devised, believing, however, that the system of equations built upon the postulated axioms are capable of an economic interpretation (cf. Clower 1995a; Walker 1997a, pp. 49 ff.). Finally, I am inclined to think that the 'elegance' or 'simplicity' (cf. Hahn 1994, pp. 246–7; 250–51) of the existence solution and the unsatisfactory state of the stability analyses led to the inattention to a 'theory of how trading can be executed given known predetermined prices'.

A non-tatonnement track of general equilibrium analysis has evolved that considers disequilibrium transactions in the convergence to equilibrium: Fisher's (1983) *Disequilibrium Foundations of Equilibrium Analysis*, conflates the main threads of this line of research, namely the Hahn Process, general monopolistic equilibrium ('non-Walrasian theory'), and 'fix-price equilibria with quantity rationing'. However, little progress has been achieved with this change of hypotheses with respect to tatonnement stability analysis (see Walker 1997a, pp. 124 ff.; Busetto 1995; Fisher 1987, esp. pp. 27–8), and neither the results nor the perspective have been integrated in the core of micro theory, as well as in state-of-the-art formal presentations of general equilibrium analysis (see e.g. Starr 1997, Mas-Colell *et al.* 1995, p. 625, n). This line of research appears to have 'died out' (Busetto 1995) or, at least, may be still too 'immature to incorporate … in the main body of the general competitive analysis' (Koizumi 1991, p. 166). In fact, '[t]he difficulty with showing a tendency to equilibrium was and is, of course, that we have no agreed theory of adjustment' (Hahn 1994, p. 250).

The whole research agenda became dependent upon the existence problem, a mathematical exercise whose method of solution has no economic interpretation. And consequently, the nexus between the problems that have been analytically defined and distinguished by Walras (the mathematical solution, and the solution attained in the market by way of bargaining and trade) was reversed, and the theory of general exchange transmuted into a diverse program, the mathematical proof of the consistency of choices defined in the form of a set of axioms. This logic of choice is devoid of behaviors, or actions by individuals, and institutional rules with empirical correspondence, even if at a high level of abstraction, and the mechanisms of interaction in markets not any more an 'essential point' (cf. Townsend 1987, esp. p. 382 [3]).

It is true that during the last two decades, after the Arrow–Debreu edifice had gained its formal structure, information and incentive issues have enriched price theory, and models have been elaborated that deal with several exchange mechanisms and institutional arrangements. Different methods have been used, from model constructions to simulation or experimental studies. Among others, some relevant developments have occurred in the fields of the theory of auctions and double auctions, or the theory of bargaining. As to the logistics of trade, a few descriptive studies are helpful, but a theory on the decentralized execution of exchange is missing. Also, the study of the effects of information and transaction costs on the explanation of the organizational forms of economic activity (as the firm, intermediation or monetary exchange), or the implications of adverse selection and moral hazard on the working (or not) of various markets, has flourished in the same period of time. No doubt these models and contributions to a 'theory of price determination' and a 'theory of how price is achieved' in particular set-ups, have broadened the picture of microeconomics but have had little repercussion on the core of the subject (cf. Weintraub 1985, Chapter 7), or are still too poorly developed to deal with the stability and execution problems. A clear instance of this is addressed by Arrow (1994, p. 5) when referring to Gale (1986a; b [4]) on the formalization of bargaining in a 'noncooperative-game-theory model of competitive equilibrium':

> The most realistic-sounding noncooperative-game-theory model of competitive equilibrium I know of is due to Douglas Gale (1986a,b), though in its present form it applies only to a pure exchange economy. Pairs of individuals meet at random and bargain (bargaining is itself formulated as a sub-game). With the endowments obtained as a result of the bargaining, they again meet in pairs chosen at random, and so forth. The bargaining at any time is, of course, affected by the (rational) expectations of the results of future bargains. These expectations are, in effect, prices. ... However, prices never appear as objective phenomena, they are only subjective, that is, expectations held in the agents' minds. (Arrow 1994, p. 5).

The general equilibrium approach dominates standard economics, as Walker (1997a) scrutinizes at length, and its core remains basically untouched as the more utilized recent textbooks in microeconomic theory continue to testify. These more applied microeconomic developments may eventually turn out to have an effect on the redefinition of the core of the general equilibrium theory of exchange in a competitive economy, but there are no signs that this has yet happened. In any case, for the most part, these applications may not be warranted.

The present research agenda has been set by the formal problems created by the proposition of the existence of a set of equilibrium prices as the solution to mathematical exercises, and not by the questions that Walras originally intended to tackle. This problem of existence was raised by Walras, but for him this was a starting point; that it became 'essential' is intriguing, it reveals that in this concrete aspect, the ideas of the past played a role in defining the formal problems only, and not the theoretical perspective. Research in the neowalrasian approach eventually crystallized in logical formalizations, and a change in perspective took place away from the real world into an absorption in logical solutions.

In the face of both the discomfort of many in the profession, and the critical appraisals conducted by a few, it might seem surprising that the general equilibrium approach strengthened in the wake of the Arrow–Debreu models has resisted a reformulation of its analytical procedures in order to bring its attention back to actual economic questions. As long as this research agenda is seen fitting as an abstract general equilibrium theory, the neowalrasian code – as Howitt defines it – has proved remarkable in its ability to incorporate such specific or applied developments in microeconomics that impinge on the exercises that have defined the general theory, without prompting the redefinition of the research procedures, that is 'without violating the code'.

The fact that many economists are working on more concrete problems and on more applied theory, and that this work is providing new knowledge in basic fields, has yet to prove to have some reflection on the core of price theory. Recent work on general equilibrium analysis has mainly contributed to inflate a vacuous program, and the positive use of doing it, or of attempts at it, have been to help evince the alienation of the mathematical exercises from the actual problems it means to deal with. In fact, as we will see below, the inclusion of features of the reality of exchange in markets we know, e.g. intermediation and money, have helped reveal the ineffectiveness of the dichotomization of the two analytical exercises, the determination of equilibrium prices and the analysis of adjustment and trading processes.

My view is that the prosecution of substantive research in the neowalrasian core has proved hopeless. It being undeniable that a critical view permeates the discussion in this book, I decline to concede, though, that this view is not substantial. My doubts and criticisms have become framed in an organized way, after my recognition that the absence of 'markets' is pervasive in both general equilibrium analysis and micro theory. The attention to exchange mechanisms and markets has provided a tool, a sieve through which several contradictions, dilemmas and paradoxes could be spotted. I do not claim that the perspective is novel, or innovative. I would just claim to have put many materials under a new critical organized light.[5]

It should be obvious that many important aspects of price theory are outside the aim of my study, even when related to it. It should now be clear that my primary concern is with the coherence of the neowalrasian construction, and with the paths to development which its dominance in price theory have barred or obstructed. Moreover, it should be clear that my concern is with the analytical procedures pertaining to the core of the neowalrasian general equilibrium approach as it is – and continues to be built and understood – and not as it might have been if all the promising present developments had been absorbed in that core. Given this, I am interested in discussing whether recent developments, namely in information theory, have proved adequate towards a reformulation of a general theory (or are only appropriate to deal with particular behaviors, or markets, that have motivated them). Therefore, the question that must be raised is whether and how these evolutions and developments in micro theory during the last two decades have influenced the way in which the theory of general exchange has been conducted.

On potentially constructive aspects, the role of information and transaction costs are present throughout, and the central question of bargaining is also tackled in Section 4.3.4, below. Yet, there is also a dead end to these evolutions. As to the implications of adverse incentives and adverse selection, the only relevant detectable development concerns 'incentive compatibility', and again it is not new (cf. Aumann 1964; Hurwicz 1972).[6] This hinges on how perfect competition can be distinguished from the existence of Walrasian equilibrium, and consists in the question of parametric pricing in supposedly 'competitive' conditions. Somehow the notion that 'perfect competition' describes a situation where transactors not only *believe* they don't, but *in fact* do not have any effect on price has become common, and so 'competitive behavior' has been defined as the rule that individual traders adhere to passive price-taking. It has been suggested that interdependence creates a strategic, or incentive compatibility problem that is inconsistent with so-called 'competitive behavior'. The presence of private information creates a moral hazard problem: by anticipating the effect of his offers to buy and sell on the formation of prices, a trader would have an incentive to misrepresent his offers in order to alter prices to his benefit. In order to preserve parametric pricing, 'continuum' economies replace 'finite' economies: infinitesimal 'individuals' are randomly paired up to bargain and trade; furthermore, the question is raised whether for such a large economy, a 'continuum' of commodities compromises competitive behavior (cf. Ostroy and Zame 1994[7]). This is another instance of confusion of a mathematical with an empirical economic question, which refinement in recent years has created new conceptual puzzles (see Sections 4.3.2 and 4.3.4, below). Such developments are an excrescence of the prominence of the existence problem, and of the underlying centralized exchange in the general equilibrium approach: this could not possibly be the case, and the paradox would be seen as false, if the formalization of bargaining and trading had belonged in the determination of the end result of the exchange mechanism.

It should also be clear that my aim is not to deal with all the ramifications of the lack of decentralized exchange in general equilibrium. The case of the representative agent in macro models would be an obvious critical extension. But I am primarily interested in interdependence in exchange, and the determination of an equilibrium price set through trade. Therefore, the question of the representative agent in macroeconomic models is outside the scope of my analysis. If in those models, a price set is presumed to exist, it is not obviously given by means of a coherence of trading plans, it is purely envisioned as the result of mental dispositions as derived from preferences and costs by the representative agent. Or, alternatively, it assumes aggregation feasible, and thus requires that the economy satisfies such assumptions (cf. Kirman 1989; 1992; see Sections 4.3.2, 4.3.3.1 (i) and (v) for related questions).

To sum up, it is intriguing that nearly three decades have passed since Hahn's words were spoken, and in that time general equilibrium analysis seems to have developed into a sterile logical exercise. It has been perfected to the point where the question is no longer so much its alienation from empirical facts, as its blind concentration on problems posed by purely logical concerns. The ascendancy of 'existence' in general equilibrium theory has largely been emphasized, but this kind of confusion of a mathematical with an empirical economic question extends much further, for instance as referred to above, to the question of parametric pricing in supposedly 'competitive' conditions. This is probably one of the extremes of unreasonableness reached by the Arrow–Debreu approach.

But my concern in this dissertation is with older 'unsettled questions'. I am interested in confronting the Walrasian program with its neowalrasian diversion (where such riddles arise more naturally). The questions I raise are, first, how the neowalrasian paradigm evolved and led to the omission of trading and markets, and second, how it constrained understanding of the execution of trades.

General equilibrium models on the Arrow–Debreu track deal with the logic of choice and do not supply any concrete treatment of mechanisms and institutions of interaction. Walras was willing to deal with this process of interaction – with logistics of transactions as an element of the explanation of the determination of prices in exchange. However, between early and later editions of the *Eléments,* Walras moved from an attempt to discuss the economy in terms of exchange models analogous to the Paris Bourse, where trade involved bargaining and information exchange, to an idealized construction where 'pledges' replace actual interaction; as Walker's *Walras's Market Models* shows, the idealized construction points in a different direction. I agree with Walker's appreciation of why Walrasian theory failed 'to be useful as even a highly abstract analysis of economic behaviour': 'the pledges model is designed to be consistent with certain mathematical conditions – that is, with the solutions of a set of equations – rather than being a set of assumptions and mathematical conditions designed to explain economic behaviour' (Walker 1987b, p. 860). This later phase is embodied in the definitive edition to which later work by Hicks (1934; 1939), Arrow and Debreu (1954), Debreu (1959) and Arrow and Hahn (1971) are all related. So the post-war literature of general equilibrium theory presents a distorted view of the early Walras's desideratum of providing models of the workings of exchange arrangements with empirical content (cf. Clower 1995a). In fact, it has long been recognized (Veendorp 1970a; Starr 1971; Clower and Leijonhufvud 1975; Ostroy and Starr 1990) that the Hicks–Arrow–Debreu version of neowalrasian theory 'limits itself to characterizing a *state* of trading equilibrium. It says nothing ... about the process by which agents exploit opportunities for ... exchange' (Kohn 1995, p. 3).

Walras was concerned with the workings of markets, though he abstracted from complications and focused on 'a hypothetical régime of absolute free competition' (Jaffé, ed. 1954, p. 40) in his exposition of equilibrium as a state of maximum satisfaction in exchange; and his theory of tatonnement was meant to be 'the demonstration of the attainment of that equilibrium through the play of the raising and the lowering of prices until the equality of the supply and demand quantities are established' (Walras 1895, p. 630; as in Walker 1987c, pp. 159–60). In short, the Walrasian program consists of describing how the mechanism of free competition 'among sellers of services who underbid one another and among buyers of products who outbid one another' (Jaffé, ed. 1954, 40, n) leads to the generation of a set of equilibrium prices in general exchange.

The neowalrasian reinterpretation, though intendedly portraying a description of relevant features of the real world, concentrates on the question of existence of equilibrium as 'coherence' of trading plans. Decentralized interaction between individuals, bargaining and transactions are sidetracked and replaced by a notional state whereby equilibrium prices are posited as determined, given, and known, and exchange is presumed feasible, even though no account of trading is supplied in the model: 'trade never takes place' (Arrow and Hahn 1971, p. 324; cf. Starr 1971). And as to the execution of trades, the model can only be supported by multilateral barter with a clearing house, the central 'market'. Hence, the neowalrasian diversion.

Given these general considerations, the argument in this book is as follows. In Chapter 2, it is shown that the program set forth by Walras, of providing an explanation for the convergence to equilibrium in competitive exchange, is still today an unresolved question. Walras's attempt to explain convergence to equilibrium in exchange dealt with bargaining and the logistics of trade. But, unable to carry forward (beyond the case of special markets in Chapter 11 of the *Eléments*) to the general model his view of the workings of free competition in markets where bargaining and trading take place in the course of the adjustment process, Walras introduced 'pledges' in his description of tatonnement in the fourth edition of the *Eléments*. But if Walras settled matters upon the assumption of no-arbitrage, the neowalrasian formalization entirely lost sight of trading and pursued tatonnement as if it described real adjustment in a competitive economy.

Chapter 3 begins with a comparison of adjustments to equilibrium in Walras and Marshall, to conclude that both authors are basically in agreement, and that the separation to be established is with Arrow–Debreu. Next, a line of evolution in price theory, from Marshall to Chamberlin and on to Triffin, is described; when the general equilibrium edifice was topped by the proofs of existence (and stability) by Arrow–Debreu in the 1950s, the

Marshallian tradition in price theory had become engulfed in a purification by means of which general interdependence does without markets.

Decentralized trading arrangements become thereby an oversight in theoretical analysis and this is why Chapter 4 opens with a discussion of whether a theory of markets and intermediation is available, and how the consideration of transaction costs by Coase sidestepped the issue. Moreover, transaction costs have been called to explain both the emergence and the impediment to the formation of markets. 'Markets' are a misnomer for 'prices' in the theory of general interdependence, and an unnoticed confusion between exchange and markets ensues.

A broad distinction between brokered and non-brokered markets is attempted and, next, decentralization is characterized in its dimensions, which regard information, the determination of the price signal, and logistics. In this perspective the Arrow–Debreu model of general exchange fails in all three aspects: first, because convergence is not computable; second, because for consistency of trading plans exchange rates are required to be common, given, and freely known; third, because only with centrally coordinated multilateral barter can the theory preclude bargaining by traders in attempts to transform planned trades into feasible executions.

The consistency of informationally decentralized trading with predetermined equilibrium prices has often been questioned (e.g. Ostroy and Starr 1990), and analyses of execution have been attempted with unsatisfactory results. Direct barter at equilibrium prices hardly meets full execution under decentralized information, that is, it is not feasible. The introduction of intermediation or a medium of exchange (monetary exchange being a special case of indirect barter, and one of central interest here because it is potentially decentralized) is shown to enable feasibility of execution. In spite of hardly fitting a world of costless exchange, the consideration of these facilitating devices helps expose the contradictions carried by attempts to dichotomize pricing and trading.

Given these negative findings, the doubt arises whether and how the Walrasian program can be furthered to include and treat logistics of exchange. Were we to stay within the Walrasian program, two possible solutions are discussed, but both face obstacles. One approach is to formalize trading in the process of bargaining, but consideration of the feasibility of decentralized execution raises doubts about the adequacy of the established notion of equilibrium (as a notional state) as a basis for understanding trading. The other possible approach is to start with logistics of transactions in an informationally decentralized setting, without postulating equilibrium prices as pre-existent to trade.

To conclude Chapter 4, comments on Arrow's (1959) contribution to the theory of price adjustment are presented, which reinforce my earlier arguments showing that existing theories of price and quantity adjustment which attempt to dispense with 'the auctioneer' have been unsuccessful in defining alternative theoretical trading schemes that would satisfactorily describe trading phenomena in the decentralized non-brokered markets that are a ubiquitous feature of every modern economy.

Finally, Chapter 5 offers a discussion of some perspectives on the directions for redefining the scope of a general theory of exchange in a competitive economy, as pointed out in the literature and suggested in the previous chapter. Our perspective is that the way should aim at rekindling Walras's program. We believe, however, that some clarity would be gained if the Walrasian program were to be disentangled from the accomplishments of both Walras and the neowalrasians, and, moreover, if the notion of a general model of exchange were defined independently of the exchange setting that has been chosen to formalize exchange, namely organized brokered markets – even though none of the models has acceptable foundations in this regard (cf. Walker 1997a).

In this final chapter, some questions will be raised. First, whether models designed upon working and factual assumptions, and not upon *ad hoc* simplifying postulates, may aspire to the degree of generality that the Walrasian program defines. Second, whether for the construction of an empirically relevant model of exchange, the organization of markets of reference should be set within a frame of 'perfection' as (explicitly) Walras, and (implicitly) Arrow and Hahn and many others did, without falling in the methodological traps that have hindered the neowalrasian approach. Finally, whether for the purpose of understanding exchange in actual decentralized economies, the construction of a model, or models, should attempt instead to formalize the workings of non-brokered markets, with the attendant institutional features. Interdependence in exchange, decentralization and markets are different notions, and I gather that in the study of a decentralized economy those concepts must have implication, and that this has not received adequate treatment in the theory of general equilibrium. Furthermore, in order to analyze the feasibility of exchange in the case of non-brokered markets, there is no escape to a clear confrontation with the institutions of intermediation and money, for the explanation of which information and transaction costs cannot be 'hidden in plain sight'. These institutions would be 'explained in the model', as part of the understanding of the pricing mechanisms and the logistics for exchange. In this set-up, then, pair-wise exchange involving intermediaries and money could be formalized in order to analyze the configuration of the result of the convergence of these processes, and to inquire whether and how interaction among decentralized decision makers attains a coordinated outcome.

Conformity with the tenets of the neowalrasian approach may be, in our perspective, a surrender to the difficulties, and the challenges, of reconstructing an empirically relevant general theory of exchange and markets.

The obstacles to the Walrasian program notwithstanding, its rekindling may, however, provide a new light on the construction of a theory of decentralized exchange. The analytical tools may be different,[8] general proofs may be unwarranted or not formally achievable, and the results not as clean, but it is now conceded by many that the existence solution is too light, though embarrassing, a foundation for the understanding of exchange in markets.

My main conclusions are then, first, that the neowalrasian model of general equilibrium cannot deal adequately with decentralized markets, either theoretically or empirically and, second, that the modeling of decentralized mechanisms of exchange and trading are in a very unsatisfactory state.

NOTES

1. In referring to neowalrasian, instead of the usual 'neo-Walrasian', I follow Clower (1995a, p. 307, n). Given that the links to the original model where the neowalrasian approach departed from (Walras's and Pareto's numeraire model) are lost, 'the word "neowalrasian" ' is regarded 'as an *impersonal* noun that requires no capitalization'.
2. I switch here from the French word *tâtonnement* to the word *tatonnement* now in common use in written English. The same applies to *numéraire*.
3. In Townsend (1987) *Arrow–Debreu Programs as Microfoundations of Macroeconomics,* we read: 'The class of general equilibrium models of Arrow, Debreu, McKenzie and others is a useful starting point for the study of actual economies. The idea is to start with a stylized Arrow–Debreu environment; impose Pareto optimality, the competitive-markets hypothesis, or the core hypothesis; and then make predictions about the methods of interaction of economic agents or the outcomes from that interaction' (ibid, p. 382). The whole article is a good example of the reversal of analytical perspective that the neowalrasian approach brought on. It labors though in some confusions as, for instance, in Sections 6 and 9 on 'private information' and 'limited communication' (see Section 4.3.1, below).
4. Notice also Gale's analyses of the effects of adverse selection on general equilibrium, namely, Gale (1992) on the determination of general equilibrium, and Gale (1996) on the efficiency properties of competitive equilibrium.
5. Beyond the instances emphasized in this Introduction, I would indicate, as examples of this sifting, the comments on: (i) the theory of the firm in Coase (Section 4.1.1), (ii) 'missing markets' (Section 4.1.3), (iii) the dimensions of the decentralization problem (Section 4.3.1), and (iv) an attempt at the demarcation of the notion of feasibility in trading (Section 4.3.3.1). It is in the basis of critical comments on search models of trade (Appendix E), as well on a preliminary attempt at laying out the grounds for the decision of the firm on price and quantity, in a decentralized environment (Appendix F). It also allowed some clarifications, e.g. on a tentative distinction of the notions of thick-markets, parametric pricing, and price-taker (Appendix D).
6. Debreu (1986b, pp. 1262–3) and Vickers (1995, p. 6, n) indicate the historical origin of the problem. For a list of references on the subject, specifically on the question of how perfect competition can be distinguished from the existence of Walrasian equilibrium, see e.g. Anderson and Zame (1997, pp. 226–7), Ostroy and Zame (1994, p. 594) and Gretsky and Ostroy (1985). When referring to continuum economies, beyond the latter I have also in mind another strand of literature that led to McLennan and Sonnenschein (1991).
7. Like Aumann (1964), Ostroy and Zame (1994) somewhere got the notion that 'perfect competition' described a situation where transactors *in fact* have no effect on price. This is inconsistent (logically) with the existence of a mathematically continuous market demand function unless a transactor's contribution to relevant quantity is vanishingly small. The

right response to this is neither Aumann's nor Ostroy and Zame's (both assume a continuum of commodities and transactors), but rather to reject assumption that transactors cannot 'believe' in continuity unless that belief corresponds exactly to 'reality'. That is why I would distinguish between perceived and actual demands; perceived demands govern behavior in the first instance. In absence of theory of actual trading (neither Aumann nor Ostroy and Zame offer one), only 'first instance' behavior is relevant.

8.   The analytical tools towards such reformulation may be different: they may be found to lie in other fields unrelated to standard microeconomics, namely computation theory, or other non-axiomatic branches of applied mathematics.

2. Walras's program and the neowalrasian diversion

This chapter addresses the question: How did the promising program set out in Walras's early writings come to be taken as laying the ground for a totally different line of problems in his later writings and in modern microeconomic theory? The study of Walras's early works (cf. Walker 1996) offers an instructive object lesson in the way in which an interesting line of enquiry leads gradually to analytical difficulties, and then to 'solutions' that evade issues and constitute a major diversion of analysis down roads not initially contemplated by its originator. This chapter attempts to trace the development of that detour from the main road of economic analysis in early Walras, to the sideroad of abstract exercises in contemporary neowalrasian literature. To assess how this happened, a review of the literature is conducted, starting with Walras's own struggles to put together a model of general exchange, and going on to attempt to understand how later formalizations of the theory of exchange led to the omission of trading and markets.

2.1 WALRAS'S PROGRAM

Walras tells us at the end of the purely theoretical portion on his *Eléments*, that his object was to present a 'scientific formulation of pure economics', and for that purpose 'it did not matter whether or not we observed [free competition] in the real world since, strictly speaking, it was sufficient that we should be able to form a conception of it' (Jaffé, ed. 1954, p. 255; cf. p. 157 [1]); and he adds 'we never attempted to predict decisions made under conditions of perfect freedom; we have only tried to express the effects of such decisions in terms of mathematics' (ibid., p. 256). In an early chapter (Lesson 5, p. 83) of the *Eléments*, Walras observes: 'Value in exchange, when left to itself, arises spontaneously in the market as a result of competition. ... The more perfectly[2] competition functions, the more rigorous is the manner of arriving at value in exchange'. Continuing, he describes three kinds of markets, according to how well competition works:

1. The best organized markets are those in which selling and buying are made 'à la criée', i.e. by being cried out, through the intermediation of agents such as brokers, commercial agents, or criers who centralize purchase and sale offers in such a way that no exchange takes place

without its conditions being announced and known, and without the sellers being able to lower the price and the buyers to raise it. Examples are stock exchanges and organized commodity markets, the markets for grain, fish, and so on.[3]

2. There are other markets, such as those for fruit, vegetable and poultry, that are less well organized, but still function in a fairly effective and satisfactory way.

3. Third, markets where competition appears to be 'somewhat defective', but that nevertheless operate remarkably well: city streets where an abundance of stores and shops can be found – bakers, butchers, grocers, tailors, shoemakers, and so on.

More broadly, Walras asserts that

the whole world may be looked upon as a vast general market made up of diverse special markets where social wealth is bought and sold. Our task is to recognize the laws to which these purchases and sales tend themselves to conform. To this end, we shall suppose that the market is *perfectly organized in regard to competition*, just as in pure mechanics we suppose, *to start with*, that machines are frictionless. (Jaffé, ed. 1954, p. 84; with adaptations from the French edition, italics added).

In fact, '[p]ure political economy is essentially the theory of the determination of prices under a hypothetical régime of absolute free competition' (ibid., p. 40), by which Walras means competition 'among sellers of services who underbid one another and among buyers of products who outbid one another' (Jaffé, ed. 1954, p. 40, n; see also pp. 83, 223–4, 255, 478). Here we have undeniably a depiction of the freedom of individuals to offer 'bid' prices or 'ask' prices, at will. [4]

Since we are here concerned with what was to become the enduring Walrasian legacy, the neowalrasian approach to general equilibrium analysis, our aim will be the general model. In building his theoretical apparatus, Walras proceeds by steps, constructing, sequentially and cumulatively, theories of exchange, of production, of capital formation and credit, and finally of circulation and money. Exchange theory comprises basically two barter models, an introductory one of exchange of two commodities for each other (ibid., Part II), and another of exchange of several commodities for one other. In the latter general model (ibid., Part III, especially Lesson 12), two features are introduced. One is that each trader holds several commodities, and the other is a numeraire. As an attempt to link the first with the general model, Walras presents his arbitrage model, which is developed in three sketchy steps. First, there is the case of exchange of three commodities (ibid., §§ 105–7); next, there is the case of 'trading posts' exchange with m commodities and $(m \ (m-1)/2)$ 'special markets', where the prices of commodities are taken two at a time (ibid., §§ 108–13); and, finally, considering the possibility of an imperfect equilibrium – unbalanced cross rates of exchange – in 'trading posts' exchange. Walras introduces indirect barter ('arbitrage'), also with m commodities and with each trader holding initially one commodity (ibid., §§ 114–16; for a detailed characterization of Walras's barter exchange models, see Walker 1993). A note in point is that there is nothing in the following that relates to intermediaries, or to money in exchange,[5] but only to exchange between individual transactors involving bilateral trades, whatever the exchangeables might be. In fact, as Bridel (1997) shows at length, 'from the very first phase of its inception [Walras's *Eléments*], general equilibrium analysis cannot offer a formal account of the role of money as a medium of exchange' (ibid, p. 40).

Walras emphasizes that the construction of his theory involves two exercises.[6] The first is the mathematical solution to a set of equations of offer and demand. This is the theoretical solution to the (static) general equilibrium model, in which the calculated prices ('prix du calcul') are the equilibrium prices (Jaffé, ed. 1954, pp. 184–5). The second exercise is meant to show that the assumed mechanism of free competition in the market provides a solution identical to the mathematical solution. In Walras's words (ibid., p. 162–3; also p. 169), 'there remains only to show – and this is the essential point – that the problem of exchange for which we have just given the theoretical solution, is the selfsame problem that is in practice solved on the market by the mechanism of free competition'. To prove that 'we need only show that the upward and downward movements of prices solve the system of equations of offer and demand by a process of groping [par tâtonnement].' (ibid., p. 170).[7]

An important shortcoming undermines the proposed second exercise. It concerns the consistency of the two solutions, the mathematical one and the one asserted to be reached by way of tatonnement. This is meshed with a discussion on whether tatonnement is an exercise in statics or dynamics, but this is an inadequate way of phrasing the question. To avoid possible confusions about the meaning of these notions in mathematics and in current looser economic reasoning, I prefer to distinguish between 'solutions to equation systems' and 'model description of real-time processes,' which for brevity will henceforth be referred to as the 'equilibrium' and the 'real-time' views, respectively. This is the main question to be addressed here because I am only concerned with Walras's proposed line of inquiry and with his struggle to make sense of it. It is a discussion about 'what Walras really said' – and a tentative one at best, made more difficult by Walras's failure to give a clear account of the workings of any actual economy. Other shortcomings, which Walras entirely failed to envision, will be addressed later. One is the logical consistency of his theory of price adjustment in exchange; another is Walras's failure to specify information requirements that impinge upon the construction of models that are meant to deal with the workings of markets.

Conflicting interpretations have been proposed as to whether Walras's work on tatonnement deals with a model description of real-time trading processes ('real-time' view) by which competitive markets move towards equilibrium, or is purely concerned with a solution to equation systems ('equilibrium' view), and is not intended to describe the behavior of real markets (cf. Walker 1987a, p. 758–59; 1996, Chapter 12, where these are called 'dynamic' and 'static' interpretations, respectively). Before Walker (1987a) this debate had mostly been settled in favor of the 'equilibrium' interpretation. Patinkin (1965, pp. 531–40), Jaffé (1967), and Morishima (1977, pp. 27–45) stand out as the influential proponents of the 'real-time' view, though meanwhile Jaffé suddenly became dissatisfied with his earlier interpretation and (Jaffé 1980; 1981) embraced the 'equilibrium' view. Finally, and mostly from 1987 on, Walker formulated a critical assessment of Walras's complete writings and of former interpretations of tatonnement, to conclude that in reference to the 'mature models' (2nd and 3rd editions of the *Eléments*)[8] Walras intended to show the behavior of real markets. But let us go into some detail, first dealing with pure exchange, and next considering exchange and supply flows.

2.1.1 Tatonnement in Walras's Exchange Models

Walras's theory of tatonnement in exchange is based on the workings of actual brokered markets, namely the Paris Bourse (see Walker 1990a, p. 653: 'le marché type'; 1990b, p. 967). The first important feature – and this is trivial for the two-commodity case – is that all traders are in direct communication and thus are able simultaneously to learn each other's offers. A broker knows his demand curve (which we assume is a net demand curve if the broker has carried out all matching trades between his customer-buyers and customer-sellers). This demand schedule is composed of the cumulated price–quantity orders received from individual traders. As far as supply is concerned, he only has access to the counter-offers (price–quantity points) of individual brokers he is proposing to deal with. If we presume that each individual broker-buyer (broker-seller) has full knowledge of every other prospective trader's effective supply (demand) at any given price (i.e. that he knows each individual prospective trader's demand [or supply] schedule), then we would be led to posit a trading scheme between every pair of brokers in the same manner as if the orders to buy or sell of both of every belonged in the book 'list' of orders to transact of the broker proposing the trade. We require less-than-perfect information about brokers' (or traders' in general) 'effective' demands and supplies at each price in order to make sense of (and allow for) exchange, but imperfect information is a standard assumption of decentralized exchange, and there is not much to add, although it may help to make this clear: without decentralized information about other traders' willingness to trade, exchange vanishes.

The second feature is that bargaining occurs by way of announcement by traders of offers to purchase and sell, and price bidding takes place so that at a certain price (equilibrium price) orders to buy and orders to sell are in balance. The third is that transactions occur only when the market equilibrium price is obtained for the day. Notice that, in his description of the workings of the Paris Stock Exchange, Walras does not allow for trading at disequilibrium prices. He is led to exclude trade 'until offer equals demand' and '[a] new stationary state is thus found at a higher price'. 'Theoretically, trading should come to a halt', and '[t]rade stops.' (Jaffé, ed. 1954, p. 85; see Walras 1885, p. 312 and 1895, p. 630). These aspects of his model actually differ considerably from the workings of the Paris Bourse, as Walker (1997b) describes.

After talking about arbitrage in the three-goods case, Walras seemed to lose interest in trading processes and also in processes of price adjustment that might precede it. He proceeds as follows. First, he raises the possibility of an imperfect equilibrium – unbalanced cross rates – and considers indirect trades (Jaffé, ed. 1954, p. 157). For the three-goods case, he shows (ibid., pp. 158–60) that a trader will not trade directly in the trading post (AC), say, if through successive indirect barter in the (AB) and (BC) trading posts, he could obtain a more favorable exchange rate: $p_{ab} \times p_{bc} > p_{ac}$. Instead, a holder of ($A$) demanding ($C$) would replace direct exchange of (A) against (C) by indirect exchange of (A) against (B), and (B) against (C), so that the 'true price' (that is, the rate of exchange at which the final transactions are expected to take place) of (A) in terms of (C) will be ($p_{ab} \times p_{bc}$). If we suppose that a given trading post displays an 'imperfect equilibrium', arbitrage opportunities will be sought. By way of substitution of two trades for one direct barter, the imbalance in cross exchange rates would be transmitted to any third trading post presumably in partial equilibrium, let us suppose, to the two neighboring trading posts.[9]

Here Walras faces a problem: if, given posted prices, there are advantageous arbitrage opportunities among certain trading posts, there will be either no demand or no offer forthcoming at any of these trading posts. This spillover from one trading post to the next would call forth bargaining, that is, changes of asking or bid prices, as is accounted for in the two-goods case. The problem is not easy to tackle: the fact that no agent or broker can have a full picture of the market for a commodity (all the trading posts where one commodity is exchanged) prevents any simple way of formalizing adjustment of exchange rates at any trading post. With respect to Howitt's (1973, p. 490) summary assessment of a two-goods, one-market case, as considered in Walras's description of the Paris government bond market, one should not be misled into thinking that the 'short' side can be ascertained in more general cases, although the problem is trivial in a two-goods market (see Appendix C, below). The possible confusion is related to an aspect of Walras that is unclear. He leads us into thinking (Jaffé, ed. 1954, pp. 84–6, 87 ff.) that the 'short' side can be ascertained, which requires the possibility that each and every broker in the course of trading can come to realize total demand and total supply forthcoming in the market at the announced price. In the case of a set of special exchanges (trading posts), one for each pair of commodities, no 'specialized broker' will be able to gather information on the 'market' excess demand of any commodity; that is to say, brokers cannot ascertain market conditions.[10]

Unable to tackle this bargaining question, in order to achieve a 'final' and 'general' market equilibrium, Walras bypassed arbitrage by assuming it is done by the market impersonally. '[A]rbitrage operations will be effected' (ibid., p. 160) in order to 'generalize the equilibrium established for pairs of commodities in the market' (ibid., p. 161). In place of an explicit account of arbitrage between trading posts, Walras introduces a set of no-arbitrage conditions.[11] Having postulated these conditions, Walras replaced his collection of special markets (trading posts) with a 'single general market', and introduced the numeraire so that a single numeraire price is associated with each commodity, thereby introducing *by assumption* the highly special condition that a single rate of exchange prevails for every admissible pair-wise commodity exchange, independently of the location at which it occurs or the individuals who execute it (this creates serious interpretation problems because, for example, if two different money prices for gasoline are observed at a single street intersection, that 'fact' can be fitted to the theory only by treating gasoline at different stations as different commodities [cf. Debreu 1959, p. 30], a type of intellectual contrivance that effectively insulates the theory from empirical confrontation). In effect, Walras thereby eliminated *by assumption* the possibility of explicit discussion in subsequent argument of competition or bargaining. The economics profession subsequently has somehow overlooked this savage emasculation of the intuitive concept of rivalrous competition, as conceived by all earlier economists including Walras's 'sainted' father Auguste Walras. The 'simplification' introduced by Walras's no-arbitrage conditions, i.e. the introduction of numeraire prices, may go a long way to explain why Marshall, Edgeworth, and other contemporaries of Walras showed so little respect for Walras's supposed 'creation' of scientific economics (cf. Bridel 1997, p. 144).

In the Preface to the *Eléments* (Jaffé, ed. 1954, pp. 40–41), a picture of exchange is presented for a 'market' where only consumers' goods and services are bought and sold, where once the prices of all goods and services have been cried in terms of the numeraire, and quantities offered and demanded of every good having been determined in this way, new prices are cried and the process continues so that finally 'the prices will be the *current equilibrium prices* and exchange will effectively take place'. In the general equilibrium model, the relevant question is not as much whether it is a realistic account of the dynamics of the equilibrating process in markets, which Walras took for granted, but whether it is logically sound (on this, see Section 4.3, below). Even though we should be aware of the dissonance between Walras's attachment to understanding tatonnement as a real procedure, and his formal account of it, an assessment of Walras's exposition of tatonnement in general exchange may be helpful (see Jaffé, ed. 1954, pp. 169–72; Jaffé 1981, pp. 317–21). A formal analysis of the Walrasian tatonnement process can be found in Uzawa (1960, pp. 186–8), Arrow and Hahn (1971, p. 305), and in Patinkin (1965, p. 535).

Jaffé (1981) searches through the literature on the two views, 'equilibrium' and 'real-time', and collates rather disputable evidence from discussions that Walras entered into with contemporary economists, in order to defend his contention that Walras intended his theory of tatonnement to be understood as a virtual and mechanical solution, adhered to for analytical convenience. Jaffé's view points in the same direction as Goodwin (1951) as well as a remark in Arrow and Hahn (1971) that Walras's formal account of tatonnement apparently is conceived of as a mathematical process of solving a set of simultaneous equations.[12] Similarly, in Arrow (1968, p. 378) we read: 'Walras did not literally suppose that the markets came into equilibrium in some definite order. Rather, the story was a convenient way of showing how the market system could in fact solve the system of equilibrium relations'. Walras could not be describing the workings of the markets, yet was intending to give a 'representation' of how the result obtained by the market could be achieved. But this is just what Walras himself wrote in the context of adjustments in the production model: 'We must picture to ourselves as taking place [Qu'on se représente comme s'effectuant ...] simultaneously all the operations that, for the needs of the demonstration, we have had to assume taking place successively' (Jaffé, ed. 1954, p. 477–8; as translated in Walker 1988, p. 313; 1996, p. 276).

Walker (1987a, pp. 762–5) convincingly dismisses Jaffé's interpretation. He defends the opposite view that Walras – at least by the time of the third edition (1896) of the *Eléments* – had not surrendered his conviction that he was describing an empirical solution on the market under the regime of free competition; and that tatonnement in exchange demonstrates 'the attainment of ... equilibrium through the play of the raising and lowering of prices until the supply and demand quantities are made equal' (Walras 1895/1965, p. 630; in Walker 1987a, p. 763; cf. Walker 1988 [13] and Edgeworth 1889 [14]). The argument was then basically centered on the production model, which before the 4th edition (1900) displayed indisputably disequilibrium tones. Nonetheless, one conclusion seems to emerge: Walras's (and later followers') mixing of mathematics with reality is a road to serious confusion.

2.1.2 Tatonnement in Walras's Production Models

However suggestive the conjectures just discussed might be, the origin of the two views of tatonnement, 'equilibrium' and 'real-time', lies in the theory of tatonnement in production. Such a demarcation in its actual form can be traced to Jaffé's change of view from 1967 to 1981, and to Walker's (1987a) critique and appraisal. Having no clear idea of the theory of production, Walras's own views evolved over time, and thereby both interpretations could find exegetical support. There is, however, a clear line of continuity. In the summary explanation of the theory of production in the Preface to the *Eléments* (Jaffé, ed. 1954, pp. 41–2) (first introduced in the 2nd edition) Walras apparently saw no need to introduce any correction in the text after a change in the mechanism of trading was introduced in the 4th edition (ibid., p. 37). Exchange and production are here understood to take place in the process of adjustment towards equilibrium prices, and this may allow only the inference that Walras did not finally attach much relevance to the mechanism of trading. His concern seemed to be above all with the generation of a set of prices leading to maximum utility in exchange. As indicated above, Walras lost interest in the mechanics of trade before he shifted attention to the 'general' numeraire model of multiple-commodity exchange. If this be the case, one cannot help reading some aspects of the discussion on the subject as a little more than 'hen scratching' (Fowles 1983, p. 32), which is not to say that Walras is blameless for his unsatisfactory account of price adjustment and for his superficial account of the logistics of trading in the general model. However, this remark better fits later writers. If Walras was beaten by the trading problem, it has been mostly evaded since.

Nevertheless, let us elaborate on the arguments the discussion involves. In the second and third editions of the *Eléments*, equilibrium in Walras's theory of production is portrayed as the result of a series of tatonnements in production, with transactions occurring at non-equilibrium prices and production at non-equilibrium quantities (see Walras 1889, p. 235; as in Walker, 1987a, p. 761). The numeraire price of each commodity is changed according to the Walrasian pricing rule, i.e. it is changed in the same direction as the sign of the excess demand quantity for the commodity. At each new set of disequilibrium prices, a new set of disequilibrium quantities of services is hired and a new set of disequilibrium quantities of commodities is produced. Prices are changed at each round of the tatonnement process, and the continuation of tatonnement is thought to lead the system of new quantities and new prices closer and closer to equilibrium, until the equilibrium set of prices and quantities is purportedly found (cf. Walker 1987a, p. 761). Walker (1994b) argues that in the 2nd and 3rd editions (Walras's 'mature phase'), Walras considers out-of-equilibrium transactions, and has 'demanders and suppliers' that 'quote and change prices' (ibid., p. 1375; see also Walker 1994a; 1996). Apparently, there is a real dynamic account of equilibrium in production, as a prior condition for the otherwise 'instantaneous' equilibrium to be obtained in exchange.

Walras struggled with this question in his theory of production. The fact is that in the 4th edition tickets or pledges (*bons*) were introduced: Walras abandoned the view that the preliminary groping in order to establish equilibrium occurs effectively, but supposed 'instead, that it was done *by means of tickets* ['*sur bons*']' (Jaffé, ed. 1954, p. 37; see also p. 242). By doing so, Walras eliminated disequilibrium transactions and production from his system. Thus, in an economy in which production occurs,

> transformation of productive services into products takes place. Certain prices of services being cried, and certain quantities being produced, if these prices and these quantities are not equilibrium prices and quantities, it is necessary not only to cry new prices, but to produce other quantities of products. In order to achieve a rigorous tatonnement in regard to production as in regard to exchange, all while taking account of this circumstance, it is necessary only to suppose that the entrepreneurs represent the successive quantities of *products* with *pledges* ...; and that landlords, workers, and capitalists represent the successive quantities of *services* with *pledges*. (Walras 1900, p. 215, as in Walker 1987a, p. 767).

Therefore, production, as well as exchange, only takes place after a tatonnement process finds the equilibrium prices, which are the same as those determined by the theoretical solution. Introducing the fiction that 'groping' in production is done by means of pledges (*sur bons*), Walras was able to prevent any change in asset holdings until the equilibrium price is found, and thus to circumvent the problem that, in case non-equilibrium production took place, at each step of the tatonnement process the amounts of assets held by traders would be altered, thereby changing the parameters – hence, also, the solution – of the system of equations (cf. Walker 1987a, p. 766; 1971, pp. 1173–74; Jaffé 1967, p. 9).[15] Production brought in a problem different from exchange only because of Walras's supposition (provisionally ignored in the theory) that '[p]roduction [as contrasted to exchange] ... requires a certain lapse of time' (Jaffé, ed. 1954, p. 242) so that intentions of economic agents would have to be reconciled *ex ante*.

In the theory of exchange the exact same complication is present, but since traders were in an idealized, organized type of market – in direct communication – there would be no need for pledges to be recorded; the simple crying out of (new sets of) prices would work it out. Walras's model of exchange logically is subject to 'complications' related to endowment effects (much the same as Hicksian income effects); but Walras's approach in the theory of exchange allowed him to dispense with pledges and assume the complication away, leaving no room for the possibility that decisions might not be reconciled *ex ante*. All the same, there is some possibility that Walras realized disequilibrium trading might invalidate his equilibrium equations in exchange (cf. Walker 1987a; Bridel 1997[16]). Whatever the case may be, having postulated the suspension of trading until prices are equilibrium prices, redistribution of endowments in exchange in disequilibrium could not occur.

In fact, the theory of exchange is liable to a much richer set of dynamic questions than Walras acknowledged. Walker's allegation 'that Walras devoted his attention almost exclusively to the conditions of static equilibrium in an abstract model devoid of institutional detail, economic facts and dynamic behaviour, is a misrepresentation of his work' (1987b, p. 854) is true with respect to his mature modeling, but not with respect to his written pledges model. Walras's abstraction from complications in dealing with tatonnement in his final account of the subject (4th editions) led him far from any reasonable representations of the workings of general exchange; here, institutional detail is a product of sheer imagination and the equilibrating mechanism does without the market. In his account of Walras's work, Walker seems occasionally to bring himself to the edge of historiographical imagination (e.g. Walker 1990b, pp. 967–8.)

However, Walker's contention that the pledges model was inserted as an afterthought to his former construction provides a good explanation for the apparent inconsistency between the formal presentation of the model and several descriptions of the working of actual markets, not only of perfectly organized markets but also of decentralized ones. In fact, Walras often has in mind tatonnement as working in non-brokered markets:

> The rapidity and reliability of the market solution leave no room for improvement. It is a matter of daily experience that even in big markets where there are neither brokers nor auctioneers, the current equilibrium price is determined within a few minutes, and considerable quantities of merchandise are exchanged at that price within half or three quarters of an hour. (Jaffé, ed. 1954, p. 106).

Summing up, Walras's 4th edition reformulation of the tatonnement process operates with pledges in both the exchange and production models, so trading at disequilibrium does not occur.[17] Equilibrium becomes determinate (Kaldor 1934), and the outcome independent of the path by which it is reached (Arrow and Hahn 1971, p. 334).

Walras's attempt to provide a demonstration that 'the mechanism of competition in the market is nothing but the practical determination of the calculated prices [prix du calcul]' (Jaffé, ed. 1954, p. 184; adapted) led him to abandon his earlier and better thought-out consideration of markets as undergoing a process of adjustment whereby transactions and production take place, and is thus more conducive to the understanding of the functioning of real competitive markets. Those are two separate theoretical goals, hardly reconcilable, and hence the two conflicting aims of a theory of tatonnement (cf. Bridel 1997[18]). That the disequilibrium production model was incomplete and the pledges model obviously farfetched, can be adduced as the reasons why Walras's second exercise did not succeed.

The second exercise is 'the essential point', as Walras remarked, for the understanding of competitive markets. In this second exercise, the working of markets cannot be frozen (trade cannot be suspended) during the adjustment process, or else we end up circumventing it, as Walras's theory of tatonnement in general exchange tacitly did.[19] We should, however, acknowledge in passing that Walras's analysis was pointing in a promising direction in his 'trading posts' model, where trading 'of several commodities ... for one another' takes place through pair-wise exchanges between traders (or trader agents) in a market 'divided into as many sectors as there are pairs of commodities exchanged' (ibid., p. 158). This is a first step into direct pair-wise (barter) exchange,[20] but the same bargaining problem that Walras attempted to deal with when he introduced indirect barter remains basically unresolved today, be it for pure barter or a money economy (see Starr and Stinchcombe 1993; 1997).

2.2 THE NEOWALRASIANS

Walras envisaged an explanation of convergence to equilibrium in exchange whereby bargaining and trading were to take place. His program was not, however, brought to completion; in the 4th edition of the *Eléments* he sidetracked it in the pledges model, which points in the direction followed by the neowalrasians. Somehow, after Hicks (1939) and more specifically with Arrow–Debreu, the formalization of general equilibrium became obsessed with consistency of plans, and overlooked bargaining and the logistics of trade.

General equilibrium analysis along the lines of Arrow and Debreu in the 1950s is usually viewed as 'an almost literal description of an idealized economy in which the notional economic plans of individual economic agents are costlessly coordinated by a central intelligence unit – the so-called auctioneer' (Clower and Leijonhufvud 1975, p. 183). This neowalrasian theory provides the solution to Walras's mathematical problem. As to the second exercise, the question raised is not Walras's, 'but rather whether we can conceive of an economy that is *completely* characterized by equilibrium relations of the kind identified by Walras' (ibid., p. 184). The adjustment of market prices to the mathematical solution is obtained by Arrow and Hahn's model, since their question is raised under the belief that the solution to the model is a proper representation of the relevant states of the real world. Differently, Walras departs from 'real-type concepts' drawn from experience and then proceeds to abstract 'ideal-type concepts' and reasons on the basis of these returning to reality only with a view to practical applications upon completion of a pure science of economics (cf. Jaffé, ed. 1954, p. 71). Furthermore, when envisaging an approach to the real workings of the market, Walras stays within his view of the 'rational' method, where he goes 'back to experience not to confirm but to apply ... conclusions' (ibid., p. 71).[21] The following quotation can be so read:[22]

> Finally, in order to come still more closely to the reality of things, we must also drop the hypothesis of an annual market period and adopt in its place the hypothesis of a continuous market. Thus, we pass from the static state to the dynamic state. ... Such is the continuous market, which is perpetually tending towards equilibrium without ever actually attaining it, because the market has no other way of approaching equilibrium except by groping, and, before the goal is reached, it has to renew its efforts and start over again, all the basic data of the problem ... having changed in the meantime. (Jaffé, ed. 1954, p. 380[23]).

In the neowalrasian approach there is nothing of the sort. The steps of the present explanation are based on Arrow and Hahn's (1971) account of general equilibrium analysis, which can be simplistically – or even abusively (see Hahn 1970, p. 2) – identified as neowalrasian. Debreu (1959) stands apart in this respect, as he clearly asserts that 'the axiomatic form of the analysis' implies that 'the theory, in strict sense, is logically entirely disconnected from its interpretations' (Debreu 1959, p. viii). Clarifying that 'there is a difference between ... the construction and examination of the workings of a model and ... the relation of the model to reality', Walker (1997a, pp. 49–50; cf. Clower 1995a) is of opinion that '[t]hat is not, however, the distinction made by Debreu. He believes that equations and mathematically expressed postulates can be used to construct the basic elements of a model, and that the resulting mathematical system can then be given various economic interpretations'. In fact, in a recent review of the theory of economic equilibrium, referring to Walras's mathematical analysis in the *Eléments*, Debreu (1986a, p. 405) starts this way: 'The observed state of an economy can be viewed as an equilibrium resulting from the interaction of a large number of agents with partially conflicting interests'. Arrow (1994, p. 5) is skeptical, however, about the 'relation to real-life phenomena' of the use of a non-cooperative game in the 'purely mathematical construct' in Arrow and Debreu's (1954) proof of existence of Walrasian equilibria. Notice, however, the more balanced view by Hahn (1973a). After defining the Arrow-Debreu equilibrium, he adds that:

> this construction ... makes no formal or explicit causal claims at all. For instance it contains no presumption that a sequence of actual economic states will terminate in an equilibrium state. However it is motivated by a very weak causal proposition. This is that no plausible sequence of economic states will terminate, if it does so at all, in a state which is not an equilibrium. ... [N]o description of any particular process is involved. It is also clear that weak as this claim is, it may be false. (Hahn 1973a, p. 7).[24]

Be that as it may, the world of the neowalrasians is an invented world, that purportedly mimics relevant features of the real world,[25] and the questions raised are 'not only whether it *is* true, but also whether it *could be* true' (Arrow and Hahn 1971, p. vii).

A world was invented. The task neowalrasians propose to undertake, in a line of inquiry reminiscent of Adam Smith's 'Invisible Hand', is 'to show that a decentralized economy motivated by self-interest and guided by price signals would be compatible with a coherent disposition of economic resources. ... Moreover, the price signals would operate in a way to establish this degree of coherence' (Arrow and Hahn 1971, pp. vi–vii). Thus, price signals would allow a decentralized economy to attain coordination, or coherence, whatever that might mean – 'notional', 'feasible', 'potentially real', 'optimal', or something else? How is 'decentralized' defined? How does decentralization affect the working of price signals? Is guidance by price signals sufficient for a 'coherent' disposition of economic resources in a decentralized economy? This sequence of questions leads to the doubt about which world – real or imagined – is depicted in general equilibrium analysis.

Equilibrium in the Arrow–Debreu world has the strict meaning of a rest point, in which the optimal plans of individuals, given a vector of known accounting prices, are in harmony ('mesh' perfectly) with each other. That is to say, 'the language is not equilibrium *is* a supply–demand balance,' but rather 'when in equilibrium, supply and demand are in balance' (Weintraub 1991, p. 107). This means that the Arrow–Debreu equilibrium is a solution to a set of implicit mathematical assumptions.

Stability of a general equilibrium set of prices is shown by means of an exercise whereby a central mediator selects prices and changes them until supply and demand plans of agents are balanced. That is to say, the equilibrium set of prices, if it exists, is asserted as the result of a virtual adjustment as conducted by a central market-maker, the auctioneer,[26] and bargaining is correspondingly out of the picture. Besides, no question is raised as to how individual agents might determine that prices are equilibrium prices, how 'long' a time must elapse before individuals conclude that the auctioneer has lapsed into inaction? We could think of this convergence to equilibrium as an 'as if' mechanism 'by which agents compare notes to see whether they are going to be satisfied' (Weintraub 1991, p. 107). There is, however, no room, and no economic incentive, for agents to devote effort to such communication. Since centralization of information gathering and dissemination is at the root of the mechanism, every attempt at 'market' imagery is in vain.[27] The neowalrasian model can be seen as an exercise dealing with an 'invented world' where, in the presence of a correct set of prices, plans are harmonized.

Arrow and Hahn's proposed claim is broader. In the study of stability, their goal is framed in the context of the Marshallian argument 'that there are forces at work in any actual economy that tend to drive an economy toward an equilibrium if it is not an equilibrium already' (Arrow and Hahn 1971,

p. 263). However, for analytical reasons, realizing how difficult the problem was, they stay within the bounds of an 'artificial process of adjustment', 'laboratory situation', and 'unrealistic analysis [by supposing] ... there is an auctioneer'[28] (ibid., pp. 264, 282, 324).[29] Of special interest is Arrow and Hahn's attempt to analyze 'trading' out of equilibrium. Here the authors relax the assumption of tatonnement, i.e. the mechanism of price adjustment 'in which no contract is binding except in equilibrium' (ibid., p. 282).[30] Thereby, 'extra realism' is gained, because instead of 'supposing that prices are moved by target excess demands, we now ensure that active excess demands are responsible' (ibid., p. 340). Nevertheless, when introducing out-of-equilibrium trading, they stick to their fiction of the auctioneer: 'at any moment of time he establishes unique and public offers on which goods may be traded, and he adjusts these terms in the light of market observations by some particular rule' (ibid., p. 324).

We should not deny the analytical difficulties under a less stringent informational basis, but we must question the merit of solutions to problems, the range of which is set by analytical technique. In fact, Arrow and Hahn's detour from the defined goal of analysis stems from the imperative of tractability: 'What is happening now is that, having decided on one idealization (perfect competition), we run into what must be taken to be logical difficulties unless we import a further idealization: the auctioneer.' (ibid., p. 325).

Therefore, the condition imposed that trading cannot occur at non-equilibrium prices should not be traced to the early Walrasian stability exercise which attempts to show that tatonnement produces a result the same as the solution to a set of equations. Walras's view of the working of the organized market of reference, the Paris Stock Exchange – however unclear or wrong – allowed him to conduct analysis as an 'as if' mechanism. In neowalrasian models, the reason for ignoring disequilibrium trading lies in tractability and an unsupported faith in correspondence between their models and 'the actual world'.

The final construction is self-contained and purely logical, yet it is believed to exhibit some correspondence with 'features of the world regarded as essential in any description of it' (ibid., pp. vii, 265). Despite Arrow and Hahn's oft-asserted reservations about the verisimilitude of assumptions, however, the overall purport of the analysis is towards an optimistic stand that consideration of features omitted from their model does not disconfirm the claims they set forth. If the 'actual market forces' that the authors summon to support the stability of tatonnement would not prove effectual, there should be another mechanism that might accomplish the analytical proof (ibid., p. 265). Arrow and Hahn are not dealing with a decentralized economy, and their exercise in stability is valid only for a world with no decentralized communication between agents, where information, and planning and execution of trades involve no set-up costs.[31] The auctioneer is thought to perform this function of finding and announcing equilibrium prices only because, since trading is costless and centrally coordinated, execution can be dealt with separately. Thus, Arrow and Hahn's question of whether the world they create 'could be true' (ibid., p. vii) is misplaced and misleading. If the execution of communication and trading is supposed to fall under the free services of a central market organizer who monitors direct trade with the central market place, as if by means of direct multilateral trades (as Arrow and Hahn [ibid., p. 329] put it: 'it is part of the auctioneer's job to freely disseminate offers to buy and sell'), also the other function of the auctioneer of finding equilibrium prices stands only as a representation of an ethereal world of centrally coordinated individual trading plans.[32]

NOTES

1. 'It should be recalled, moreover, that what we have in mind throughout this volume is not to pose and solve the problem in question as if it were a real problem in a given concrete situation, but solely to formulate scientifically the nature of the problem which actually arises in the market where it is solved empirically.' (Jaffé, ed. 1954, p. 157).

2. 'Selon que cette concurrence fonctionne plus ou moins bien ...' (Walras 1926, p. 70). We should beware of the intrusion of 'perfection' with its later connotations; see, for instance, Schumpeter 1954, p. 1026, n.

3. See Walker (1997b) on an 'archaeological' digging into the workings of the Paris Stock Exchange. The author reveals how thoroughly decentralized trading was in the nineteenth century Bourse, which ought to put an end to a piece of folklore that, like any other, has long been based on repetition. A recent instance of such is Kregel (1995; also 1992).

4. This is not a feature of modern 'competitive' models (e.g. Arrow and Hahn 1971). As Stigler (1957) shows, long historical survival can be adduced as evidence of the ubiquity and viability of competition in 'city streets'. The same cannot be said of 'organized' commodity exchanges (Cassady 1967, Chapter 3).

5. 'If, on the other hand, money intervenes in these exchanges – which is a hypothesis closer to actuality – the result is different. Let (A) be silver, (B) wheat, (C) coffee, etc. In the real world, the producer of wheat sells his wheat for silver, and the producer of coffee does the same. With this silver the first producer will buy coffee and the second wheat. ... We are assuming at this stage of our argument that the buying and reselling of (A) as a medium of exchange take place in a way that does not exert any influence on the price of commodity (A). In the real world the matter presents itself quite differently.' (Jaffé, ed. 1954, p. 190).

6. Yet the construction of each model involves four parts (cf. Walker 1987b, pp. 854–5): (1) the structure of the market, (2) the process by which adjustments take place when the market is in disequilibrium, (3) the conditions of equilibrium, and (4) comparative statics. Basically, the first exercise corresponds to part (3), the second to part (2).

7. Walras's general program in regard to this second exercise is defined in the preface to the 4th edition as: 'that the mechanism of increase and decrease of prices in the market, in conjunction with the fact of shifting of entrepreneurs from enterprises showing a loss to enterprises showing a profit, is nothing but a way of resolution by groping of the equations involving these problems.' (Jaffé, ed. 1954, p. 44).

8. This expression was coined by Walker (1994a; 1994b). Walker's (1996) book *Walras's Market Models* presents a thorough appraisal of Walras's models, where the 'mature phase' and the 'phase of decline' are the building blocks of the exposition. I will be referring mostly to the papers from which this book originated.

9. 'This condition [for stable equilibrium] was first stated by Walras. Walras, however, formulated it in a way which limits its applicability to partial equilibrium analysis. Within the framework of general-equilibrium theory the stability conditions must take into account the repercussions of the change in price of a good upon the prices of other goods as well as the dependence of excess demand (or excess supply) of a good on the prices of the other goods in the system. This has been done by Professor Hicks' (Lange 1945, p. 91). But Hicks (1939/1946) only accomplished his stability proof (save for instability due to asymmetrical income effects [ibid., pp. 66, 316–17]) through the presumption that 'p_s is adjusted so as to maintain equilibrium in the market for x_s, but all other prices are unchanged; ... p_s and p_t are similarly adjusted; and so on' (ibid., p. 315). Whose 'market' information for each commodity is it that allows for adjustment?

10. The same imperfection in the communication and assessment of market conditions extends to the possibility of non 'single valued' transaction prices (cf. Osborne 1965, p. 112).

11. Walras's introduction of 'no-arbitrage' conditions (and the numeraire) does not complete the basis upon which the edifice of general equilibrium analysis would be built later. The key element here was Pareto's introduction of a budget equation in his *Manual of Political Economy* (1909/1927, pp. 160, 412), a concept not found in Walras, that was adopted, apparently without serious reflection, by Slutsky (1915), and then by all later interpreters of Walras, including Allen (1932, pp. 210, 212, 216), Hicks and Allen (1934), Schultz (1935, pp. 434–6), Hicks (1939), and Samuelson (1947). Notice, however, Schultz's (1935, p. 434) recognition of the question: 'These prices are assumed unaffected by the individual's trading, so that his budget always balances: he gives (supplies) in proportion to what he receives (demands), and receives in proportion to what he supplies'. For further comment, see Appendix A, below.

12. Goodwin hinted at the similarity between 'the traditional mathematical device of solving equations by trial and error' and economic dynamics regarded as 'a series of iterated trial solutions which actually succeed one another at realistically great, regular intervals of time' (Goodwin 1951, p. 4; in Jaffé 1981, p. 332). Further, the remark is that 'in his more formal account of [tatonnement, Walras] seemed to conceive of it as the Gauss–Seidel process' of solving a set of simultaneous equations, which being neither 'a particularly attractive computational means' nor an imitation of the market 'has rather little to recommend it'. (Jaffé 1981, p. 329; from Arrow and Hahn 1971, pp. 306, 322). None of these writers seems to have any awareness of the impossibility of arriving at an *exact* solution by *any* computational technique (Manin 1977, Chapter 5). Had any of them recognized this, their discussions of tatonnement would surely have been seen to be puerile as well as logically and empirically pointless (cf. Velupillai 1991, pp. 32–5).

13. See also Walker, 1988. Most of the article is devoted to showing that 'rightly or wrongly, [Walras] thought [his theory of economic tatonnement] was an abstract account of real economic behavior' (ibid., p. 304).

14. Edgeworth expressed strong doubts on the possibility of giving a general solution to the dynamic behavior of markets (cf. Walker 1987c, pp. 160–61). Furthermore, he attacked Walras's generalization of tatonnement as *the* rule of price adjustment in markets (the choice of free competition being only one among a variety of actual market structures): 'Prof. Walras's laboured lessons indicate *a* way, not *the* way of descent to equilibrium' (Edgeworth 1889, p. 435). This rejection of tatonnement as important to the theory of determination of prices was received acrimoniously and provoked Walras's reiterated affirmation of his position, as above (cf. Walker 1987c, pp. 160–64).

15. In any iteration the system would be in 'temporary' equilibrium (cf. Archibald and Lipsey 1958).

16. Walker (1987a) presents fragmentary evidence thereon in a piece of correspondence from Walras to Bertrand, according to which Walras had 'rightly maintained' that his model of exchange was determinate because 'exchange was suspended in the case of the inequality of the quantities supplied and demanded' (Walras 1895, p. 630; in Walker 1987a, pp. 766–7). See also Bridel 1997, p. 33, referring to Walras 1885, and p. 144.

17. On trading at 'false prices', see Hicks's *Value and Capital* (Chapter 9 and related note), where the assumption of 'an easy passage to temporary equilibrium' sweeps complications under the rug. For critical comments, see Appendix B, below.

18. See Bridel (1997, p. 34), who contends that 'from Walras's earliest 1874 venture into pure theory, the two interpretations of tatonnement are both present'.

19. I agree with Walker's appreciation of why Walrasian theory did 'fail to be useful as even a highly abstract analysis of economic behaviour': 'the pledges model is designed to be consistent with certain mathematical conditions – that is, with the solutions of a set of equations – rather than being a set of assumptions and mathematical conditions designed to explain economic behaviour' (Walker 1987b, p. 860).

20. By pair-wise exchange, or bilateral exchange, I mean a transaction between two individuals involving two goods. The term 'barter' is often used as a synonym for 'primitive' non-market exchange, or as an implicit indicator of the absence of 'money'; I use the word 'barter' only to mean pair-wise exchange (thus, in my sense, pair-wise exchange of cash for food would be an instance of 'barter' [cf. Thornton 1802, p. 81]: 'gold and silver coin ... may be considered merely as instruments for facilitating the barter' of one sort of goods for another).

21. Notice the similarity to Colander (1992, p. 195), borrowing from John Neville Keynes, on the 'art of economics' – to be differentiated from positive economics, and empirical work in positive economics. 'The purpose of empirical work in the art of economics is not to test theories: it is to apply theories to real-world problems. ... Empirical work in the art of economics should be designed to apply a theory by adding back the contextual reality'.

22. Notice Jaffé's (1981, p. 325) opinion that this quotation appears in a final part of the *Eléments*, dealing with distinctly dynamic phenomena structurally separated from the theory of pure competition. On this, see Bridel (1997, p. 40).

23. See also Walras on equilibrium as 'an ideal and not a real state', yet it is 'the normal state, in the sense that it is the state towards which things spontaneously tend under a régime of free competition in exchange and production.' (Jaffé, ed. 1954, p. 224).

24. On these two different questions, first, that 'equilibrium cannot be claimed to describe properties of all potential terminating points of any actual process', and second, that the weak claim may be false, see Hahn (1973a, pp. 6–16). Also, referring to the mistaken, commonly maintained, implication of general equilibrium analysis that the price system ensures the 'proper' use of exhaustible resources, Hahn remarks (ibid., pp. 14–15): 'This negative role of Arrow–Debreu equilibrium I consider almost to be sufficient justification for it, since practical men and ill-trained theorists everywhere in the world do not understand what they are claiming to be the case when they claim a beneficent and coherent role for the invisible hand. But for descriptive purposes of course this negative role is hardly a recommendation' (cf. Starr 1997, p. 194).

25. See the Introduction to Arrow and Debreu (1954) on the reasons for studying the question of existence of an equilibrium for a competitive economy, which is considered of interest both for descriptive and normative economics: 'Descriptively, the view that the competitive model is a reasonably accurate description of reality, at least for certain purposes, presupposes that the equations describing the model are consistent with each other' (Arrow and Debreu 1954, p. 265).

26. The representation of market forces is assigned to the 'market participant' in Arrow and Debreu (1954, p. 274), the 'chairman' of a 'central registry' in Patinkin (1956, p. 37), and the 'Secretary of Market' in Uzawa (1960, p. 184). On the introduction of the figure of the auctioneer, see Walker (1972, p. 356) and Fisher (1987, p. 26). Koopmans (1951, pp. 93–5) has a 'helmsman' (representing the 'one' consumer) determine the initial prices of final goods, and a set of rules for price adjustment by the commodity 'custodians' (cf. Hurwicz 1973, pp. 8, 12); later, Koopmans (1957, p. 179) became critical of 'the view that impersonal market forces can generate the *tâtonnement* properties' and of the 'mechanical use of the Walrasian pricing rule' in tatonnement models (cf. Walker 1972, p. 357, n). Clower (1955) appeals to the marketor function in either competitive or monopolistic market forms (see also Clower 1994b, p. 377, n), and Haavelmo (1958, p. 29) summons a 'market administrator' to make sense of the 'demand–supply cross'.

    Edgeworth (1881, p. 30) invoked 'a sort of market-machine' to evaluate the *price* in a state of perfect competition; but he was not dealing with convergence. Walras had also referred to calculators (see Walker 1990b, p. 966).

27. 'The "supply–demand balance" ... serves, simply put, as a reference point for some fictitious market-maker to tell players to keep on playing, for they are not yet coordinated.

If, indeed, all agents were to get this information for themselves, from their own actions, then the supply–demand balance idea would not be associated with equilibrium except after the fact; that is, if the message "lack of coordination" could be triggered directly by the lack of harmony among agents' plans, and that message would lead to a revision of those plans in a self-correcting manner, then there would no longer be any need for the "market" to function as an information–dissemination device that says "keep on trading." ' (Weintraub 1991, p. 107).

28. Elsewhere Arrow and Hahn (1971, p. 256) refer to their auctioneer as following rules that 'however remotely, mimic what we believe goes on in actual markets'.

29. See Debreu 1959, p. 89, n; p. 36, n

30. In fact, this 'serious enough restriction on reality' (Arrow and Hahn 1971, p. 285) 'seems to carry the logical implication that trade never takes place' (ibid., p. 324). But, as will be seen below, there is no trading, or at least no decentralized execution of trades; see also proportional 'rationing' in the case of a monetary economy (ibid., p. 340). This is just an exercise on convergence.

31. Hicks (1967, pp. 6–7) raises the question of non-proportional transaction costs. '[I]f the cost is proportional to the volume of the transaction, it is the same as if the transaction were subjected to a tax.' A Walrasian equilibrium could be attained, even though it could be 'a Walrasian equilibrium after tax'. On a related but different issue, the consideration of set-up costs of transaction – entailing economies of scale in transacting – has more serious consequences for the Walrasian model (Hicks 1967, p. 6, n). An attempt to explain the effect of both types of transaction costs is given in Hirshleifer, 1973. See Section 4.1.2, below.

32. For a discussion of the missing of exchange in the neowalrasian approach, see Clower and Howitt, 1996 and Kohn, 1995. For an assessment of Debreuvian axiomatics, see Clower 1995a.

3. How standard price theory became predominantly neowalrasian

In this chapter I discuss some evolutions, dissatisfactions and solutions in price theory that led to the dominating role of the neowalrasian approach, and hint at some abandoned tracks along the way.

First, the basis for the accepted division between Marshall and Walras as foundations of economic analysis is questioned. Adjustments to equilibrium in Marshall and Walras are compared, and the conclusion is that both authors can be interpreted along the same lines and that the contrast should be established with Arrow–Debreu. After this clarification of the distinction between Marshall and Walras on the one hand, and the neowalrasians on the other, regarding the choice variables pertaining to the definition of stability conditions, this chapter attempts next to draw a historiographical outline concerning mainstream price theory, from a partial to a general equilibrium approach. This line of evolution begins with Marshall and from there moves to Chamberlin and on to Triffin, whose criticisms of the monopolistic competition theory set the analysis of competition in a general equilibrium framework, backtracking to the Walrasian perspective. However, along the way, this unification of price theory in the general equilibrium mold rendered the concern with markets to the sidelines of theoretical analysis and, as a consequence, sight of market interaction and the logistics of exchange is lost in standard microenomic theory. The way is paved for the acceptance of equilibrium states brought on with the Arrow–Debreu–McKenzie models, as descriptive of real decentralized economies, and processes of interaction and the analysis of convergence to equilibrium only studied as subsidiary to the results of the existence question.

3.1 MARSHALL, WALRAS, AND THE NEOWALRASIANS: SOME DIVIDING LINES

Marshall and Walras stand rather often as labels to be thought of in opposition. In fact, this is misleading. The contrast should be established with the neowalrasian construction, which as seen above, evolved out of Walras's and Pareto's no-arbitrage or numeraire models.

This is not to deny that there are differences between the authors. In a broader perspective, Hicks put it this way:

> For a considerable part of the way Walras and Marshall go together; and when they separate it is a difference of interests, rather than technique, that divides them. While Walras was seeking for the general principles which underlie the working of an exchange economy, Marshall forged an analytical instrument capable of easier application to particular problems of history and experience. (Hicks 1934, p. 338).

There is another apparent difference, and this regards exposition technique. My interpretation is, however, that to contrast Marshall and Walras in terms of content is a mistaken perspective: in fact, I shall attempt to show that there is basically no contrast as to their descriptions of adjustment to equilibrium in exchange, as well as in production.

Before that, however, let us point out a common view of market economies that underlies the analytical developments in both authors. Searching for the empirical presuppositions underlying the *Principles* and the *Eléments*, we may say that these are basically the same, and this is that markets exist, and that they work almost perfectly, almost always. In the first edition of the *Principles*, Marshall (1890, Book VII, Chapter 1, pp. 540, 542) says that: 'the position of normal equilibrium at any time is rather to be regarded as one towards which the forces of demand and supply at the time are tending, than as one that is ever actually attained', and 'the adjustment will not be perfect any more than the surface of a viscous fluid, which has been left a long time undisturbed, will be absolutely level. But as that surface will have become sufficiently level for all practical purposes ...' And Marshall goes on. He uses the image of the sea surface which is always tending towards a level, but never attains it. This is just the picture presented by Walras of what he calls 'the continuous market':

> Finally, in order to come still more closely to the reality of things, we must also drop the hypothesis of an annual market period and adopt in his place the hypothesis of a continuous market. Thus, we pass from the static to the dynamic state. ... Such is the continuous market, which is perpetually tending towards equilibrium without ever actually attaining it, because the market has no other way of approaching equilibrium except by groping, and, before the goal is reached, it has to renew its efforts and start all over again, all the basic data of the problem ... having changed in the meantime. Viewed in this way, the market is like a lake agitated by the wind, where the water is incessantly seeking its level without ever reaching it. (Jaffé, ed. 1954, p. 380).

In both authors there are markets, and the market forces operate such that markets tend to work well all the time. Both authors are concerned with how underlying forces lead to normal equilibrium (short- or long-run). The difference is that Marshall does it in words, while Walras has a reach that exceeds his grasp.

However, Marshall and Walras refer their theories to different markets. Most probably as a consequence, with respect to the statement of stability conditions the two authors apparently explain the determination of equilibrium in a slightly diverse fashion, Marshall in terms of demand and supply prices and Walras in terms of net excess demands. This might mean that they were dealing with different choice variables, in Marshall agents choosing prices, and in Walras quantities; that is to say, in Marshall agents regarding quantities as the independent variables and demand and supply prices as dependent, and in Walras agents considering prices as independent variables, and quantities demanded and supplied as dependent (cf. Clower 1996, pp. 36–7). Nevertheless, in their explanation of adjustment to equilibrium either in exchange or in production their language is very much compatible, even though much confusion envelops the interpretation of Walras's view on the subject. The fact that Walras does not allow for trade to take place in disequilibrium, and that the bargaining process is not explained in the general barter model (with prices set as a result of bargaining among agents, as he does, or attempts to do, in the case of the other barter models) do not imply, however, that Walras did not mean the finding of prices to be obtained by means of bargaining among agents in the general model (even though this might be infeasible).

The case is different in the neowalrasian view. Here the function of finding equilibrium prices is clearly viewed as requiring a central price-maker, the 'auctioneer'. Strangely, although Walras had started from decentralized bargaining, and general equilibrium analysis is barren in the understanding of adjustment processes, in fact the neowalrasian view of central coordination has been thought to deliver a logical and complete account of the working of Walras's general model.

In order to compare the description of adjustment to equilibrium in the two authors, the clue is to attempt to separate the functions of exchange and supply. Doing this, we gather that in both Marshall and Walras, adjustment to market period equilibrium is explained by way of variation in price, with agents bidding against each other. Dealing with normal equilibrium, where supply flows are also considered, if the two functions (the determination of prices in exchange and the choice of output in production) are separated, we have a similar picture in Marshall and Walras: in both authors exchange is conducted by traders, and transaction prices determined through bargaining; and in addition, these prices operate as signals which serve as the 'active force' for producers to change quantities to supply. Thus, a first conclusion is that equilibrium in exchange is arrived at by means of price adjustments, and equilibrium in production by quantity adjustments in both authors. And second, that in both Marshall and Walras, the determination of prices is carried out by traders, whereas in the neowalrasian approach, on the contrary, equilibrium prices are obtained in the models as a solution to equation systems, no bargaining involved.

3.1.1 Markets and the Definition of 'Market' Equilibrium

Starting off with the dissimilarities, some differences are notorious between Walras and Marshall, and the first one regards the choice of market of reference for the understanding of competition. As we have seen, in the construction of his barter models, Walras always supposes the markets to be well organized in regard to competition.[1] Marshall, on the other hand, has an encompassing perspective of markets; he establishes only a gradation regarding how much traders are in close communication,[2] and the consequent definition of perfection of the market in terms of 'the tendency for the same price to be paid for the same thing at the same time in all parts of the market' (Marshall 1920, p. 325). Marshall distinguishes the wide markets such as those of securities and of standardized commodities like valuable metals (or grain in America) and, on the other extreme, basically local markets, where competition is, however indirectly, felt: 'those secluded markets in which all direct competition from afar is shut out, though indirect and transmitted competition may make itself felt even in these' (ibid., p. 329; see also p. 328). Moreover, 'about midway between these extremes lie the great majority of the markets which the economist and the business man have to study' (ibid., 1920, p. 329). For the purpose of the analysis of adjustments to equilibrium, Marshall chose as expository examples, 'a corn market in a country town', or the fish market, specifically for price adjustment in the market period. According to Kregel (1992, p. 536), Marshall may have had in mind stock markets as the markets of reference for his description of adjustments: 'Marshall's description ... corresponds quite closely to the system of price determination which is employed in British and American stock markets, continuous auction broker-dealer markets'.[3] But to infer this conclusion by way of noting that '[i]n all three volumes of the *Principles*, Marshall repeats the idea that the stock market is the archetypal organized market' seems to me an unsupported platonism. Be that as it may, it should be granted that Marshall relies on the 'broad relations which are common to nearly the whole of [economic science]', assuming 'that the forces of demand and supply have free play; ... and there is much free competition; that is, buyers generally compete freely with buyers, and sellers compete freely with sellers' (Marshall 1920, p. 341).

Another aspect about which the two authors apparently diverge regards the variables on the basis of which equilibrium is defined, which can be related to the choice variables. Here Marshall and Walras rely on different definitions, and mathematical or graphical formalizations. In Marshall's temporary market-period equilibrium, equilibrium price is plainly defined as that that equates supply and demand:

> The price of 36*s*. has ... some claim to be called the true equilibrium price: because if it were fixed on at the beginning, and adhered to throughout, it would

exactly equate supply and demand (*i.e.* the amount which buyers were willing to purchase at that price would be just equal to that for which sellers were willing to take that price) (Marshall 1920, p. 333).

As to the equilibrium in production, however, Marshall does not start out as clearly. He states: 'when the demand price is equal to the supply price, the amount produced has no tendency either to increase or to be diminished; it is in equilibrium' (Marshall 1920, p. 345).[4, 5] But he immediately adds: 'When demand and supply are in equilibrium, ... the price at which it is being sold may be called the *equilibrium price*'. Thus, overall we may infer that, in Marshall's (partial equilibrium), net excess demand, $Q \neq 0$ unless $p^s = p^d$. In Walras, equilibrium in exchange requires that net excess demands be zero for every commodity (cf. Jaffé, ed. 1954, pp. 41, 109, 253).

The relevant question is whether these are just mirror images or whether they carry implications for the analysis. First, we may refer to Cournot who, when passing from monopoly to competition of producers, replaces the demand curve ($D = F(p)$) with the 'inverse notation' ($p = f(D)$) (Cournot 1838, p. 80); without however changing his exposition, and continuing to refer to adjustments in price (ibid., p. 80 ff.). In Cournot, the demand function is invertible,[6] and this is all there is to this change in notation. We know, however, that this is not just a question of notation. In the theory of oligopoly it is clear that price competition and quantity competition have, for a broad class of game configurations, distinct results, the reason stemming from prices being strategic complements and quantities strategic substitutes (cf. Bulow, Geanakoplos and Klemperer 1985; Klemperer and Meyer 1986). Second, for a competitive economy, if strategic interdependence is left out of the picture, and no single agent realizes he is able to influence the prices of the market, then prices can be used as economic parameters. In the study of competition, this was clearly used by Walras, and also, but less so, by Marshall. For both authors, this must have derived from Cournot's analysis of unlimited competition (both authors acknowledge the influence of Cournot, in general terms). But then we have a problem in both Walras and Marshall: if agents are thought of as bargaining over prices how can we also treat prices as parameters? Be that as it may, the relevant point is that the neowalrasian approach is only clearly understood with individuals choosing quantities on the basis of given equilibrium prices. And as standard price theory stands, '[i]t is not explained whose decision it is to change prices' (Arrow 1959, p. 43).

3.1.2 Adjustments to Equilibrium

Despite this different assertion of equilibrium conditions, we are very much led to the conclusion that this has no recognizable consequences for the exposition of adjustment to equilibrium by Walras and Marshall. Notice, however, that we are not looking at the consistency of bargaining and trading execution; in fact, we are looking only at bargaining and pricing in exchange. In order to compare adjustments to equilibrium in Marshall with adjustments in Walras's exchange model we must, first, look at *temporary equilibrium*, and next, to fully understand Marshall's view, we have to ask how he fits bargaining and pricing into the analysis of normal equilibrium (specifically, short-run equilibrium).

In Marshall, the relation of forces of demand and supply leading towards equilibrium in the market period, are explained on the basis of adjustment of price such that net excess stock demand is zero. Also in Walras, adjustments to equilibrium in exchange are assessed by way of variation in price, with agents bidding against each other (Jaffé, ed. 1954, pp. 40–41, 83, 223–4, 255, 478), the rule applying that '*to the left* of the point of equilibrium, *the demand for the commodity in question is greater than the offer*, which must result in a *rise* in price, that is, in a movement towards the point of equilibrium' (ibid., p. 109). Therefore, in Walras, equilibrium prices are 'obtained' through competitive bidding among buyers of products (or among sellers of services), according to the Walrasian rule (cf. Walker, 1994b). Exactly the same picture of price as the adjustment variable is depicted in Marshall's temporary market-period equilibrium, but for the fact that Marshall is clearer than Walras in allowing for trades during the equilibrating process (Marshall 1920, p. 333–4).[7]

Moving on to *normal equilibrium*, where supply flows are introduced, Marshall is still concerned with movements of price (ibid., p. 338), but adjustments here involve both price and quantity.[8] The function of adjusting quantities clearly concerns the producing unit, the representative firm. The marketor function in Marshall's short-run period is carried out by sellers[9] who bring goods to market. Their function in the working of the market is twofold: one is supposedly trading ('higgling and bargaining'), the other is to issue a signal, to represent the 'active force' that tends to change quantities to supply, or to produce:

> When ... the amount produced (in a unit of time) is such that the demand price is greater than the supply price, then sellers receive more than is sufficient to make it worth their while to bring goods to market to that amount; and there is at work an active force tending to increase the amount brought forward for sale. (Marshall 1920, p. 345).

Now, let us consider the relationship between the two functions, the determination of prices in exchange, and the choice of output in production. Exchange and supply (production) are better separated in order to understand the working of the market. In both Walras and Marshall, exchange is dealt with by agents – buyers and sellers – and prices obtained by means of bargaining. Further, the effect of the price signal given out on the goods markets is the same in both authors, it impinges on the producing units, which choose outputs. In Walras, exchange and production are dealt with separately, one a stock equilibrium, the other a flow equilibrium. We are led to conclude that the same is true in Marshall, that is to say, in Marshall's normal equilibrium, exchange plans are not specifically at stake, only production plans are; hence the reasonableness of Marshall's postulating 'perfection' in regard to price in the case of normal equilibrium: 'we assume that there is only one price in the market at one and the same time' (Marshall 1920, pp. 341–2 [10]). If this is the case, pricing refers to temporary equilibrium, and supply or production planning distinctly to normal equilibrium. By any means, this is not to say that Marshall did not allow for supply flows to have an effect on pricing. Marshall acknowledges this influence by means of anticipations; the anticipation of the effect of the increase in supply on future prices leads buyers to intertemporal substitution, and 'by waiting they help to bring the price down' (Marshall 1920, p. 333), and dealings or contracts for future delivery (ibid., pp. 337–8). And consequently, expectations of future prices by dealers will affect supplies (cf. Kregel 1992, pp. 534–5).[11] Thus, given prices and expectations, production decisions ensue and short-run normal equilibrium is asserted. (This is not so simple; see Leijonhufvud [1974, esp. pp. 32–3] on Marshallian and Walrasian microfoundations, namely his discussion of the *ex ante* / *ex post* character of normal equilibrium in Marshall.)

Walras has the same types of adjustments in the case of the establishment of equilibrium in a production economy. Price adjustments are supposed to bring about equilibrium in exchange, and quantity adjustments equilibrium in production (for the conditions of equilibrium and adjustments, specifically in production, see Jaffé, ed. 1954, pp. 40–42, 253–4, 478; Marshall 1920, pp. 345, 807, n).[12] This is consistent with Walker (1994b, esp. pp. 1361–8) in his interpretation of 'adjustment of output markets in the consumer commodities model', as referring to Walras's 'mature phase' (2nd and 3rd editions of the *Eléments*).

Summing up, the marketor function is played by traders in both Walras and Marshall. This is not so, however, in the neowalrasian construction where prices are determined in abstraction from bargaining.[13]

Furthermore, we may now be ready to resume and conclude the discussion on choice variables in Walras and Marshall. The problem is one of logical coherence between adjustment of price by agents in exchange, and the role of prices as parameters in the analysis. First, we have to bear in mind that both authors rely on the assumption of 'perfect' information on market prices in the process of adjustment, in the planning of production, even though Walras also specifically assumes this in bargaining (which is possibly due to his assumption on markets of reference). And this is where the view of prices as parameters comes in. It does not mean, however, that there is no room for adjustment of price; that is to say, pricing is viewed as the result of bargaining in exchange, but all other prices in the market are taken as given 'in the interim'. Second, convergence to equilibrium prices in exchange is meant to happen quite fast (Walras), or without consequence, although fast as well (Marshall). Therefore, quantities exchanged are decided on the basis of these known prices, and the planning of output to produce can take place, based on prices determined in exchange (equilibrium prices, in Walras's pledges model). This is so in Walras. In Marshall we have seen that the distinction between temporary and short-run equilibrium brings in anticipations of future supplies. So that prices determined in exchange are not independent from expectations regarding the 'normal' situation, which is not so in Walras's theories of exchange, or of production, where the market 'day' is seen in isolation from past or future events (cf. Hicks 1967, p. 3). But the question of the role of prices as variables of choice by agents, or as parameters, should by now be more clear, and interpreted on fairly similar terms in both authors.

3.2   FROM A PARTIAL TO A GENERAL EQUILIBRIUM APPROACH

From the 1930s on, general equilibrium analysis was following its own course along two fairly separate routes. One is traceable to Cassel's *The Theory of Social Economy* (1918/1932) and it led to the Arrow–Debreu–McKenzie models.[14] The other arises following Hicks's learning of the general competitive model in the writings of Pareto (and Walras), and its exposition in *Value and Capital* (1939) – in a form, as much readable as lacking in precision and clarity.[15] This had a thoroughly undermining influence on both sides of the economics' new divide. On the aggregative side (macroeconomics) Hicks originated a reformulation of Keynes's *General Theory* along Walrasian lines.[16] As to price theory, *Value and Capital* sidetracked the recently proposed theories of imperfect or monopolistic competition, and eventually helped to bring forth Triffin's appeal to general market interdependence. Those theories of imperfect competition had evolved, though, from a different approach, Marshall's partial equilibrium (and the welfare analysis of Pigou), which dominated standard price theory in Britain and the United States. Let us elaborate on this last point.

3.2.1 From Marshall to Chamberlin

Studies of price adjustment by firms in competitive markets (of which Arrow's *Toward a Theory of Price Adjustment* is paradigmatic) view the individual firm as facing a downward-sloping particular demand curve. Thus, in the background of any of these analyses, lies the question of monopoly, monopolistic competition or imperfect competition, whatever the setting of such models. In the early 1930s, these subjects were brought to the fore mainly with a view to solving Marshall's gap in the explanation of long-run equilibrium of firms displaying increasing returns.[17] Industries were thought to conform either to conditions of the theory of competition or to the theory of monopoly, only the case of duopoly presented a special embarrassment, and was deemed in an unsatisfactory state.

Marshall's attention was directed to the equilibrium of a competitive industry. Even though he was also concerned with the equilibrium of the firm (the 'representative' firm, an equilibrium firm[18]), his method stopped short of the posterior definition of a perfect market, which was put in terms so strict as to entail the necessity for the equality of marginal costs and marginal revenue of the individual business. The conditions imposed on the long-run supply curve of the individual firm that are compatible with equilibrium within a competitive industry, were questioned on the grounds that increasing long-run returns were taken as the common situation in manufacturing. The solution to this problem of the determination of equilibrium at the firm level, took primarily the way of postulating that marginal revenue should fall, with increasing output, faster than marginal costs fell; hence, the introduction of the concept of the individual demand curve (cf. Andrews 1964, pp. 20–21). Downward-sloping demand curves bring about falling marginal revenue curves and the presence of increasing returns is no more the problem. The problem is then the economic basis for such downward-sloping particular demand curves. Joan Robinson's demand curves were sketched as a ready-made 'implicit' device, to allow in theory the equilibrium of the firm, but rather than solving the problem it just concealed it.[19] Although issuing from reasons unrelated to the above controversy, Chamberlin explained his falling demand curves in terms of underlying consumers' preferences for the products of individual producers, on the basis of product differentiation within the group (of products that are close substitutes for each other). He distinguishes, though, the 'perceived' demand curve (*dd'*) from the 'share-of-the-market' demand curve (*DD'*), which were instrumental in the explanation of adjustment to equilibrium, either of the firm in isolation or of the group.

Chamberlin's solution was received as a complete answer to the problems of the day: equilibrium of a competitive industry had become compatible with decreasing costs at the level of the firm. His success in getting a determinate solution for the large group as well as for the individual firm, regardless of cost conditions, made *The Theory of Monopolistic Competition* the most influential work in the attack on the dichotomy of competition and monopoly. Firms are partially isolated from their competitors, with product differentiation as a monopolistic element, and the preferences of consumers for variety, and the possibility of firms changing their product, or of new firms entering the market, as the competitive elements. Thus, the Marshallian gap in the explanation of the long-run equilibrium of the firm was filled by making monopoly and competition compatible in a partial equilibrium set-up.

Several criticisms were immediately addressed to the new theories, but we would have to wait until the 1960s for its demolition. A first set of critiques points towards the internal consistency of the functioning of the model.

First, let us consider an exercise in comparative statics. As to the relationship between the elasticity of the *dd'* curves and the number of firms in the group, Kaldor (1935; 1938, pp. 84–6) pointed to the likelihood that the density of product varieties will increase the elasticity of each producer's *dd'* demand curve. Therefore, with entry of new firms (brands), if we assume that demand doesn't change, then the shift of the *DD'* curve to the left goes with the *dd'* curve becoming more elastic. If we consider an increase in demand, however, the *DD'* curves move to the right, but the entry of new firms shifts them back to the left; the direction of the effect on equilibrium price and size of plant depends on the effect of market share on the *dd'* curves, which is not known (cf. Archibald 1961, pp. 16–18). The reason for this inability to predict arises because the relationship between the *DD'* and *dd'* curves is not specified. This argument is limited, though, to the variables price and quantity (capacity) and it omits advertising expenditure or quality, which are integral variables to the monopolistic competition model. Comparative statics dealing with two variables at a time failed to recognize for a long time that the model is empty in regard to predictive power. If these other variables are added to the analyses, as they should be since they belong in the model, problems with comparative static exercises become compounded. In fact, Archibald (1961; 1967) showed that this model is unsuitable to qualitative comparative static predictions, either for the case of the equilibrium of a firm taken in isolation, or for the equilibrium of the group.

Second, Chamberlin's recognition of differentiation notwithstanding, his assumptions[20] of 'uniformity' of demand and cost conditions throughout the group, and of 'symmetry' (the effects of the adjustment by one firm having an even impact throughout the group) clearly affected his construction. And the reasons are that uniformity is only compatible with product homogeneity and, hence, horizontal demand curves; and that symmetry is incompatible with competition among heterogeneous products. If the first assumption is abandoned there will be profits throughout the group in equilibrium, and if the second is abandoned the uncertain outcomes that are characteristic of oligopoly, are present, and we are unable to define equilibrium for the group. Both assumptions in conjunction imply that 'we cannot have downward sloping demand curves *and* the tangency solution together' (Archibald 1961, p. 6; on Stigler 1949, pp. 313–14).

Also, the concept of industry fades away when differentiation, and 'general' impact of each firm's adjustments on competitors, are brought together. Since the distinction between large and small cross elasticities is an empirical question, the critique goes that theory is left with no intermediate concept between the firm and the general market. This is where Triffin's argument takes hold, even though his proposed solution does not escape exactly the same problem of mixing together differentiation and the symmetry assumption; allowing for differentiated units as the molecules of the general market, he only pretends the problem soluble by posing it on a larger scale.

Furthermore, beyond the methodological choice of partial versus general analysis, a real problem is whether the individual firm is theoretically viewed as facing a horizontal or falling demand curve. And here there is no basic change from Chamberlin to Triffin. As seen in this perspective, the question would boil down to parametric pricing in competition versus pricing on the basis of full information about demand schedules in an economy made up of competing monopolies.

Another line of criticism to monopolistic competition stems, however, from the use of the perceived, subjective or conjectured demand curve. Hicks (1935) surveys the state of the art immediately after the main contributions towards the solution of the above-referred Marshallian gap had been proposed.[21] Hicks is very skeptical about these innovations. His doubts on the usefulness of the new apparatus derive mainly from the subjective character of individual demand curves confronting a monopolist, or for that matter any competitive firm that cannot maintain the belief that output has no limits, for demand reasons.[22] In monopolistic competition, the perceived demand curve is introduced in order to explain adjustments to equilibrium; the question arises whether the firm is supposed to perceive demand correctly at equilibrium only, or whether information of the full schedule is necessary (this is dealt with in more detail in Section 4.4 and in Appendix F).[23]

Despite Hicks's undermining the bridge from Marshall to Chamberlin by exposing the problem of uncertainty, construction went forward. In fact, Hicks played a double role for the reason that his critique of the apparatus of the falling demand curve goes with a defense of the sufficiency of the perfect competition and the monopoly models for the analysis of markets, and consequently he stands for Marshall's dichotomy (Stigler's view is more clearly so). But, meanwhile, since he comes to subsuming competition under general equilibrium, his criticism of imperfect competition was without consequence, even in his own research.[24] This time Triffin advances to underpin the argument with the Walrasian framework, so that we come circling back from Marshall to Walras.

3.2.2 From Chamberlin to Walras

Triffin's role was to draw the logical consequences of what he thought was the main contribution of monopolistic competition theory, the interdependence of firms:

As soon as substitutability becomes imperfect, each competitor may choose to charge either a higher or a lower price than any of his rivals. Although the range of freedom may be more or less narrow, this is only a matter of degree. Monopolistic competition throws us into the stream of general competitiveness between non-homogeneous products. In kind, the theoretical problems to be dealt with will be the same, no matter the degree of that heterogeneity, no matter whether the firms would be classified as belonging to the same or different industries. Particular equilibrium methodology is no longer of any help. We may just as well face immediately the problem of general economic interdependence, as presented by Walrasian theory, rather than sacrifice generality without being rewarded by any gain either in simplicity or in definiteness. (Triffin 1940, p. 86; see also pp. 3, 88).

That is to say, the argument goes that given the theoretical difficulties of confining an industry, the abandonment of partial equilibrium analysis was thought theoretically inadequate and 'the general theory of economic interdependence has to be constructed so as to encompass interrelations among all firms in an economy' (Negishi 1987, p. 535). This solution, by pushing the argument forward for the sake of generality, goes at the high cost of rendering meaningless the concepts upon which he bases the argument. Triffin is not referring to firms and to industries, these are only 'dummy' indices; even the concept of a firm may not withstand his critique to the question of the group, for with general product heterogeneity it seems that only the single unit fits; moreover, Triffin fails to realize that rivalry is an empty concept in his purely virtual construct of purely virtual competitiveness; and his reference to the Walrasian theory seems misplaced, since in general equilibrium analysis there is no direct awareness of competition, or choice of 'a higher or a lower price' by competitors, only of a central market-maker.

However, the consequences of Triffin's purification of price theory were profound. 'Modern theories of monopolistic competition and general equilibrium such as Negishi (1961), ... Arrow and Hahn (1971), ... should be seen in this historical perspective' (Negishi 1987, p. 535). Thus, there is a deflection towards general equilibrium, which certainly eventually came to hamper the development of standard economics along the Marshallian tradition (cf. Weintraub 1991; also Leijonhufvud 1974).[25]

Markets (the group, or industry, in Triffin's words) are entirely dispensed with for theoretical purposes and relegated to empirical observation:

In the restricted place where it is now confined, the concept of group, or industry, acquires a significance entirely foreign to the significance it had with the classicists. ... It is now seen to be merely the outcome of an empirical investigation, a summary of factual findings. It does not give us any additional knowledge. It opens no avenue to theoretical reasoning. All it does is to crystallize into convenient moulds the results of our market observations. (Triffin 1940, p. 89; see also p. 188).

Theory and factual analyses are compartmentalized (Triffin 1940, p. 189). Theory, being drawn from arbitrary assumptions, is unsuited to the analyses of the variety of concrete cases; therefore, their individual aspects would be more advantageously analyzed with attention to relevant factual information and less to general theory. Our criticism is very much in line with Triffin's coherent concluding remark that '[t]he present stage of pure theory appears undoubtedly very formal, lacking in concrete content and practical significance' (ibid., p. 189). It is a sad, though unsurprising, outcome that no place for a theory of markets would be left, and that industry analyses would be deprived of guidance from the existent standard price theory. General equilibrium can only go together with individual actors, consumption and production units, so that interactions in the economy conflate to a single marketplace (where multiple or general coincidence of wants is obtained by way of a synchronized direct multilateral barter exchange); in fact, the assessment of the logistics of trade is not easy, and may be rather long-drawn-out (see Section 4.3.3.1, below). Markets as organized by traders in order to facilitate exchange disappear, and with them vanishes the concern with the flows of information and the logistics of exchange.[26] At this time, there was no recognition that general equilibrium in the Walrasian mode left no room for any market arrangement but that provided by an 'auctioneer', and that this implied sidetracking any assessment of intermediaries in markets and, hence, adherence to centralized coordination of exchange. This was not so in Marshall's discussion of the competitive industry, where there is a crucial role for intermediaries (merchant-middlemen), which is to relay information among firms in the industry and consumers (although the role of the firm was not integrated in the working of the market). They hold inventories, place orders and attend to the bargaining process. The role of trader agents, or of firms, in creating markets so organized as to allow for the working of competition, may be the starting point in bridging the void among individuals in the market.

Triffin's endeavor to deliver a general theory, or as Fisher (1989, pp. 117–18) puts it 'generalizing, as opposed to exemplifying', may very well be perfectly legitimate. In fact, there is no general theory explaining the 'context' in which agents act and how markets operate (although the possibility of building such a general theory is an open question). Theories of monopoly, monopolistic competition, as well as all breeds of oligopoly, rely on stripped-down constructions that do not allow for generalizations. Triffin's apparent success in providing a general theory came, though, at a high cost, of totally doing without such context, of clearing any meaningful allusion to institutional settings, unless we are prepared to accept the 'Walrasian institutional setting' as such.[27] Be that as it may, we might indict Triffin for outlining the obituary of markets in standard price theory.

All could be just an outgrowth of the manner in which static theory of pricing would have to evolve if theoretical purification were ever to be attained. Why pay attention to context in formal static general equilibrium analysis? The case is different in models where 'timing and information structure faced by firms' require 'constructing' (Fudenberg and Tirole 1987, p. 176). Understanding adjustment processes quite possibly begs the definition of context and can only be worked out along such lines.

3.3 EQUILIBRIUM STATES AND ADJUSTMENT PROCESSES

Price theory evolved from the 1930s onwards in a misguided way and this is mainly due to the confinement of economic analysis to equilibrium configurations. The logical completeness of the general equilibrium approach was as much a challenge as a promising basis to frame the research agenda, and this may explain its overriding acceptance as the profession's canon. However, a derived result may have been that this predominance in focus gained currency due to a 'subtle point,' according to Weintraub (1985, p. 129): 'Specifically, perhaps the *focus* on equilibrium can lead an economist to a belief that equilibrium positions are the important states to investigate' (cf. Fisher 1983, Introduction).[28, 29]

These analyses played their role and therefore are important, no doubt, but basic assumptions and technical apparatus devised to comprehend questions of equilibrium, are not the right ones to tackle other questions of interest, namely those we are proposing to study, adjustment processes in a decentralized economy.

I am not interested in reconstructing the whole sequence of developments in price theory. The only aspect to be investigated is how the way to a refinement in economic analysis overtook some previous lines of research that are of interest to our topic. As seen above, Triffin is of interest here. His work conflates a trend towards such a restricted state of affairs. Exploring contradictions in Chamberlin's work, and setting the analysis of monopolistic competition in Walrasian terms, he helps subdue the Marshallian tradition.

The interest here is not documenting evolution of the general equilibrium approach from Walras and the Austrian tradition on to the Arrow–Debreu model; this is a marginal aspect to this study. The evolution we are dealing with is one that comes from Marshall to Chamberlin and Joan Robinson and then to a dead end. If Triffin's role was of recasting this tradition into a general equilibrium framework, it reflects also the vanishing of an interest in 'competition' and markets. As Hayek put it,

> what the theory of perfect competition discusses has little claim to be called 'competition' at all ... The reason for this seems to me to be that this theory throughout assumes that state of affairs already to exist which, according to the truer view of the older theory, the process of competition tends to bring about (or to approximate) and that, if the state of affairs assumed by the theory of perfect

competition ever existed, it would not only deprive of their scope all the activities which the verb 'compete' describes but would make them virtually impossible. (Hayek 1948, p. 92).

A complementary question regards the above-hinted fact that the study of adjustment processes requires a broadening of fundamental assumptions. Or better, it requires that some fundamental assumptions common to the Arrow–Debreu model be given a different, we would say more concrete, form. These fundamentals are knowledge and markets.

In order to understand adjustment processes of individual agents in a competitive economy (which fits into prevailing economics as adjustment to equilibrium positions, and is usually studied under stability of equilibrium), the logic of the Arrow–Debreu model is not the right choice. Assumptions on information ('full relevant knowledge') and on how individual choices are coordinated 'in interrelated markets' may have enough content in the study of interdependence in a static world as in Arrow–Debreu general equilibrium (cf. Weintraub 1985, esp. p. 109), but not so in adjustment situations. Arrow (1959) raised the question of knowledge but he did not notice that his question begged another one with respect to markets. In disequilibrium, uncertainty springs up in a deeper (no more one single price) and broader (it overflows to other variables, prices are not sufficient information for decision-taking) form that can only be made sense of in the case of non-brokered markets. Otherwise, in centralized markets such uncertainty is vacuous and the problem of adjustment has a narrower interest in theoretical terms. Thus, markets are due some content, which Arrow–Debreu models dispense with.

From this broad picture, two lines of inquiry arise. One is to explain how inattention to markets evolved, as well as to show how exercises on price adjustment were proposed and solved without regard to this logical gap, that in disequilibrium states, information and market arrangements need content; another is to explain how agents and markets would work in adjustment situations.

NOTES

1. In fact, the wording Walras uses is 'perfectly organized', but this should probably be avoided on grounds of misleading connotations, which however were not present before the 1920s.
2. Beyond space, Marshall emphasizes the element of time in the working of a market, and he distinguishes temporary equilibrium (market period), the short-run and the long-run, the first where supply is fixed (stocks offered for sale are a given), the second where supply is variable given capacity, and the third where capacity is adjustable.
3. On the institutional basis for the analyses by Walras and Marshall, see Kregel (1992; 1995) and Walker (1997b). Kregel's interpretation is deficient with regard to Walras, and at points totally wrong, as Walker shows.

4. However, the exposition based on demand price and supply price as the variables to be equated in order to define equilibrium, stands coherently with his view of markets of interest to investigate.

5. The definition of supply price is the following: 'the price required to call forth the exertion necessary for producing any given amount of a commodity may be called the supply price for that amount, with reference of course to a given unit of time' (Marshall 1920, p. 338); or, as to normal supply price, 'this is the price the expectation of which will just suffice to maintain the existing aggregate amount of production' (ibid., p. 343).

6. Cournot assumes the market demand function ($F(p)$) is continuous, and that 'the variations [of demand with price] will be of opposite signs, *i.e.*, an increase in price will correspond with a diminution of the demand.' (Cournot 1838, pp. 49–50).

7. Since Marshall was dealing with a particular market in isolation, he could show that if the commodity offered in exchange could be assumed to display constant marginal utility (money or 'income'), the final rate of exchange (equilibrium price) would be independent of the path through which equilibrium is reached (cf. Marshall 1920, pp. 334–6, and Appendix on Barter, p. 793). On this, and other aspects regarding the attainment of market period equilibrium, see Kregel 1995, esp. pp. 461–3.

    A detailed analysis of the assumptions on which adjustments are explained in Walras and Marshall is presented in Kregel (1992); special attention is paid to the question of time and false trading during the market day, to conclude that '[w]ith respect with these problems of time, there is really very little difference between Marshall and Walras. They both use the same assumptions and their analysis produces the same results. The more interesting point is that Marshall's analysis shows the extent to which it is meaningless to discuss "equilibrium" price in continuous auction markets and the importance of intermediaries in such markets, while Walras' analysis seems to suggest that intermediaries are imaginary constructions which can be dispensed with in reality.' (ibid., p. 543). Notice, however, Walker's (1997b) characterization of the Paris Bourse at the time of Walras, which is critical of Kregel's.

8. See Leijonhufvud (1993, p. 9), who considers that 'the market for a produced good has to have two servo-mechanisms – one regulating price, the other output. Such a Marshallian market might be represented by two differential equations: (1) the rate of change of prices as a function of excess demand, and (2) the rate of change of output as a function of excess supply price'.

9. The discussion is worded in terms of sellers, the fact that they are possibly the same people as the producers being theoretically irrelevant here: 'The amount which each farmer or other seller offers for sale at any price' (Marshall 1920, p. 332). We are concerned with functions, not people.

10. This is an implication of Marshall having 'assumed provisionally to be true both of finished goods and of their factors of production, of the hire of labour and of the borrowing of capital' that: 'though everyone acts for himself, his knowledge of what others are doing is supposed to be generally sufficient to prevent him from taking a lower or paying a higher price than others are doing.' (Marshall 1920, p. 341).

11. 'Even in the corn-exchange of a country town on a market-day the equilibrium price is affected by calculations of the future relations of production and consumption; while in the leading corn-markets of America and Europe dealings for future delivery already predominate ... Anticipations of [a] rise in [price] exercise an influence on present sales for future delivery, and that in its turn influences cash prices; so that these prices are indirectly affected by estimates of the expenses of producing further supplies.' (Marshall 1920, pp. 337–8). On this, see Tricou 1994, esp. pp. 43–6.

12. Samuelson (1947, p. 264, n), first published in 1941, points out the 'historical error' of attributing to Walras and Marshall the indication of stability conditions 'in alleged contrast'. He observes that Marshall 'as far back as in *The Pure Theory of Foreign Trade*' defined stability in similar terms to Walras (a formal presentation of which the author makes on pp. 266–7); and the same opinion had been offered in Hicks (1939/1946, p. 61). Samuelson bases Marshall's adjustment in the theory of normal price on the obvious fact that 'the quantity supplied is assumed to adjust itself comparatively slowly' (Samuelson 1947, p. 264). However, he fails to establish the broader similarity between the two authors, only

because no attention was paid to the effect on adjustments of the distinction between exchange and supply. (Notice the parenthetical note on p. 270: 'This rules out in the beginning cases II ["Marshallian stability conditions require that quantity increases when demand increases in every case" (ibid., p. 264)] and IV [case of Marshall's *Foreign Trade*]'. This note refers to Hicks' stability conditions that an increase in demand increases price, and can be read as an indication that Samuelson may have been misled by Hicks.)

    In fact, the same mistake appears in Hicks (1939/1946, p. 62, n), who states that Marshall's stability condition is more appropriate to conditions of monopoly than to perfect competition. Furthermore, on what basis does this sentence by Hicks apply? 'In deciding to treat the general theory of exchange before dealing with production, we are following the example of Walras rather than Marshall.' (ibid., p. 57).

13. Let us quote these sentences from Samuelson (1947), which though drawn from a welfare reasoning, are nonetheless meaningfully innocent of the marketor role in the determination of prices: 'although each individual in pure competition takes price as given, for the market it is a variable', and '[t]he only distinguishing feature of pure competition, as compared to any other mode of behavior, is that the market conditions facing each individual are taken (by him) to be 'straight lines' involving trade at unchanging price ratios.' (Samuelson 1947, p. 204).

    Notice this comment by Kornai and Martos (1981, p. 44) on Samuelson's dynamic price formula: 'For Samuelson price changes over time are functions of excess demands. But he does not specify how the magnitude of excess demand is determined or estimated by market participants'.

14. In fact (cf. Weintraub 1985, Chapter 6), the development of ideas that proved conducive to the eventual formalization of general equilibrium analysis in the Arrow–Debreu–McKenzie models, gathered initial moment with the influence of Cassel's *The Theory of Social Economy* (1918/1932) upon a circle of Viennese economists, namely Karl Menger, Abraham Wald, Karl Schlesinger and Oskar Morgenstern. Meanwhile, by way of lectures at Princeton by the mathematician J. von Neumann (and his subsequently obtaining a permanent position there), and a 'westward movement' of Austrian economists to the United States around 1937 (Wald, Menger, Morgenstern, Tintner), this research program eventually combined with the ongoing 'studies on the general theory of economic measurement' at the Cowles Commission – which Kenneth Arrow (among others) joined by 1947.

    In the 1940s '[g]eneral equilibrium was in the air', however largely due to the influence of Hicks's rendering in his *Value and Capital* (1939) to English-speaking economists of the value theory of Pareto (and Walras) with a view to its application to dynamic problems of capital.

    Finally, with the *Theory of Games and Economic Behavior* by von Neumann and Morgenstern (1947) and its generalization by Nash (1950) to the *n*-person equilibrium, together with the development of activity analysis and programming, the ground was laid for the Arrow–Debreu–McKenzie models, which ensued in the early 1950s.

    For another account of this development, see Arrow 1968; for the contributions of K. Arrow and G. Debreu, see Feiwel 1987, esp. pp. 29–45 and Hildenbrand 1983, respectively.

15. See Morgenstern's (1941) review and strongly critical appraisal of the book. Young's (1991) survey on this and other early critiques is of interest.

16. Aggregative economics was molded into the general equilibrium framework; eventually, Lange (1945), Klein (1947), and Patinkin (1956) perfected this neowalrasian reconstitution.

17. The predominant attention to this subject was, according to Hicks, brought about mainly 'on grounds inherent in the development of economic theory itself' (Hicks 1935, p. 362), by which he meant both the interest in mathematical economics that 'turned attention back to the work of Cournot,' as well as concern about logical gaps in the work of Marshall.

    Cournot, who had adopted the monopoly solution as a starting point for the study of competition, based his analyses of markets on the behavior of the individual firm. This contrasts with the Marshallian tradition and is in line with the general equilibrium analyses of Walras and Pareto (Lausanne School).

18. Marshall's recourse to the 'representative' firm withdrew any meaning to the equilibrium of the firm, it just meant postulating equilibrium.

19. J. Robinson's demand curves were so vaguely defined that imperfect competition became in her construction indistinguishable from oligopoly. The demand curve shows what the firm will sell at each price when all other adjustments are complete: 'The demand curve for the individual firm may be conceived to show the full effect upon the sales of that firm which results from any change in the price which it charges, whether it causes a change in the prices charged by the others or not.' (J. Robinson 1933, p. 21).

20. There were two fundamental assumptions adhered to as a first step in the large-group analysis: first, '[i]t is required only that consumers' preferences be evenly distributed among the different varieties'; also, regarding the symmetry assumption as to the numbers problem, 'we assume *for the present* that any adjustment of price or of "product" by a single producer spreads its influence over so many of his competitors that the impact felt by anyone is negligible and does not lead him to any readjustment of his own situation.' (Chamberlin 1933, p. 83).

21. In its limited scope, the survey looks quite appropriate to today; see, for instance, Franklin Fisher's (1979) *Diagnosing Monopoly*, where Hicks (1935) is the only reference on the subject.

22. 'Whether competition is perfect or imperfect, the expansion of the individual firm will be stopped by factors which are purely subjective estimates ... by rising subjective costs, or costs of organization; ... by an estimated downward slope revenue curve. Objective facts give us no means of distinguishing between them' (Hicks 1935, p. 382). We are, however, interpreting Hicks's judgement in broad terms. His focus is on long-run equilibrium of the firm, and we are extending his rationale to the short-run decision problem – which is the one of interest to us, here.

23. Under the symmetry assumption, the perceived demand curve is obliterated, since no consideration is finally paid to the question of adjustment of the individual firm in isolation (cf. Chamberlin 1933, esp. pp. 89–93). Otherwise, if each competitive firm is observed facing a particular inference problem, uncertainty has to be dealt with. Arrow (1959) envisages the problem and poses the right questions. Uncertainty is pervasive since in the process of adjustment the individual demand curve is shifting while the firm is attempting to infer it; and in order to know the 'whole' demand curve (which is required of the 'now' monopolist as a profit maximizer), a premium is put on the acquisition of information, beyond that on the prices and quantities that the firm can itself gather (cf. Arrow 1959, pp. 46–7). But Arrow stops short of the question whether the demand curve is the real or a conjectured one.

    If the correct demand curve is, for whatever reason, deemed unknowable – for instance, the frequency of shifts or, (and consequently) experimental limitations, may prevent the monopolist from knowing present or lagged demand curves – the monopolist, in order to approach maximum profit, may have to make do with the adjustment of a conjectural demand curve (conjectured in the light of a sequence of sales and price data); this can be shown as tending toward the 'true' equilibrium (cf. Clower 1959).

    Nevertheless, more often than not, price adjustment is analyzed on the basis of certain information on the demand curve, be it that of the monopolist (e.g. Barro 1972) or of the competitive firm (e.g. Phelps and Winter (1970), where individual firms face a share-of-the-market demand curve; and the rate of change in each one's firm proportion of the total customers is a function of the moments of the (customer-weighted) distribution of other firms' prices; the element of subjectivity introduced being the 'simplification' of the objective law that determines customer flows, that a firm will only pay attention to the average market price.

24. See Hicks' *The Process of Imperfect Competition* for the 'assumption of a stationary state of demand for the products of the industry' (1954, p. 53) where '[i]t is assumed (for there is no advantage in assuming the contrary) that actual demand during the ... period coincides with expected demand.' (ibid., p. 43).

25. According to Weintraub (1991), a shift in the meaning of the word 'equilibrium' occurred, which may be traced in the works of Hicks, Samuelson, and Arrow–Debreu.

    'Hicks (1939) offers two images of "equilibrium." The first is associated with mechanics and is impersonal in tone (e.g., "in balance", "equally opposed forces"). The second brings to mind individuals acting as if in harmony with one another ... The first ...

speaks of a "market," and the latter of a "person"; ... the market equilibrium was associated with Marshall, whereas the more individualistic alternative was associated with Walras and Pareto' (Weintraub 1991, p. 100). 'That is,'[Hicks] believed that his method of analysis added a Marshallian dynamic theory to the static theory of Walras' (ibid., p. 101).

Also, according to Weintraub, Samuelson intervened and 'obliterated the distinction between equilibrium as a behavioral outcome and equilibrium as a mechanical rest point', 'for if one were careful in defining (mathematically) the notion of a static system, then both interpretations would collapse to a simple formal definition.' (ibid., p. 103). 'Indeed, from the standpoint of comparative statics, equilibrium is not something which is attained; it is something which, if attained, has certain properties.' (Samuelson 1947, p. 9).

Finally, with Arrow and Debreu 'the language is not "equilibrium *is* a supply–demand balance," but rather "when in equilibrium, supply and demand are in balance." ... The "supply–demand balance" is thus what remains of the older images of balance beams and forces. It serves, simply put, as a reference point for some fictitious market-maker to tell the players to keep on playing, for they are not yet coordinated. If, indeed, all agents were to get this information for themselves, from their own actions, then the supply–demand balance idea would not be associated with equilibrium except after the fact; that is, if the message "lack of coordination" could be triggered directly by the lack of harmony among agents' plans, and that message would lead to a revision of those plans in a self-correcting manner, then there would no longer be any need for the "market" to function as an information-dissemination device that says "keep on trading".' (Weintraub 1991, p. 107).

26. Rejected markets were adopted by the fledgling specialized discipline of industrial organization. Even though we should bear in mind that it is not methodologically unified, standard accounts commonly suffer from the same fault: firms and consumers are the basic elements of the analysis, the market in between conflated in an undefined way. Markets, and their intermediation structures, are sidetracked; that is to say, distribution channels and the structure of retail trade are not the objects of even cursory interest, in most accounts of them.

27. Triffin refers to Walrasian institution even though he is utterly unconscious of the clearing-house, central monitoring type of marketplace that his construction on the Walrasian foundation implies. Also, see Triffin's comment on methodology, regarding 'the claims and domains of "institutional" versus "theoretical" economics' (Triffin 1940, pp. 15–16).

28. This question arises in the sequence of several quotations of criticisms by 'Post-Keynesians' to the Arrow–Debreu–McKenzie equilibrium notion.

29. See Hahn (1970, p. 1) for stronger doubts about the attractiveness of the study of equilibria, and of the danger of restricting analyses to the refinement of equilibrium states, which possibility or likelihood of materializing is not even questioned. In this regard, Marshall's admonition is also of interest: 'The Statical theory of equilibrium is only an introduction to economic studies ... Its limitations are so constantly overlooked, especially by those who approach from an abstract point of view, that there is a danger in throwing it into definite form at all.' (Marshall 1920, p. 461).

4. On markets

In the previous chapter we have seen how standard price theory evolved from a Marshallian to a Walrasian perspective, and in the process became predominantly framed in the neowalrasian general equilibrium approach. The outgrowth of this graft of the analysis of competitive markets in a general equilibrium conceptualization was a dominant body of formal models whose unrelenting aim at 'perfection' was achieved at the cost of missing the empirical mark. The attention to equilibrium states with its concentration on proofs of existence, virtual stability and uniqueness, led the analysis of competitive markets, bargaining, feasibility of trading and, in general, of processes of adjustment to the sidelines of theoretical inquiry. This is the objective in this chapter: to gain some perspective on this state of affairs in general equilibrium analysis; to recognize the track by which it has come to a dead end; and to hint at possible ways to renew the program set forth by Walras, to describe how the mechanism of free competition in market models of empirical resemblance may help explain the generation of equilibrium in exchange.

To start with, a discussion of markets as institutional arrangements for the conduction of decentralized exchange is attempted. The importance of information and transaction costs for the formation of the institutions governing the pricing mechanism is stressed; both the emergence of the firm and of market arrangements should be explained, and not simply postulated. Coase's and others' views on markets are discussed, to conclude that a theory of intermediation and markets has not been provided to this day. Next, the 'missing markets' paradox is addressed. Our view that transaction costs should be called upon to explain the emergence and workings of market institutions contrasts with the 'missing markets' literature, which bases the non-existence of the markets that the general equilibrium theorist predicts, equally on transaction costs. The view here is that markets are to be 'explained in' the theory to start with, and that the general equilibrium theorist is mistaken in the use of the 'market' label: in the theory of general interdependence that the neowalrasian approach has devised, the theorist needs 'prices', but cannot miss markets for there is no place for these in the theory.

A broad classification of markets ensues, and the distinction between brokered and non-brokered markets serves as an empirical reference for the understanding of decentralized exchange. Next, decentralization is characterized according to features regarding information, the determination of the price signal, and logistics of trade. It is shown that the Arrow–Debreu model of general exchange fails as a decentralized mechanism when set against those features. Then, according to the tenets of the neowalrasian general exchange theory, the two functions implicitly ascribed to the central market organizer are considered separately. First, we look at the determination of the equilibrium price set and, second, to the execution of trading, presumed to occur at these predetermined prices. A summary review of existence, convergence and execution in the general equilibrium literature is conducted. This helps show the difficulties, first, in proving convergence to the equilibrium price set on the basis of decentralized information, and, second, in the analysis of execution of trading given a general equilibrium price set (assumed attained). The consistency of convergence, as well as of the execution of trading with predetermined equilibrium prices, has been hard to demonstrate. As the literature stands, attempts at dropping the functions assigned to the central market organizer and, therefore, at explaining exchange under decentralization assumptions, has been unsuccessful. Feasibility of trading at equilibrium prices has, however, been demonstrated when facilitating devices are introduced, like intermediation or a medium of exchange. That only for such cases the feasibility of execution of trading at predetermined equilibrium prices could be shown, may nevertheless help reveal the sterility of attempts to dichotomize pricing and trading as analytical exercises.

The unavoidable conclusion seems thus to be that the construction of a theory of general exchange may have to be redefined in such a way that existence is not supposed beforehand. This negative conclusion brings us back to the Walrasian program we started with, and a positive side of this is that our discipline has wide scope for progress in the understanding of decentralized exchange. Then, the obstacles that hinder the Walrasian program are highlighted and some basic reflections are expanded towards the consideration of bargaining and the logistics of trade in the process of attainment, and determination, of equilibrium in general exchange. Finally, the analysis of Arrow's (1959) *Toward a Theory of Price Adjustment* is attempted, to conclude that this singular account of the adjustments of price and quantity by firms in a competitive market in fact presumes a degree of centralization of information which does not allow this contribution to be submitted as a theory of adjustments in a decentralized economy.

4.1 MARKETS AS INSTITUTIONAL ARRANGEMENTS

In standard price theory, market stands as the organizational focus for the study of interdependence in exchange, the theoretical program of which dates back to Adam Smith's 'invisible hand'.[1] Demsetz describes the problem that the 'hand' is supposed to address as 'whether extreme decentralization leads to chaotic resource allocation'. Referring more to modern theory than to Smith, Demsetz then adds:

> Perfect decentralization is realized theoretically through assumptions guaranteeing that authority, or command, plays no role in coordinating resources. The only parameters guiding choice are those that are given – tastes and technologies – and those that are determined impersonally *on* markets – prices. All parameters are beyond the control of any of the model's actors or institutions, so these assumptions effectively deprive authority of any role in allocation. They are fully justified by the theory's remarkable yield – a compact, coherent, subtle yet simple model for deducing the equilibrium consequences of extreme decentralization of resource ownership. (Demsetz 1988, p. 160, italics added; cf. Arrow 1994, p. 4).

Despite some misplaced use of the notion of institution, as well as the hazy use of the notion of decentralization (see Section 4.3.1, below), Demsetz's point may be granted. What he presents is the bare bones of modern microeconomics: (i) firms as model 'agents', embodying parametrical technologies, and (ii) markets as institutions that impersonally determine prices. Firms maximize profit with no information, information processing or management costs. More from Demsetz:

> the model sets the maximizing tasks of the firm in the context in which decisions are made with full and free knowledge of production possibilities and prices. The worldly roles of management – to explore uncertain possibilities and to control resources consciously, where owners of such resources have a penchant for pursuing their own interests – are not easily analyzed in a model in which knowledge is full and free. 'Firm' in the theory of price is simply a rhetorical device adopted to facilitate discussion of the price system. (Demsetz 1988, p. 160–61).

Furthermore, allocation is obtained by means of an institution, markets in which no transaction costs are incurred by any agent. But, as we have seen above (Section 3.2), on these assumptions markets vanish from standard price theory to be left with only 'the general market', which can only be conceived as a common meeting point[2] where the allocation problem is impersonally solved to determine prices. Arrow's (1994, p. 4) answer to the question 'What individual has chosen prices?' in the general competitive equilibrium model is: 'In the formal theory, at least, no one. They are determined on (not by) social institutions known as markets, which equate supply and demand'. Like the firm, markets or the general market are properly envisioned in standard price theory as merely 'a rhetorical device', which for lack of being an actor could only be labeled as an institution; a similar comment about markets as 'a figure of speech' is proffered by Tobin (1980, p. 796). Since no agent can possibly solve the suggested coordination problem in this 'decentralized' setting, only some disembodied entity could be assigned that role. 'Institution' is as good a label as any other, it is just devoid of theoretical or empirical content.

It being granted that not all economic problems can be tackled with vacuous notions like 'the firm', and 'the institution' of markets, I propose to consider a further point, whether we can find a theoretical basis to understand the emergence and working of trading arrangements brought about by economic agents.

In general, my view is that both markets and firms are specialized coordination devices, respectively, the interfirm and the intrafirm modes. As Winter has stated the matter:

> Orthodox theory recognizes two aspects of the problem of coordinating economic activity, the interfirm aspect and the intrafirm aspect. Markets are shown to be the answer to the interfirm aspect. What the answer to the intrafirm aspect may be is not explicitly addressed but presumably it is contractually based authority of the 'entrepreneur'. However, since the functioning markets and the firm-qua-production sets are given data of the theory, there is no opportunity for an analysis of the division of labor between these two coordination modes. Hence, as Coase observed, there is no question of why markets do not do the coordinating that firms do, as no answer to the obverse question of why one big firm would not work as well as a market economy. In short, textbook orthodoxy provides no basis for explaining the organization of economic activity. (Winter 1991, pp. 182–3).

This raises two questions, one which Coase took up, the other which he passed by. The first question is *'which transactions would be organized by which mode of organization and why'* [3] (Williamson 1991, p. 7), and this can be addressed in terms of the comparative account of Coasian transaction costs[4] and the costs that will have to be incurred with alternative modes of coordination. This is a question of production management (or production allocation). Where are specific transactions relevant, in the market, the firm, or hybrid organization? That is to say, to what extent will costs be internalized? According to Coase, to answer this question 'we still have a long way to go' (Coase 1988a, p. 67). More to the point, we might ask why any of this is relevant anyhow; surely we economists need be concerned only with what goes on 'before' and 'after' output is produced, not with the particulars of production engineering or management.

Of course, this is altogether different from saying that Coase explained the existence of 'the firm'. In fact, Coase dealt only with the internal organization of the firm, i.e. the internalization of costs, and provided no foundation for explaining the emergence or existence of the firm, Coase's claim to the contrary (1937, p. 20; 1988b, p. 6; cf. Clower and Howitt 1997b, pp. 198 ff.); notice, however, that Coase's more recent view is different (1992, pp. 715–16). The firm is assumed to exist, and costs of coordination within or, alternatively, outside the firm (the price mechanism) are assessed. I think transaction costs are, in fact, crucial to explain the emergence of intermediation, and the organization of trading arrangements; but this may have to start from the analysis of the execution of exchange[5] (see Coase's

[1992, p. 716] mention of money as reducing search and transaction costs of barter exchange). Therefore, we cannot say that Coasian transaction costs added fresh content to the firm *as a theoretical entity.*

The second question is deeper. After transaction costs enter the analysis of the pricing mechanism and the firm is *ex hypothesi* introduced into the construction, can we still treat markets as given? And are the supposedly different entities, the market and the firm, theoretical primitives? [6] I think not (cf. Clower and Howitt 1997b, pp. 198 ff.; 1996, pp. 32–3).

For the sake of the argument, let us suppose that Coase's analysis could explain the existence of the firm. Having included transaction costs in his analysis, Coase is led to think of the firm in isolation from the price mechanism. Then we have a firm deciding[7] whether to carry out a transaction within the organization, or through the marketplace. The firm economizes on transaction costs and this allows for the definition of the scope of its activities, internalizing transactions otherwise carried out through the open market or through another firm. On this procedure markets are assumed, not explained, not integrated in a theoretical construction built upon transaction costs. There is an organized market out there through which the firm can sell its product, or from which it can obtain desired inputs. Simply put, Coase gives us no theory of markets, no account at all; and without an explanation of markets, which Coase mistakenly treats as pre-existing the creation of firms, he lacks a necessary foundation for his treatment of the emergence of firms.

4.1.1 Coase on Markets

A note on Coase's view on markets is due at this point. My first contention is that all of Coase's writings – as well as the major part of the literature that has sprung up from his insights – are centered in production rather than exchange (see *The Nature of the Firm* [1937], the Introduction to *The Firm, the Market, and the Law* [1988b], his [1988a] reflections in Williamson and Winter [1991], and his 1992 lecture). Moreover, Coase treats markets as organized markets in the fashion of the Chicago Mercantile Market or the London wheat market. As to the first aspect, his explanation of how his approach 'succeeded in linking up organization with cost' (Coase 1988a, p. 47) mainly involves the consideration of production activities of the firm. Much more significant, though, is his discussion of weaknesses in *The Theory of the Firm* (cf. Coase 1988a, p. 67). Let me put it this way: if transaction costs are considered, and firms are formed so that costs of conducting transactions through the market are thereby avoided – i.e. 'if the costs avoided were greater than the costs that would be incurred by the firm in coordinating the activities of the factors of production' – then certain transactions are carried out within the firm; and their inclusion in the internal organization of production *replaces* the market. Coase acknowledges that he did not try to indicate determining factors of that choice between organization within the firm or through the market; he just invoked grounds for the reasonable assumption that costs of coordinating factors of production within the firm could often be presumed comparatively lower. Furthermore, in order to cope with such limitations, Coase raised the need for a theory to explain 'what the institutional structure of production will be. That depends on which firms can carry out this particular activity at the lowest cost and this is presumably largely determined by the other activities that the firms are undertaking' (Coase 1988a, p. 67); yet, he admits in *The Institutional Structure of Production* (1992, p. 718) that his lack of indication of such 'factors' has made it difficult for others to incorporate transaction costs in such a way as to support construction of a satisfactory theory. Coase's focus throughout has been not the organization of markets by firms but the organization of production within firms.

My second contention is that Coase focuses too much on organized commodity exchanges and too little on commonplace entrepreneurial market-creating activities. Despite Coase's statement that '[t]he provision of markets is an entrepreneurial activity' (Coase 1988b, p. 8), his consideration of exchange revolves around organized markets. Markets are organized by traders in order to reduce transaction costs, be it 'fairs and markets' or 'commodity exchanges and stock exchanges', and only as an approximation to such 'perfect markets', is decentralized exchange called forth (ibid., pp. 8–10). Institutions are set up that require not only 'the provision of physical facilities' but more importantly 'the establishment of legal rules governing the rights and duties of those carrying out transactions in these facilities' (ibid., p. 10[8]). Nonetheless, Coase's view in his Nobel lecture (1992) is well balanced: 'It makes little sense for economists to discuss the process of exchange without specifying the institutional setting within which trading takes place', as is the case 'when trading takes place outside exchanges (and this is almost all trading) and where the dealers are scattered in space and have very divergent interests, as in retailing and wholesaling' (Coase 1992, p. 718[9]).

It being granted that Coase's explanation of *The Nature of the Firm* is weakened by his presumption that markets pre-exist the creation of firms, then in order to carry the argument to its logical completion, we should dismiss the assumed presence of the open market and explain its emergence in a decentralized economy. If we are to explain the emergence of markets as created and maintained by specialized agents, we complete the whole construction with 'firms' that are market-makers. The existence of 'markets' does not precede the 'firm's' existence, both have the same origin in the activities of agents who incur costs in order to reduce transaction costs in exchange.

'Markets are institutions that exist to facilitate exchange, that is, they exist in order to reduce the cost of carrying out exchange transactions' (Coase 1988b, p. 7), but they do not pre-exist exchange transactions. They are created by means of specialized agents, who make or devise market arrangements to earn income as the condition for their activity to succeed or survive.

4.1.2 Set-up Transaction Costs and Intermediation

In a decentralized economy, markets have to be explained and not just taken as unquestioned presuppositions. A first step toward explanation is to ask how exchange might be organized so as to be less 'clogged and embarrassed in its operations' (Adam Smith 1776, Bk.1, Chapter 4, 1–2 [10]). This is addressed in Alchian (1977), Chuchman (1982), and in Clower (1977; 1994a; 1995b), Clower and Friedman (1986) and Clower and Howitt (1996). The essential point in all these papers is that the emergence of intermediation in exchange depends crucially on the existence of set-up transaction costs, i.e. costs that are in large measure independent of quantities traded. The existence of such costs not only creates a reason for middlemen to emerge, but also encourages the provision by middlemen of specialized trading services. That is to say, set-up transaction costs not only explain the emergence of market arrangements but also explain why particular kinds of specialization ('monetary exchange') are a ubiquitous characteristic of every ongoing market economy.

An explanation of the role of transaction costs in intermediation is first attempted in Hirshleifer's *Exchange Theory: The Missing Chapter* (Hirshleifer 1973; and also 1980, Chapters 7 and 8). Hirshleifer shows that proportional exchange costs create a gap between the selling and buying prices of prospective transactors, and hence *room* for intermediation. The gap 'can be thought of as the price of "middleman" services' which 'are assumed to be competitively supplied', so that, in general equilibrium, 'the implied gap G must be such that middlemen are induced to provide exactly the requisite quantity of [demand for middleman services]' (Hirshleifer 1973, pp. 135, 137).

This point is more clearly treated in Demsetz (1968). He asks whether transaction costs are affected by the scale of trading in the New York Stock Exchange (NYSE). In the transaction cost he includes brokerage fees and ask–bid spreads; the latter are paid to specialized intermediates '[t]o cover the cost of standing ready ... to sell or buy at stated prices immediately upon receipt of a matching order'. Middlemen provide a service of 'immediacy': 'If buy orders and sell orders could be counted upon to arrive simultaneously, ... there would be no demand for the services of persons to stand ready and waiting' (Demsetz 1968, pp. 36–7). The ask–bid spread of intermediated exchange (by brokers or specialists, though we need not consider risk-taking here) will be comprised between two (theoretical) equilibrium points, which make an ask–bid spread of non-intermediated exchange. One is the equilibrium ask price, determined between 'those who desire immediate purchases' and 'those who stand ready and waiting to sell to those who demand immediate servicing of their purchasing orders'. Another is the equilibrium bid price, defined in a similar way. Among Demsetz's conclusions, the most important is that the time rate of transactions, by lowering the cost of waiting, is the main influence on the reduction of spreads in the NYSE, which is 'a *form* of scale economies' on trading in a particular security (ibid., p. 41).

But, having provided room for intermediation, Hirshleifer then seems to fail to propose a reason for the comparative advantage of intermediated exchange as provided by middlemen. A possible reason might be, for instance, any 'technological' advantage on their supply of intermediation services, which we might think of as reducing the proportional cost[11], and thus would allow for a reduction of the lag as compared with the unassisted barter situation. This is not contradicted in his argument, but there is no explicit recognition of the question.

Furthermore, Hirshleifer explains the emergence of stocks of inventories of transacted goods when 'costs of exchange take the form of a fixed lump-sum *charge per transaction*' (1980, p. 246)[12], and '[a]s before, some individuals will find it advantageous to use some or all of their resources to provide middleman services' (1973, p. 141). Corresponding to this lump-sum character of exchange costs is the bunching of acquisitions and sales (and, as a consequence, holding of inventories). This creates a demand factor for intermediation, even in a world of perfect information of trading partners and their offers: if we assume a given dispersion of endowments among individuals, a buyer benefits from bunched purchases and sales, thus saving on fixed costs of exchange.

Therefore, for intermediation to emerge, we may need either a technological advantage of intermediated supply or set-up transaction costs, independently of the consideration of another factor also involving fixed costs, e.g. imperfect information, which is beyond the case considered by Hirshleifer. Hirshleifer makes room for intermediation in the case of proportional costs of exchange but he fails to discuss the benefits brought about by middlemen in this case; we might then tentatively propose that, in order to explain intermediation and markets, we need set-up costs of exchange of informational nature.

4.1.3 Missing Markets

I presume that Hirshleifer is absolutely right on 'missing' exchange, but he takes markets for exchange. He seems to mix the question of existence of markets due to the presence of transaction costs, with the (observable) effect of changes in the magnitude of such costs on the survival of markets, and thus is mistaken in concluding that 'given that trading costs exist, markets can easily disappear or become non viable' (1980, p. 245).[13] Once lump-sum costs of transacting are brought into the picture, a change in perspective is required. It is relevant here to mention an apparent contradiction between the view in Clower and Howitt (1996) and Coase (cf. Coase 1992, p. 716), and the literature on 'missing markets' (cf. Hahn 1989a, esp. pp. 1–2). The first view is that the existence of set-up costs of transaction fosters the emergence of markets – so organized by traders as to economize on such costs. In contrast, the literature on missing markets argues that the existence of set-up costs explains the non-existence of markets – as provided by godly decree. As Arrow puts it, '[t]ransaction costs are the costs of running the economic system', which 'in general impede and in particular cases completely block the formation of markets' (Arrow 1969, p. 48; from Williamson 1987, p. 590).

Hahn refers to 'gaps in the traditional theory. In particular, it is now widely recognized that it postulates there to be many more markets ... than we observe. "Missing markets" lead to reformulations and questions. The economy has to be studied as one in which there is trading at every date' (Hahn 1989a, p. 1; cf. Starr 1997, p. 193). More specifically, Hahn notes that 'the more finely time is divided, the more goods and transaction dates there are. If we had allowed for set up costs (and increasing returns), we could argue that to have markets at every t for all goods dated $t' \geq t$ must always use more resources when time is more finely divided. In that case one may be able to show that in any equilibrium many markets will be inactive' (Hahn 1971, p. 436; see also 1973a, pp. 15–16). But this only begs the question of why they should be active in the first place. However, before this question is tackled two comments are in order. First, without explicit consideration of the logistics of exchange[14] there are no *a priori* grounds to believe that an Arrow–Debreu economy where all contracts, for present and future exchange, are carried out at a single date, involves a smaller number of contacts (both contracts and transactions) than one with contracting at every date. Second, that markets may vanish, as have brokered markets in case of hyperinflation, is an empirical fact that is good to explain, but is not the same question as this one. Here the question is why do we see markets to start with, not why exchange in some dynamic juncture may suffer certain adaptations, which compromises the viability of a market. In any case, let us attempt an explanation inspired by Demsetz (1968). To begin with, let us assume that transaction costs have a lump-sum component. If we imagine a world without specialized intermediation in exchange (e.g. commodities or securities markets), in case of increased uncertainty in hyperinflation conditions, the willingness of traders to stand ready to meet counteroffers to trade immediately (cf. Demsetz 1968, pp. 35–7) would be drastically reduced, so that the (theoretical) spread between the (unassisted, or non-brokered) equilibrium ask price and the equilibrium bid price could contract to such a degree that it would lie within the bid–ask spread that pays for the survival of brokers. The organized market is, therefore, compromised. (A broader and deeper explanation is summarized in Leijonhufvud 1995, pp. 1506 ff., referring to Heymann and Leijonhufvud 1995.)

Be that as it may, the aforementioned distinction between the literature on 'missing markets' and the view here is simply false. One perspective is that the world, as envisioned in its purity, should conform to the needs of the theorist (its creator); if we lack a few prices, and consequently a few markets where they presumably would be asserted, then (an oversight by the theorist?) some factor must explain that omission: transaction costs, i.e. 'the costs of operating markets themselves' (Starr 1997, p. 193 [15]). The other view is that the economy is opaque to individual traders, and that we attempt to bring some order to what we perceive in it. If we have markets at all then we must think in the first place that their working is paid for by costs they supersede; and the costs we can make sense of for their emergence are set-up transaction costs.

There is a more interesting implication of this argument. Everything would be just right if, instead, we talked about 'missing exchanges' (or even, with a different meaning, 'missing prices'). The trivial fact that transaction costs of the set-up type reduce the volume of transactions, has nothing to do with markets, or impediments to their functioning. If transaction costs were absent why would any organization of trade be necessary, what would trading posts, and specialists, merchants or even brokers be doing there?

The economy envisioned in Debreu's account of general equilibrium analysis relies on m entities who maximize utility by planning a set of trades *given* the accounting (numeraire) prices of n commodities, for t market dates in a single 'general market'; ignoring contingencies and locations, we have $((n-1) \times t)$ exchange rates. For aggregate consistency of plans, prices must be the same for all prospective transactors, and for this it is also convenient that they be given independently of the quantities proffered for trade, and known; independently of the specifics of the logistics of trade, we might accept that the $((n-1) \times t)$ prices are freely known and adhered to in exchange. Now, in a world without transaction costs, it is a matter of indifference whether there is centralized multilateral barter (cf. Jaffé, ed. 1954, Lesson 12; Hicks 1939/1946, pp. 58 ff.: 'multiple exchange'; Patinkin 1965, esp. pp. 11–12, 36–8), or a set of $(n (n-1) / 2 \times t)$ trading posts, at each of which the individuals may trade two commodities (cf. Jaffé, ed. 1954, pp. 157–60); or simply presume that pair-wise or larger combinations of individuals, can somehow meet and conclude desired barter (spot or future, alike) transactions as a kind of 'do it magically' affair! After all, if every aspect of trading activity (search for prospective opposite parties, bargaining and closing deals) is truly costless to prospective transactors, intermediation of any kind serves no purpose that is worth paying for, so it will not be provided (neither is it needed), so literally anything would be admissible in 'the organization of trade'.[16] In a world without transaction costs there is no room for any notion that could have any resemblance to the markets we know in experience (cf. Clower 1995a, p. 312, n, commenting on Hahn's 1973a, p. 15 'empirical confrontation'). We might see multilateral barter, successive encounters in trading posts, pair-wise meetings of each with everyone else in any fashion our wildest fancies might suggest (cf. e.g. Ostroy 1973; Diamond 1982a and 1984a; Kiyotaki and Wright 1989; Aiyagari and Wallace 1991). Therefore, in the absence of any goal, the problem of 'missing markets' is a shot in the dark.

We could acknowledge that in a world with transaction costs there is economic incentive for lumps of intermediation to shape amorphous exchange. In this light, the proposition that transaction costs prevent the proper crystallization of trade in organized markets is unsound. (The wonder is that the amorphous mass has gained some shape, not that crystals don't pervade the universe.) Markets are to be explained in, not explained out, for without set-up transaction costs there is no reason to have them to start with.

If something is missing that the theorist needs, this is prices as given to traders. This is clear from Hahn (1971, pp. 430–31): 'many markets will be inactive in an equilibrium', but 'one is asked to suppose that prices are established for all possible markets, active or not'; also 'adjustment without prices (markets)' (Hahn 1982, p. 746). But if we believe that this is the right state of affairs, to explain consistency of plans for a given common price set, then we are constructing our theory as if it were based on a certain sort of ideal brokered market, where traders know current *market* prices (spot or future, alike) and use this as a signal to issue their decisions to trade.

4.2   BROKERED AND NON-BROKERED MARKETS: SOME GENERAL CONSIDERATIONS

The objective here is to lay some basis for the understanding of the working of decentralized markets, the interest of which stems from the difficulty to answer 'such basic questions as who sets prices and under what motivation, and why transaction-quantities are determined the way they are' (Howitt 1986, p. 77).

Standard microeconomic theory is founded upon a fictional market arrangement derived from a cleaned-up version of Walras's theory of exchange without bargaining, and 'naturally' without disequilibrium trading, i.e. as an auction that precedes actual trading. The adjustment of prices, as orchestrated by the central auctioneer, is the only equilibrating mechanism, and equilibrium is ascertained as a matter of logic as a notional consistency of plans. There is no account of pricing or trading interactions among economic agents, and market organization is not considered; decentralized mechanisms of control are therefore of interest for the simple purpose of exploring an alternative to the established, empirically blind and theoretically obscure, foundation of standard economics.

Thus, a set of questions arises which will be the unifying line of our query, throughout: How are markets organized? Who creates and runs markets in a way that facilitates the interaction among the trading decisions of the economic individuals? That is to say: Who creates and runs markets in a way that the interaction among willing traders is rendered less costly than it would otherwise be if trading decisions of economic units were left to their unassisted endeavor to make double coincidence of wants and timing possible?

I believe that markets are not given and are costly to set up and to run. Therefore, bringing them in to an analysis of exchange begs the question of the benefits they purvey, or the opportunity costs they supersede. Robert Clower's *The Fingers of the Invisible Hand* (1994a) lays out a basis for understanding how self-interested economic agents may be led to specialize as middlemen and set up trade arrangements, whereby markets evolve and become so organized as to reduce both search costs and transaction costs of willing transactors. Otherwise, they would tend to be autarchic.

At this point our objective is humbler. Since there is no coherent view of the workings of markets, and only very tentative theoretical accounts have been advanced that may provide a basis toward the replacement of the neowalrasian fiction, we will be content only to identify market organizations of empirical relevance that may help us bring the question of decentralization to the fore.

A mass of literature, all factual, is available on the workings of markets, but no analytical basis can be sifted from it. Of interest in this regard is a classification of price-making mechanisms defined in R. Cassady's *Auctions and Auctioneering* (1967) and *Exchange by Private Treaty* (1974), who distinguishes take-it-or-leave-it administered pricing, private treaty pricing through negotiation, and competitive bid pricing (on this, see Appendix C, below).

On auctions, which are 'direct extensions of the usual forms of bilateral bargaining', theory is abundant (Wilson 1992, p. 228). However, specifically on dynamic double auctions ('bid–ask markets') to which commodity markets and some financial markets comply, little theoretical work has been accomplished (cf. ibid., p. 271 [17]). Among these we should notice Daniel Friedman (1984), Wilson (1987a[18]), and, on commodities exchanges, Working (1967), Telser (1967), and Telser and Higinbotham (1977). Development in this area has been chiefly motivated by experimental studies. As recent examples, notice Friedman and Ostroy (1995) on double auctions and Cason and Friedman (1997) on 'two-sided sealed auctions', and, for other references, see Wilson (1992, pp. 260–61). Among this growing literature, I would select Davis, Harrison and Williams (1993) where convergence to 'nonstationary' equilibria is studied, to conclude that double auctions tend to converge quite fast, and are relatively efficient.

Furthermore, it is most typical of financial markets for double auctions to be conducted by specialists 'who maintain inventories and order books of bids and offers in order to sustain continual trading opportunities and price stability' (Wilson 1992, p. 259). Factual references to securities exchanges can be found in Osborne (1965; 1977); for some theory, see Wilson (1992, pp. 255–6) and, for dealer quotation markets specifically, Reiss and Werner (1994, p. 6).

Some attempts at formalization on alternative intermediation contracts (merchants versus brokers) are found in Hackett (1992; 1993), though most refer to financial markets. Townsend (1978) is of interest, and a notable (more general) exception is Rubinstein and Wolinski (1987) on endogenous middlemen, as a 'time saving institution' as derived from a search theoretic basis.

Factual literature is also vast on non-brokered markets. On market places, studied especially by anthropologists and geographers, see Hill (1987) for references. On negotiated pricing, Cassady (1974) is an excellent reference. In contrast, the non-factual literature on non-brokered markets is meager, but a few remarkable exceptions attempt some theory (elements of which will be of great help in Appendix F, below, in order to give body and behavioral content to the 'market-maker'):[19] these include Okun (1981) on 'customer markets', Daniel Friedman (1989) on 'producers' markets', and Clower and Friedman (1986) on 'trade specialists'. The latter stands in a category of its own since it brings to life figures that take on the function of organizing and running bilateral exchange, i.e. specialist traders who, acting as middlemen, lead to a decentralized working of the market.

It should be evident that with regard to market organization, several types of markets of empirical relevance exist. Our goal now is to establish a broad distinction concerning the collection and dissemination of information as well as the degree of decentralization of the price signal. Two types of market organization of empirical relevance are sufficiently contrasted for our purpose, namely brokered markets and 'decentralized markets'.

First, we consider brokered markets, where trade is conducted through agents who gather information of offers to buy or sell and match transactors at their bidding and asking prices, so that the price at which each transaction takes place is announced to other traders and is therefore the 'running price' before a next transaction is completed at a different price. Such a ruling price is produced as a result of trading among buyers and sellers, although transactions are carried out through trader agents – brokers[20] – who trade on behalf of their customers. Buyers and sellers communicate their bidding and asking prices to brokers, and each broker has the possibility either of carrying out trades between his customer-buyers and customer-sellers (i.e. crossing buy and sell orders for his customers), or of dealing with any other broker that is an agent of a buyer or a seller, in order to match the orders given to him, to buy or sell, by his customers.

Attempting a general approximation, when a certain broker is on the market as a supplier he will attempt to trade with whoever has the highest bidding price, be it his or other brokers' customer-buyers; when he is arranging a purchase for a customer he will have a bid price and he will face asking prices by other brokers acting on behalf of their customer-sellers – he will take the lowest asking price so that he can obtain his commission (or otherwise make the largest margin).[21]

Several kinds of market exist that conform to this picture, although the characteristics and the degree of organization vary a lot. In all of them, however, the volume of trade may be such that it will seem to the individual participant that price is produced anonymously by the workings of the organized market. But this is only achieved either by means of auction, or set as a result of a bargaining process among a number of middlemen who at every moment concentrate a fraction of the information conveyed to the market by acting as agents or brokers (or otherwise, acting as trade specialists, merchants, or dealers who change their bidding and asking prices to take advantage of arbitrage or speculation opportunities).

Second, we consider 'decentralized' markets that lack any central mechanism of information-gathering and production. These are non-brokered markets where the matching of willing transactors is not provided by a specialized trading agent. And besides, where there is no ruling price, asking prices are posted by sellers and not a single buyer in the market has costless information about ongoing transaction prices. Transactions imply a search process for trading partners, for prices, or for other information.

As a familiar example, let us consider the case of an imaginary hamburger vendor called Old MacBurgher. Like his competitors, he opens his shop sometime in the morning and serves people at a price he has posted on a bright display over the cash register. Our consumer has an idea of the price paid on his last few visits and even has a fuzzy recollection of an advertisement on television some days before. On his way he also comes across some other hamburger vendors, the quality and price of which he has some expectation too. Anyway, he enters Old MacBurgher, pays the price and has a hamburger. Here, the asking price is also the transaction price and this is typical in customer markets. Other examples exist where transaction prices may vary from customer to customer, and a large fraction of trade may occur below the posted price. In some markets for homogeneous goods like, for instance, cement and some metal commodities, many transactions appear to fit this case; for some of these commodities two market systems coexist, organized exchanges for spot or future trading, and merchant trades, usually on a long-term supply contractual basis (see Hubbard and Weiner 1992).

Now let us look specifically to the degree of decentralization of the price signal. The price signal is the most commonly studied control mechanism in price theory, and the only one in the Walrasian tradition standard textbook (micro)economics is imbued with. I shall attempt a distinction regarding the origin of the price signal as a control mechanism in the workings of markets, which is intended to bear correspondence with the distinction above between brokered and 'decentralized' markets.

First, the price signals are formed by individual transactors, and no mechanism is available currently to transmit this information to other prospective transactors in the market. One example might be a market where individual transactors post their price for the good, and admit no negotiation. Another example is when (regardless of there being or not a posted price as a starting point) transaction prices are asserted as a result of communication and bargaining between prospective transactors; i.e., the information available to traders is obtained only by means of communication between transactors when a prospective transaction is meant to take place (or, alternatively, as a result of costly search). Either buyer and seller communicate bidding and asking prices to each other, or each individual trader posts an asking price and a bid price for the good(s) he is willing to sell or purchase, in the case of a bilateral market for the good.[22] Common to these pricing schemes is the pervasiveness of set-up costs: go to a familiar seller to avoid them.

Second, a price signal is produced by the participant transactors, in such a way that each transaction price becomes currently available to broker agents as well as to buyers and sellers (or at least to a subset of these, including specialist or middlemen traders).[23] Transaction decisions to buy or sell are therefore guided by this current 'running' price – so that this price works as a signal for transactors to decide on the bid or asking prices at which they are willing to buy or sell a certain quantity. One example is provided by the 'running' market price in relatively thick organized markets (see Appendix D, below). Even though the market may be atomistic, the control mechanism is not decentralized. In the first case, on the other hand, independently of how thick the market is, the control mechanism is decentralized: price signals are formed by individual transactors without guidance from currently communicated transaction prices – which is not to say, without knowledge of market conditions, or expectations about price(s) deemed relevant for their businesses.

Broadly, the first case is typical of non-brokered markets and the second of brokered markets. But such a stark distinction between brokered and non-brokered markets is only tentative. For further elaboration we need a clearer idea of decentralization.

4.3 DECENTRALIZATION OF EXCHANGE: INFORMATION AND FEASIBILITY

Next we analyze decentralization. First, decentralization is defined, and the Walrasian model of general (barter) exchange is characterized as the centralized model of reference. Second, we attempt to follow the common procedure of dropping the functions assigned to the central market organizer in the neowalrasian general market. One is the handling of the logistics of trade. The other is the finding of the equilibrium prices and its communication to traders. If we drop these functions of the auctioneer of providing costless 'disequilibrium coordination', and attempt to explain exchange in a decentralized setting, we end up in an impasse. Logical inconsistencies and analytical difficulties leave us with only a few threads aiming at a proposal to coherently understand decentralized exchange.

4.3.1 The Dimensions of the Decentralization Problem

Decentralization is not an established concept in economics. Hahn's (1970, p. 2) dissatisfaction seems to apply as much today: 'When we talk of decentralizing a plan we think of agents maximizing at given shadow prices and not of the design of decentralized information systems and responses which have only recently begun to be discussed'. As to the common view, reference is often made to 'decentralization of resource ownership' (Demsetz 1988, p. 160; in line with Debreu 1959, p. 79 and Arrow and Debreu 1954, p. 266). Other senses that are suggested by this one, but are more operative and may be conducive to substantiate Hahn's proposed aim, concern the following three aspects: information, the origin of the price signal, and logistics.

4.3.1.1 Informational decentralization

Decentralization of information happens when we allow only for a limited exchange of information among economic agents. Specifically, it comprises two elements:[24] One regards the 'initial dispersion of information', i.e. the nature of the information each trader is assumed to have prior to any market interaction is considered. Information about each trader's characteristics or situation (resource endowments, preferences, technologies) is private, and its communication is (too) costly.[25] And, therefore, decentralized information implies that each trader's net excess demands are private information. The second aspect regards 'limited communication', and has been called the 'privacy-preserving' property,[26] which implies that information of other agents' characteristics is only conveyed through explicit or 'formal' messages (cf. Calsamiglia and Kirman 1993, p. 1157). When two traders meet, communication to the other of each one's information on net excess demands, and/or proposed exchange rates comprises the sort of explicit or 'formal' messages that are relevant here. Or, as Hurwicz (1969, p. 514) puts it: 'This communication is accomplished in the competitive mechanism through bids (representing quantities supplied or demanded) and prices attached to those bids'. Limited communication precludes centralization of information, both the 'initial' information on endowments and preferences, as well as the proposed actions of all other traders, viz. their net excess demands. These two elements of decentralized information signify incomplete information, and this is common to brokered and non-brokered markets of empirical resemblance. These features of decentralized information do not imply, however, that knowledge is not 'complete' in the 'market', as Stigler, elaborating on Knight's assumptions of perfect competition, explains:

> Consider first complete knowledge. If each seller in a market knows any *n* buyers, and each seller knows a different (but overlapping) set of buyers, then there will be perfect competition if the set of *n* buyers is large enough to exclude joint action. Or let there be indefinitely many brokers in any market, and let each broker know many buyers and sellers, and also let each buyer or seller know many brokers – again we have perfect competition. Since entrepreneurs in a stationary economy are essentially brokers between resource owners and consumers, it is sufficient for competition if they meet this condition. That is, resource owners and consumers could dwell in complete ignorance of all save the bids of many entrepreneurs. Hence knowledge possessed by any one trader need not be complete; it is sufficient if the knowledge possessed by the ensemble of the individuals in the market is in a sense comprehensive. (Stigler 1957, pp. 258–9).

The following aspects focus on communication of information in the market by means of messages sent and received (e.g. prices), or as a result of trade interactions.

4.3.1.2 The determination of transaction prices, and/or their communication to prospective transactors

Standard microeconomics implicitly separates these two functions, the determination of prices as a result of the adjustment to an equilibrium set of prices, and the information about these, assumed at the command of individual traders. The first function is conducted by the 'market' or the 'price mechanism', and is supposed to require only the aggregate of individuals' net excess demands. But, as we have seen, excess demands are private information by adherence to the tenets of informational reasonability of pure competition. Thus, the determination of prices relies on information individuals have no way to convey to the market: their excess demands, as required for the computation of equilibrium prices, are planned, notional or target, hence private information. They are not effective, which could only occur in case trade out-of-equilibrium was not assumed away.

The second function is not explained, it is just postulated that individual traders know the equilibrium set of prices. This is meant to be a virtue of decentralization of the market mechanism that individual participants in the economy need only information about prices, beyond their own knowledge of resources, preferences and technology, privately held. This is hardly so, and only as an 'as if' market mechanism. In fact, the adjustment to the equilibrium price set is based on aggregate information, which cannot be known to any market participant (unless it is a central one); and the process of dissemination of this information (prices signals) is not even contemplated. The notion of decentralization is mistaken in general equilibrium analysis, as the following quotation may reveal: 'the information needed by firms and consumers consists solely of their technologies or utility functions plus prices, while the adjustment of prices is based only on the aggregate of individuals' decisions. It is the minimization of information requirements for each participant in the economy which constitutes the virtue of decentralization' (Arrow and Hurwicz 1960, p. 42; see also Demsetz 1988, p. 160).

Thus, we must rework the definition of decentralization at this point. The control mechanism is completely decentralized[27] when each and every individual agent is not endowed with information about prices (or about proposed prices and/or proposed quantities to trade) either that each agent has obtained in pair-wise meetings with prospective traders, or that he has sought. Decentralized price determination should, as a starting point, be thought of as coming about by pair-wise bargaining (cf. Rubinstein and Wolinski 1990, p. 63).

A less strong, and the most commonly used, understanding of decentralization is that implied in pure competition: individual traders making their decisions 'based on a fairly small body of universally communicated information (e.g. prices)'. This is the definition in Ostroy and Starr (1990, p. 33). It is also unreservedly followed by Veendorp (1970a, p. 2); this author sees, however, the need to justify this assumption, which he does mainly by reference to Hayek (1945), even though his other assumption of organized exchanges does not play a lesser role. The notion of known prices, commonly espoused, is erroneously based on Hayek's demonstration of the informational efficiency of the price mechanism. Hayek never presupposes anything like universal communication or free information, rather he only asserts that the price system works like a mechanism for the communication of information, so that 'only the most essential information is passed on, and passed on only to those concerned'. Moreover, relevant information is transmitted through market interaction of individuals possessing only partial knowledge: 'The whole acts as one market, not because any of the members survey the whole field, but because their limited individual fields of vision sufficiently overlap so that through many intermediaries the relevant information is communicated to all' (Hayek 1945, pp. 526–7, 530).

This misconceived notion of universal knowledge of prices will be present in the greater part of the analysis to follow. However, we should be aware that it is only good for constructions that freeze the function of finding market-clearing prices to focus on the execution of trades; its purpose is exclusively for analyzing the logistics of decentralized barter exchange, given equilibrium prices. However, this is not a suitable definition; the information about the market-clearing price set cannot be assumed to be costlessly known to traders (as first pointed out by Stigler 1961), for a consistent comprehension of decentralized exchange.

4.3.1.3 Logistical decentralization

For the logistics of trade to be decentralized, the trading arrangement is required to be based on decentralization in the first of the above senses, specifically that information about each trader's net excess demands be private information. The precise assumption on knowledge of market prices is left open. One possibility is that agents are endowed with information on the set of current market prices, supposedly equilibrium market prices. Another might be that information of each agent about ongoing prices is limited to the degree of search he does accomplish.

In any case, logistical decentralization involves bilateral trade and search for transactors. Absence of a central authority in charge of trading coordination is a necessary first step, but in order to focus on the logistical problems of exchange we have to let individual traders on their own conduct transactions pair-wisely. Exchange occurs in the course of transmission of information between traders on proposed price and/or quantities to transact, and is reasonably thought of as involving bargaining; or alternatively, under certain suitably specified institutional settings, the posting of an asking price by the seller, or of an offer price by the buyer (prices set on a take-it-or-leave-it basis).

4.3.1.4 A typification of decentralization in models of exchange

Summing up, with a view to a broad classification of trading schemes as to the degree of decentralization, we may present a set of assumptions regarding the three aspects of decentralization we have considered: 'initial' information, predetermination of the price signal, and logistics.

The assumptions about communication of private information are common to all the trading schemes that are set out below, namely:

a. *Information* on endowments and preferences of individuals *is private*; also, net excess demands are private information. Also, *communication of information* on net excess demands or proposed exchange rates *is limited to the parties trading*, i.e. limited to bilateral meetings between prospective traders.

Regarding the two other aspects, the price signal and execution of trades, we make the following distinctions. As to the determination of transaction prices and its dissemination in the market two possibilities are considered:

b1. *Equilibrium prices are predetermined*, as the solution to an aggregate consistency of trading plans by means of an implicit auction. Moreover, *information on the equilibrium set of prices is costlessly available to all traders.*

b2. This second case does not allow for a centralized computation/determination of equilibrium prices. *Rates of exchange* (prices) *are contracted by way of bargaining*, or are adjusted by trading post specialists. Another feature is that *communication of transaction prices,* as well as asking and/or offer prices if bilateral bargaining is presumed to occur, *is limited to the participants in the transaction.*

As to the logistics of trade, let us distinguish centralized and decentralized execution:

c1. Execution is carried out with a central market place, so that trading can properly be seen as *multilateral exchange* mediated by the services of a central agent.

c2. The execution of trades is left to *pair-wise meetings* between traders.

A typical model involves a mixture of the assumptions in all three aspects. Combining these assumptions, we arrive at the following trading schemes:

1. Assumptions (a), (b1), and (c1) correspond to the *centralized neowalrasian model.*

2. Assumptions (a), (b1), and (c2) correspond to a situation of *logistical decentralization*, where, however, we allow for knowledge by each trader of the set of relevant equilibrium prices contemporaneously prevailing elsewhere in the economy. Ostroy and Starr (1974; 1990), and the search models of trade fit this pigeonhole.

3. Assumptions (a), (b2), and (c2) make up a more radically decentralized scheme: *decentralized bargaining and execution.* Individuals only gather information and determine transaction prices by way of bilateral meetings with prospective transactors. Besides, logistical aspects is all there is to this case, obtaining information and contacting trading partners is part of the same logistical process. Or, the other way around, potential trades are assessed in the process of obtaining information, either through search, pre-assigned cycles of meetings, or through consultation of trading-post agents.

This framework of trading schemes is a good basis for organizing this section. As a reference, it is pardonable to introduce the neowalrasian model, since every theoretical attempt at decentralizing exchange could hardly escape the fetters of general equilibrium analysis. Then the consistency of informational requirements of convergence and execution will be questioned. Next, I shall try to make sense of the progress made by a few authors to decentralize the logistics of trade, maintaining equilibrium prices as given. Finally, a few steps will be discussed that may be required towards the construction of a theory of decentralized exchange in all three aspects.

4.3.2   The Neowalrasian Model of Centralized Exchange

As we have seen, Walras depicted exchange in markets where free competition takes place by means of bargaining whereby price bidding among traders leads to equilibrium prices, and, given those prices, exchange takes place. A few drawbacks weaken his construction. Even if we take for granted the dichotomy between the determination of the equilibrium set of prices and its execution, we will have to raise doubts regarding, first, the determination of those equilibrium prices, second, their assessment by or communication to traders, and third, the logistics of trade. All three regard the degree of decentralization of the market mechanism Walras envisioned but was unable to complete logically. The irony is that, though outwardly the neowalrasian theory is a reconstitution of the Walrasian system, it is thought to represent a complete rendition of general exchange – yet for a world of imagination, as we have seen, without exchange – while Walras's was not for a market 'perfectly organized in regard to competition'.

Before a critical appraisal of those drawbacks, referring to disequilibrium coordination, I shall attempt to characterize succinctly the neowalrasian model of general exchange as basically centralized, and present a few notes on equilibrium coordination.

The neowalrasian model of general exchange relies on a centralized market mechanism. The two following functions are commonly assigned to the fictional auctioneer. The first is finding market-clearing prices, and their communication to traders. The second is providing the organization of trade, i.e. the execution of trade, by means of a clearing house; or, as Arrow and Hahn (1971, p. 329) put it, 'that it is part of the auctioneer's job to freely disseminate offers to buy and sell' (cf. Walker 1997a, pp. 23–5).[28]

Both these functions regard *disequilibrium coordination*, according to Howitt (1990, p. 4): 'Perfect disequilibrium coordination – the fact that all trades occur at equilibrium prices – reflects two basic sets of assumptions. One is the set of technical assumptions guaranteeing existence. The other is the set guaranteeing that everyone knows the equilibrium prices'.

The first function performed by the auctioneer is that of coordinating the beliefs of traders (through prices). Tatonnement is supposed to converge to a given equilibrium set of prices, and since the process of gathering and disseminating this information is costless, traders are, therefore, informed of equilibrium prices.

The second function has the auctioneer guaranteeing that buyers' and sellers' proposed transactions match by means of direct 'multilateral' barter exchange with a central clearing-house. The auctioneer is in charge of keeping records of disposals and acquisitions so that trading plans are carried out, the single budget constraint enforced, and no trader's proposed trade is left unmatched. Buyers and sellers transact directly with a central clearing-house, 'simultaneously' and at no cost, and therefore the logistics of trade bring no impediment to a full consistency of trading plans, as assessed in the course of the determination of the equilibrium set of prices. In fact, traders have communicated to the central market-maker their net excess demands, which are dispositions to trade on the basis of the pre-announced prices. If, given this set of prices, buyers' demands and sellers' offers are equalized on the aggregate for each and every good, then the auctioneer stops; he has concluded his first function. This will be a signal for traders that their last decision on dispositions to demand and to offer will be their effective trades. And this is the case. Plans to trade coincide with effective trades, as warranted by the frictionless execution of exchange. The auctioneer's second function allows dispositions to eventuate. Notice, however, Arrow and Hahn's (1971, p. 264) comment about tatonnement as sidestepping the difficulty that 'some agents will find their plans cannot be brought to fruition'; in fact, only under the implicitly posited execution will traders be spared disappointment, and therefore this is not the whole story. Coordination problems arise when minimal decentralization features are introduced in the setting for the execution exercise, maintaining however the assumption of central pricing. In Appendix E, a reference is made to such a case, where the conclusion is that 'traditional Walrasian models of general market clearing do not formalize and cannot analyze the allocation problem inherent in decentralized exchange' (Meyer *et al.* 1992, p. 295).

There is also the question of *equilibrium coordination*. Perfect equilibrium coordination, 'the fact that plans made at equilibrium prices constitute a Pareto-optimal allocation' (Howitt 1990, p. 4), is a property of the Walrasian general equilibrium. Equilibrium coordination means that decisions of individual traders are based 'on mutually consistent beliefs' (ibid., p. 2), this involving agreement upon a common set of priors (as to the model of the economy), and the requirement that all interactions between economic agents be exclusively mediated by prices, of which each trader is informed and which he takes as given. However, even if disequilibrium coordination obtains as regards the determination of equilibrium prices, information by every individual trader of the equilibrium price set is not sufficient to guarantee an optimal allocation, i.e. equilibrium coordination.

4.3.3　Execution Given Convergence: Two Exercises at Odds

In the Walrasian setting, we have to distinguish existence, convergence, and execution.

Proofs of existence of equilibrium of a competitive economy were obtained on the basis of a fixed-point theorem for an economy that satisfies appropriate axioms, like convexity and monotonicity of preferences (see Uzawa 1962a, Debreu 1982, and Scarf 1982; for references on variants and alternatives, see Debreu 1982, pp. 697–8). Existence has been asserted either based on the preference relations of individual consumers (e.g. Arrow and Debreu 1954), or just on the excess demand correspondence (e.g. McKenzie 1954; see 1981). Constructive proofs of the existence of an equilibrium price set were developed, starting with two main contributions. One was the computation of fixed points, by Scarf (1973; see 1982) on combinatorial algorithms for the computation of 'approximate' fixed points; a recent account of applied general equilibrium is Shoven and Whalley (1992). The other was Smale (1976a) who proposed a 'differential process' – following the return to calculus by Debreu (1970) – which was elaborated in Smale (1981) and given a systematic presentation in Mas-Colell's (1985) 'differentiable approach'; this is based on the definition of a differential equation applied to equations of supply and demand, called a 'global Newton', which can be transformed into an algorithm analogous to Scarf's (see Smale 1976c, p. 293). In both of these procedures, the question of existence of an equilibrium price set is given the underpinning of computability. In fact, if the proof of existence is mathematically equivalent to the proof that a fixed point exists that is computable, it also allows its 'approximate' computation. Hildenbrand (1974, pp. 162 ff.) describes the meaning of 'approximate' equilibrium price. However, when discussing 'the sense of approximation' of an algorithm for the computation of a fixed point in the general Walrasian model, Scarf (1973, p. 93) concludes that 'if the grid is sufficiently fine, the discrepancy between supply and the market demand at prices $\hat{\pi}$ will be small for all commodities. Unintended inventories, arising from a price vector that does not clear all markets precisely, will be insufficient to provide a signal for the revision of prices'. We have to ask: Signal to whom, the auctioneer? And for decentralized pricing, how could this be maintained? But these questions, such as Scarf's reference to signal, are wide of the mark; the computation of a fixed point cannot be interpreted as any economic mechanism.

These constructive proofs of existence are not, however, the same as proofs of stability of the price adjustment process. In any case, the purposefulness of existence exercises is problematical (Clower 1995a, esp. pp. 316–18; cf. Punzo 1991, p. 36). Constructive proofs of existence or the analysis of stability of convergence processes may eventually be all there is to it, since the question of local uniqueness is closely tied to convergence analysis for purposes of comparative statics (cf. Debreu 1976, p. 233; Dierker 1982, pp. 796–7; see also Hahn 1989b).

Referring to multiple equilibria, Debreu admits that '[t]he pathology [of infinite equilibria] is due to the manner in which the agents are matched, a situation entirely different from that of existence theory where it was possible to give general conditions on the behavior of each agent separately' (Debreu 1976, p. 233). In fact, since even the 'market imitative' processes (Arrow and Hahn 1971, p. 307) are notional and involve no activities or transactions, on strict logical grounds stability analyses add little to proofs of existence. Even though at variance with the prognosticated descriptive realism in Arrow and Debreu (1954, p. 256), existence proofs do not deal with exchange.

It is Scarf's opinion that 'the price adjustment mechanism can be used neither to provide a proof of existence of competitive equilibrium nor an effective computational procedure for the general case' (1982, p. 1012). In the case of Smale (1976a)[29] the distinction between existence and convergence becomes hazy since the algorithm for the computation of equilibrium prices uses an adjustment process, where the price change of a commodity depends on the properties of the excess demand for all other commodities (Hahn 1982, p. 767; cf. Ingrao and Israel 1990, p. 356). This is even more so in Saari and Simon (1978), and Saari (1985a), where the rate of adjustment of a price is proportional to the (market) excess demand of that commodity only.

Stability deals 'with endogenous processes operating in an economy which may bring about an equilibrium. Indeed, the latter is often implicitly or explicitly defined as a stationary point of such a process' (Hahn 1982, p. 745; thorough surveys on stability of the competitive equilibrium are Negishi 1962, Hahn 1982, and Weintraub 1991). Of these processes the most commonly considered is 'the law of demand and supply', and the price mechanism in general exchange is that of tatonnement of Walrasian extraction – which will be our main concern. However, other mechanisms have been proposed (cf. Hahn 1982, pp. 745–6 and 772–85; Fisher 1983, Chapter 2) that allow for exchange at out-of-equilibrium market prices. One possibility is to keep the auctioneer but assume that markets are 'orderly'[30] at each date. This is the Hahn Process, as in Hahn and Negishi (1962). 'Markets are orderly if no agent is restrained in his planned demand (supply) of a good when that good is in aggregate excess supply (demand)' (Hahn 1982, p. 746). An interesting comment is added:

> Exchange is now with an anonymous market. At all times (including $t = 0$) markets are *orderly*: no agent has excess demand (supply) for a good which is in aggregate excess supply (demand). The idea is that there is very good information in all markets so that (instantaneously) agents know of all supplies and demands. It is not a very convincing assumption but it has lately become popular in rationing models (e.g. Drèze (1975)). (Hahn 1982, p. 781).

Moreover, as will become clear in the following, this mention of trading out-of-equilibrium is mistaken: for feasibility, the orderly rule implies central allocation of trading opportunities, or even the possibility of central enforcement of certain transactions (Veendorp 1969; see Koizumi 1991, esp. pp. 188–90). This is purely an exercise on convergence, and for that matter, one that fails the requirement of information decentralization.

Another problem with this process is that 'the equilibria ... are themselves path-dependent. Consequently, *the inability to specify agents' disequilibrium behaviour* also prevents determining the equilibrium position towards which the adjustment process eventually converges' (Busetto, pp. 100–101, italics added). In such cases of indeterminateness of equilibrium, the existence of equilibrium is not independent of convergence even in strict formal terms, as is the case in Fisher's (1983*) Disequilibrium Foundations of Equilibrium Analysis*, and therefore the specification of agents' disequilibrium behavior is a necessary component of the analysis. In fact, in Fisher (1983), although neither central nor market price setters are posited, this issue is eventually sidestepped, and, in this respect '[w]ork on disequilibrium transactions ... has proceeded ... in the same way that is true of the virtual models' (Walker 1997a, p. 125; also pp. 33–4 and 124–5): [31]

> So far, this discussion has concerned how price offers get made. There is another question involved in price adjustment, however, that of how price offers get accepted. Here too I shall be general and vague, although such vagueness seems less important in this context.
> I assume that institutions are such that some set of agents in each market explicitly set prices and the remaining agents, if any, decide which prices to accept. (Fisher 1983, p. 189).

Furthermore, Herschel Grossman (1969, p. 478) concedes that Hahn and Negishi (1962) have developed a theory of disequilibrium transactions, but notices that this 'model incorporates only distribution effects, and thus does not seem to get to the essence of the recontracting assumption', since spillover effects are not considered, be they due to 'price adjustment relationships' (Patinkin 1965 spillover effect) or to effective market transactions relationships (Clower 1965 dual decision hypothesis).

A second possibility, the Edgeworth Process, which was considered by Uzawa (1962b) and Smale (1976b), dispenses with the auctioneer: common prices are not given, and exchange occurs if, and only if, it is 'budget feasible' and a transaction between each pair of individuals takes place whenever it is utility improving (cf. Hahn 1982, pp. 772 ff.; Uzawa 1962b, p. 219). It is Walker's (1997a, pp. 123–4) opinion that the 'mathematical adjustment process associated with a disequilibrium transactions model' as in Smale (1976b) 'displays the same defects that characterize the virtual models'. Again the informational requirements may be large, and arbitrage is not easy to accommodate, given the non-decreasing utility constraint in every trade (cf. Fisher 1987, p. 27).

4.3.3.1 The stability of tatonnement equilibrium

Let us concentrate now on the stability of tatonnement equilibrium. The Walrasian tradition poses tatonnement as an iterative calculation of the set of equilibrium prices. This function is generally assumed realized in the model of general exchange by an external entity, the auctioneer – though the question of whether it is tractable, and under which informational assumptions, is seldom and only marginally appended.

First, we have to question convergence. Commonly, analyses of general equilibrium assume that a set of equilibrium prices can be computed and announced to traders, and therefore is taken as a given. And the conclusion is that it cannot be shown – in general, it is not true. Then we intend to question the beliefs of traders, i.e. their reliance on this information in the workings of the general barter model. Next, the analysis proceeds by analyzing the feasibility of trades, execution, or logistics. For this purpose, the informational assumptions are chosen to be as close as possible to those underlying pure competition, the informational efficiency of which is thought to be a central property. Decentralization of information is, thus, a starting point in the study of the feasibility of trades, only to arrive at the conclusion that execution of planned trades is generally not feasible.

I am not denying that analysis should be decomposed in manageable steps. The question I am raising here is whether those analytical steps are informationally congruent with each other. Dichotomization between convergence to the equilibrium price set and execution of trading leads to analytical inconsistencies in decentralized exchange: given the different informational set-up, there is no clear logical point in relating or comparing them. Only in centralized exchange does the problem of convergence to an equilibrium set of prices mirror that of convergence to a set of coordinated trades, and therefore the whole exercise can be curtailed to getting prices right.

Now, the argument is developed in detail. The objective is to analyze the consistency of the three exercises: existence, convergence and execution.

(i) Convergence

The traditional and most commonly considered price mechanism is a tatonnement process whereby individuals take centrally determined prices as a given to assert their planned trades, and only consider trade if planned trades are consistent in the aggregate, i.e., if net excess demands for every commodity are zero. The auctioneer is supposed to cry out a set of prices, to collect information on aggregate excess demands for the communicated set of prices, and change prices if excess demands are not zero. In the limit of this process, prices are supposed to converge to equilibrium. The problem of convergence in the neowalrasian world is limited to getting prices right. However, as the Walrasian program predicates, tatonnement is meant not only to get prices right but also the right prices: the same prices for the 'theoretical' and the 'practical' solutions, i.e. to achieve a determinate solution. According to Gandolfo (1987, p. 462), stability analysis here is a case where a disequilibrium dynamics is 'superimposed' on 'a model whose solution only determines the equilibrium'.

Stability analysis was initially dealt with on continuous time, and proofs were obtained only under special restrictions, like the cases of gross substitutability or of a 'representative' consumer (cf. Arrow and Hahn 1971, esp. pp. 322–3; Hahn 1982, pp. 754–70). Yet, configurations of excess demand functions have been constructed (e.g. Scarf 1960; Gale 1963) for which this tatonnement process is unstable; by simplifying the construction of such (counter)examples, these results were strengthened by some theorems of Sonnenschein–Debreu–Mantel 'which, roughly summarised, show that any arbitrary set of excess demand functions continuous on the interior of the simplex and satisfying Walras' Law, can be generated by utility maximising behavior of agents for some utility functions and [distribution of] endowments'. These results 'established that there are economies based on the actions of utility maximising agents which have equilibria that are not locally asymptotically stable' (Hahn 1982, pp. 745 and 763; cf. Sonnenschein 1972; 1973; Debreu 1974; Mantel 1974). For a review of the negative results of Sonnenschein–Debreu–Mantel on proofs of uniqueness and stability – proofs of asymptotical local stability of general equilibrium of an exchange economy – founded on 'decomposed' excess demand functions,[32] i.e. on 'individualistic assumptions', see Kirman (1989, esp. pp. 128–33) and Hildenbrand (1983, pp. 25–7). This literature concludes, for the case of finite economies, that models of general exchange – built on individuals' excess demand functions as derived from standard behavioral assumptions – do not have enough structure; i.e., aggregated excess demands cannot be generated that present sufficient restrictions (beyond continuity, homogeneity, and Walras's identity) for a well behaved convergence. The work by Sonnenschein–Debreu–Mantel is extended in Saari (1992) who concludes that with respect to aggregation procedures, such as implied in stability proofs, 'anything can happen'.

Given this general introduction to the questions that the stability analysis raises, let us now deal with the accomplishments of recent convergence exercises. Proofs of convergence to the equilibrium set of prices have been sought on the basis of informational decentralization (endowments and preferences are private information).[33] Thus, the first question concerns the information required to assert stability. Another question is of convergence 'time'.

As to the first question, the most complete answer is provided by Saari (1985a). He develops the case of a tatonnement process for discrete time, which was initially dealt with in Uzawa (1958), and presented in Arrow and Hahn (1971, pp. 307–309) for the special case of gross substitutes (for the case of continuous time, see Saari and Simon 1978[34]). He attempts a more general conclusion, which however is basically the same – that knowledge of excess-demand functions will not be sufficient for stability. A (traditionally) held position is that the auctioneer is not required to be endowed with knowledge of every individual's excess demands; to find equilibrium prices, only aggregate net excess demands for each commodity would be needed. The function of determining and announcing equilibrium prices would be centralized, even though information were decentralized. This is not right, though (cf. Meyer *et al.* 1992, as discussed in Appendix E, below).

Saari attempts to identify what is required in order to find a 'universal' adjustment process, one that converges for any economy which satisfies convexity ('standard concave utility functions') and regularity conditions (aggregate excess demand function is single valued and smooth), as well as one that puts *no* restrictions on the forms of the excess demand function. This is 'an unresolved aspect of the theory because the standard story of prices adjusting according to supply and demand need not correspond to a convergent process' (Saari 1985a, pp. 1117, 1119).[35] Saari considers 'any iterative procedures which can be expressed in a standard form, which depends smoothly on the aggregate excess demand function, and which stops when it reaches an equilibrium'. The basic result is that the 'informational requirements can be very large ... and they are not of the type suggested by the usual tatonnement process. This is true even in the two commodity case!' (ibid., p. 1118).

The dynamic process associated with tatonnement is more appropriately thought of as a discrete time iterative process, since a differential dynamic would require a continuous updating of information at each instant of time, which can be seen as going beyond the computational ability of the 'auctioneer'. But, given that the continuous case may be viewed as approaching, in the limit, the iterative mechanism, 'it is only natural to expect the informational requirements of the iterative dynamics to mimic those given by the differential equations' (Saari 1985a, p. 1119).

Locally converging mechanisms require information of the excess demand function $(z(p))$ and of all the marginal rates of each component of the aggregate demand with respect to each price $(Dz(p)$, the Jacobian of $z(p))$.

Given the difficulties met in the literature of proving the local stability of tatonnement mechanisms under decentralized assumptions – e.g. the information 'privacy preserving' property of the system – Saari and Williams (1986) find that:

> These negative statements are discouraging because they imply that unless unrealistic informational requirements are imposed upon the system, the standard economic assumptions need not lead to convergent, decentralized dynamics. The

instability of these economic systems must either be accepted, or else the hypotheses that lie behind them must be reexamined. (ibid, p. 153).

In this article, the authors attempt such an exercise, whereby it is identified which additional local information can be communicated by agents in a decentralized way that is amenable to building a stable dynamical process (an extension to iterative processes is also conducted): 'If economic models with a *single* dynamical system lead to impossibility results, then the models need to be based on a *set of dynamical systems*' (ibid, pp. 153–4); that is, 'different mechanisms and procedures are required for different economic settings' (Saari 1992, p. 362).

For globally convergent mechanisms, Saari (1985a) shows that there does not exist an iterative mechanism 'which depends upon the information obtained solely from z, Dz, ..., $D^N z$, where N is any positive integer' (ibid., p. 1120). There are problems with the mechanism. The main one lies in lack of information about price points at which to start the iteration, and that there is an uncountable number of these points whose dynamic is not convergent (cf. Saari 1985a, pp. 1122–4). In order to obtain convergence, the choice of the iteration function (step size) may have to be restricted (for an equivalent conclusion, see Uzawa 1958 and Hahn 1982, pp 768–9)[36] but this would be incompatible with a universal mechanism since it requires global information about the underlying differential function. But '[t]his type of information is a long way from the usual story where the information is sought strictly from the reaction of the people in the market' (Saari 1985a, p. 1124). Furthermore, as to 'supplemental global information to assist the process' Saari hints at the possible need to include prices directly as in the Scarf algorithm (i.e., not only indirectly through the excess demand function).

Knowing that local information is not sufficient, which global information would be required could not be specified, in order to find a universal process. '[T]he basic reason [of the impossibility result] behind Saari's theorem ... is [that] the function space is so rich that for any given procedure we can construct smooth maps which "trap" the procedure into a small region of the domain containing no equilibria of the function' (Bala and Kiefer 1994, p. 302). Saari's impossibility result, 'that there does not exist a universally convergent mechanism', has led Bala and Kiefer (1994) to look for a generalization of the class of mechanisms in order to 'find a process which cannot get trapped in the above manner'. By enlarging the dimension of iterative mechanisms, the authors were able to show the existence of a convergent process that complies with the proposed 'admissible' criteria, namely that the mechanism is informational simple (memoriless), time stationary, deterministic and works in discrete time. 'It should be mentioned, however, that while our mechanism is universal, it is probably an inefficient procedure in practice' (ibid., p. 302; cf. Saari and Williams 1986, p. 153).

As to the second question, that of convergence 'time', for those settings where convergence is shown to exist, the speed of convergence may be very slow, be it in 'model' or 'computer' time (Hahn 1987, p. 137). Referring to stability in the short-period equilibrium as asserted by means of tatonnement processes, Arrow and Hahn frame the question properly:

> Is it possible to say that the auctioneer's rule is stable, when that notion seems to imply time going to infinity and we are confining ourselves to a finite time interval? The answer is that we have used time as an expository device so far; what is really at stake is that the number of steps – price changes undertaken by the auctioneer – goes to infinity, and that is clearly possible in a finite time interval. While in a formal way we can avoid being silly, it is true that in practice price adjustments do take time and that if the tâtonnement is to be taken seriously as in some sense connected with reality, then it must face the objection that even if the process is stable it is only asymptotically that equilibrium is attained. (Arrow and Hahn 1971, p. 310).

This same problem is implied in rules of price adjustment either in continuous time, as a limit of a function (cf. Samuelson 1947, p. 261; Arrow and Hahn 1971, pp. 274, 324),[37] or in iterative mechanisms. Saari (1985a, p. 1124) shows that convergent points exist that can take innumerable iterations to even settle into the appropriate convergence interval.

Therefore, the computation of the equilibrium price set by way of an iterative process requires information surpassing the limits of private information. And, even if such information is assumed, iteration is not guaranteed to converge in a finite number of runs.

These are negative results for the tatonnement process, or any other adjustment process for that matter, since a 'basic requirement is that [the dynamic, economic mechanism] converges to an equilibrium. If it doesn't, the mechanism's basic objective is invalidated' (Saari and Williams 1986, p. 152). Or, in general, the requirement that there should be a process capable of generating an equilibrium was asserted by Hahn (1994) quite forcibly: one of his 'most lasting convictions' has been that 'equilibrium analysis can only be applicable in economic theory if one can show that there are reliable and speedy feedbacks which ensure that an economy does not stray far from equilibrium' (ibid., p. 249).

(ii) Beliefs

The communication of prices presents two problems, one the means by which it takes place in general exchange, and the other, whether, being known to traders, these beliefs play any role. As to the first, this is appropriately dealt with neither in Walras nor in other accounts of general exchange. As Walker notices, Walras's general model lacks the definition of the means by which information is produced, and by whom, and how it is disseminated in the market among prospective transactors. Information requirements, and the logistics of information gathering and communication that underlie trading, are just postulated: Arrow and Hahn (1971, p. 264) assume that the auctioneer 'receives transactions offers from the agents in the economy'; or, in most cases, they are implicitly assumed away as relevant features of the intermarket adjustment problem (cf. Walker 1997a, p. 22).

Furthermore, if this failure impinges in the first place on decision taking on planned quantities to trade during the equilibrating process, the informational problem is also present in equilibrium transactions after the general equilibrium set of prices is reached:

> Even if the rule existed [the rule that trade cannot occur until excess demand quantities in all markets are zero], it would not be sufficient. There would also have to be a means of collecting and disseminating information so that all traders are informed when all excess demands are zero, features that also do not exist in [Walras's] models. In short, the barter models lack the institutions, technology, rules, and procedures that would be necessary to generate the necessary characteristics of information, adjustment, and coordination. (Walker 1993, p. 1444).

The import of all this lies in the construction of beliefs that prices are equilibrium prices. In the Walrasian system, this coordination of traders' beliefs is presumed ensured by completion of tatonnement (cf. Howitt 1990, p. 4), despite the inexistence of any mechanism to communicate to traders that their plans are coordinated *ex ante*. However, since information gathering and dissemination are costless, there is no room for the consideration of such a mechanism. The possibility that the constructed beliefs could be invalidated in the course of transacting does not exist either, since in strict logic no (direct) bargaining over exchange rates takes place. Price determination and trading are both centralized, and for this invented world no contradictions exist. Beliefs are inconsequential. All the problems arise when specks of decentralization are introduced in the mechanism.

(iii) The consistency of bilateral barter with predetermined prices

A thorough account of a pure barter model is Veendorp's (1970a) critique of general equilibrium analysis on the grounds 'that the existence of a set of positive prices at which demand equals supply on all commodity markets does not assure the existence of a set of positive exchange rates at which demand equals supply on all commodity exchanges' (Veendorp 1970a, p. 3 [38]). Further, the author contends that 'the analysis of the existence of equilibrium exchange rates in barter economies is closely related to that of the actual trading process'. The procedure by which individual traders are meant to carry out their trades is, in the case under analysis, by bartering as taking place successively in trading posts, one for each pair of commodities. (Trade within each trading post is not tackled by Veendorp; if it were, he would have to consider successive barter for each pair, both of transactors and goods.)

In order to analyze execution of trading by direct barter as carried out by individual traders, we should pay attention to two assumptions. One is that equilibrium prices have been determined, i.e. planned net excess demands for every commodity are zero. The other is the absence of a central exchange agency, i.e. a clearing center where participants would maintain an account, where excess suppliers were credited their deposits of excess supplies, and afterwards, from where excess demands were collected. However, the existence is assumed of organized commodity exchanges for the exchange of any two commodities, trading posts. At each trading post, the restriction prevails that total demand for one of the commodities in exchange for the other must balance total supply of the first in exchange for the second (ibid., p. 3), so that equilibrium exchange rates are not disconfirmed at any exchange. Hence, a 'specialized broker'[39] is assumed to attend ongoing pair-wise transactions, and to enforce the condition that total demand and total supply of each commodity in exchange for the other, are in balance at any trading post. In addition, during the execution of exchange the 'necessary condition' for market equilibrium in a barter economy is extraneously maintained 'that the total excess demand for any commodity (summed over all individuals and all commodity exchanges) equals zero' (ibid., p. 5). As may be clear, two equilibrium conditions are imposed at each step of the barter process. One is the market clearing rule, that net excess demand for any commodity be zero. And the second is a trading rule, that at any trading post total demand and total supply of each commodity in exchange for the other, match. This trading rule is equivalent to the quid pro quo condition in an aggregative form over all trades taking place at a trading post, under the assumption of known equilibrium prices. Either equilibrium prices are assumed to be known and we can presume traders enforce quid pro quo at such prices, or they are not and a 'market' restriction, as defined by Veendorp, becomes binding; this is why, if prices are assumed to be known and adhered to in every pair-wise trade, the market equilibrium condition becomes redundant. (Veendorp seems never to believe his assumption that prices are known to be equilibrium prices; it is a very sensible suspicion, but one that helped raise doubts about his argument.)

Then the author presents an example where the final result of barter, independently of the sequence in which trade takes place, shows that the existence of a set of equilibrium prices at which notional excess demands are consistent, does not assure the existence of a set of exchange rates in direct barter trading on all commodity exchanges (cf. Veendorp 1970a, p. 3).

Two main comments are due, the second built upon the first.

In the spirit of Walras and central to Veendorp's argument, we should stress, first, the condition that restricts each commodity's net excess demand – given the predetermined equilibrium price set – to be zero during the execution of barter trades; this is assumed by Walras and Isnard (cf. Jaffé 1969, esp. pp. 30, 34–35) and Pareto (1909/1927, p. 432) refers expressly to it. As seen above, it may be redundant: if transaction prices are equilibrium prices, quid pro quo implies this restriction. We should notice however that the assessment of this condition of zero net excess demands is beyond the information endowments of individual traders or the information capabilities of the 'specialized brokers' and so it is not enforceable by (each of) them. Complying with assumptions of pure competition, individual traders are assumed to have knowledge only about market prices and their own endowments and preferences (ibid., p. 2). And also, 'specialized brokers' at each trading post are only informed of proposed demands and supplies of the pair of commodities whose exchange they attend, and consequently cannot gather information on market net excess demands of these two commodities.

Barter is occurring in a direct, pair-wise, quid pro quo, 'sequential' way, which is decentralized. However, during the execution of barter trades, the working of the market is restricted by some entity who is assumed to gather and aggregate information over all individual traders, and enforce continuously the condition of net excess demands of zero.[40] So, the working of market trading is supposed to call forth centralized information, which individual traders, and 'specialized brokers' as well, have no way of knowing. Barter is assumed direct but the information required for the working of the market is not decentralized. This seems inconsistent; in effect, Veendorp has missed the problem to which he was responding in his paper.

If we envision the execution problem as direct barter and rely only on decentralized information, we have to be content to impose only such restrictions, or 'rules', as are based on market information available to individual traders (prices), or are meant to be 'enforced' by them ('sequential' quid pro quo, which in any case is a 'rule' that can be assumed 'enforced' by the trading partners, independently of knowledge of market prices). The maintenance of the market clearing assumption – reasonably logical for centralized exchange, where the relevant aspect is not only to get prices right but also the right prices – during the barter process is a product of forcing the transplant from centralized to decentralized exchange of the dichotomization between existence/convergence and execution. In order to assess decentralized exchange this may be ineffectual. For decentralized exchange, convergence to an equilibrium set of prices and existence of a coordinated set of trades cannot be separated,[41] and thus convergence and execution lose autonomy. Moreover, in decentralized exchange, the meaningful exercise is not of convergence to an equilibrium price set but the convergence to a feasible set of trades (see next section (iv)).

In fact, as traditionally defined, existence is a notional state, and convergence is a virtual exercise. Trading, however, involves not the consistency of plans but the matching of active demands and supplies. A tentative conclusion therefore seems to be, for the sake of 'conceptual coherence', entirely to subsume convergence to the equilibrium price set under convergence to (and execution of) a coordinated set of trades, relying on a coherent set of informational assumptions (cf. Veendorp 1970a, p. 6 [42]). For decentralized trading arrangements, convergence to the equilibrium price set cannot sensibly be imposed as an *a priori* postulate.

Given this, a second comment ensues. Veendorp (1970a) makes the point that a decentralized exchange arrangement like direct bilateral bartering may fail to allow trading plans to correspond to feasible trades. The author started, however, from the assumption that prices were equilibrium prices, and deduced the logical implications of such knowledge with which he endowed his traders. From this standpoint Veendorp's conclusions are devastating enough.

But now I would like to ask the reader to imagine himself not as the omniscient storyteller, but as one of the characters in the story lacking full information. Let him be a trader in a decentralized market. And now let us observe his certainties and his questions or doubts. Suppose first that the trading rule is able to accomplish feasible trade, so that planned trades are consummated. If this is the case, the quid pro quo condition (which is decentralized) is sufficient to generate this result. Let us suppose, alternatively, that direct barter in a set of trading posts is unsuccessful, given prices; i.e. predetermined trading plans cannot be accomplished. If execution cannot be accomplished by any set of trading rules of the storyteller's creation, that obeys some restrictions like informational decentralization, we say it is not feasible under such restrictions. What could our trader infer? Or what can some decentralized viewer infer from the observation of the results? That direct barter was unfeasible given equilibrium prices, or that, on the other hand, prices were not equilibrium prices to begin with? If he thought about it, he would be unable to draw any conclusion and so should the character in our story.

Full execution may be feasible under quid pro quo, at given predetermined equilibrium prices (the market clearing condition is not binding in such possible case). It may not be feasible, though (and the trading rule becomes binding). On the other hand, if we assume that prices are not equilibrium prices, full execution is not feasible (both the trading rule and the market clearing rule are binding). As a consequence, unfeasibility of trading would provide a noisy signal to any 'decentralized' market participant in our story that would care to mind. Let us put this in perspective, in the mind of the storyteller.

Under quid pro quo, inability to complete planned trades in direct barter provides a 'mixed' signal to traders and 'specialized brokers'. Their response may be to attempt to carry out some unfeasible trades at the going prices by way of bargaining. They may be leading the price signals towards equilibrium or, on the contrary, give rise to a derailment of the (notional) equilibrium price signal.

Decentralized information is compatible with quid pro quo (or its aggregative form, as in Veendorp). The market clearing rule is not – under limited knowledge of other traders' excess demands and supplies, individual traders cannot compute market excess demands at any step of barter – and accordingly we should leave it aside as a control mechanism in trading. Thus, if we postulate information decentralization, individual traders who face the inability to complete their desired trades may be led to proceed exchange and attempt to bargain, in order to further their 'gains from trade' – consequently adjusting prices. This could just potentially end up 'derailing' the price signal, which might just possibly as well be the equilibrium set of prices. We are led to the discomforting conclusion that in decentralized barter there is lack of information in the market to let individual traders infer which state they are at, whether in a notional equilibrium where exchange is infeasible, or in a situation of market disequilibrium to begin with. We aim at a world of decentralized exchange: in pair-wise meetings, transactors do not know and do not care about anyone else, about rules, or market equilibrium. Rather, the presupposition of equilibrium prices can be dropped, without harm, and possibly ease the understanding of the logistics of barter. In fact, if we contemplate barter of given quantities (g) of two goods (i and k), between two individuals (j and l), exchange means that g_{ij} trades for g_{kl}, and so we have $g_{ij} / g_{kl} = 1$ (cf. Pareto 1909/1927, p. 178). Or, in general, $g_{ij} / g_{kl} = p_{ki} = v_k / v_i$, with v_k and v_i standing as the value of goods k and i in exchange (expressed in a common unit of account).[43] Thus, barter is balance.

(iv) Feasibility of trades
As to the meaning of feasibility, Ostroy (1973, p. 609) has the right perspective: 'the term "feasible" denotes what *could* happen, ignoring individual behavior, not what *would* happen'.

It is, first, a thought experiment with no claims to deal with any facts of experience of trade, but unlike the exercise on convergence, it ascribes actions to individuals. Consequently, and second, it is not an assertion of equilibrium or notional plans, it requires the description of transactions of goods between individuals according to defined rules. Third, some criterion or restriction is needed to define feasibility. If unqualified, feasibility has no meaning, this is only given by some restriction – as we know, centralized exchange as conducted by the auctioneer, if feasible, is only trivially so. The set of restrictions of interest concern primarily information decentralization.

Mandatory 'givens' are a set of individual traders, a set of goods, the distribution of certain quantities of these goods to individuals (endowments), and the trading rule(s) with which individuals are supposed to comply in the execution of transactions; an optional given, normally postulated, is a set of common exchange rates for each pair of these goods, as predetermined, before trading starts. Then, the execution of trading by individuals in compliance with the rules is described. But, in order to assess a feasible execution, we need to ponder whether prices are predetermined or not:

a. For the most commonly considered case (e.g. Ostroy and Starr 1974; 1990), where an equilibrium price set is given, if trading can be shown to be executed to completion of the desired/planned trades without infringing the restriction, we say that execution is feasible, given the restriction.
b. For the case where no exercise precedes trading (no prices are given or 'known' and no notional trading plans pre-exist trade), a followed path (e.g. Feldman 1973; and Madden 1975) is to treat execution as a sequence of utility non-decreasing bilateral trades in order to enquire about optimality. In this case, where no predetermined equilibrium prices are assumed, attainment of execution within the confines of decentralized information has not been investigated, to the best of my knowledge;[44] but the fact that there is a trade off will become clear in due course. Another more relevant question arises here. Unlike before, we have no reference to gauge the set of achieved trades: in the Walrasian sense, the planned or target trades. But if we are unable to define *full* execution, we gain now extra degrees of freedom in the formalization of exchange. For one thing, we are now in a position to observe what *could* be attained given the posited trading rule(s), without the strings of necessary conformance with equilibrium, as notional consistency of plans. But, moreover, we are free to postulate whatever transaction rules we may choose with no (necessary) requisite that they comply with (notional) maximizing behavior by the individual – which in the case of sequentially assessed trading opportunities may have no rationale. In this situation, a window is open to view feasibility as aggregate coherence of any given trading rule. And further, if aggregate coherence under a set of trading rules is shown to satisfy relevant restrictions like informational decentralization, a boundary could be set for the behavior of individual traders.

Be that as it may, feasibility is only a first, but necessary, step towards making sense of trading. First, because it immediately invokes a next step, dealing with facilitating mechanisms of feasible trades, be that brokerage, or specialists, with or without a medium of exchange. And necessary, because only if trade is feasible according to some trading rule, can it be facilitated. According to Ostroy (1973, p. 608): 'In the standard theory, any redistribution of commodities which preserves their totals is feasible'. An instance of this is a 'solution' devised by Veendorp in order to show that, given a predetermined equilibrium price set, a direct barter economy can satisfy feasibility conditions at these prices: 'Working backwards ... one can generate feasible excess demand patterns' (1970, p. 7). Given this, let us consider the role of a facilitating device towards the feasibility of trades. Ostroy (1973, p. 9) adds:

'Monetary exchange does not enlarge the set of feasible transactions; it merely enables trades, which must be feasible in the first place to be realized'. In the same direction, Starr (1976, p. 1087) concludes: 'Barter mechanisms can succeed as quickly as monetary trade if coordination and sufficient market information are freely available. In their absence, successful barter may require much longer'. An altogether different consideration is, however, that it may happen that only the facilitating device will enable execution to comply with the restriction of informational decentralization (cf. Ostroy and Starr 1974; 1990).

These facilitating mechanisms are paid for in that they economize on set-up costs of transacting. And here we can see why it was said above that feasibility does not deal with facts of experience. None of the ensuing analyses of feasibility of trading does consider the set-up costs of transacting,[45] and this is a sufficiently revealing symptom that all that is done there is a 'contemplation' of trading. In this regard, and referring to the construction of 'a model which can serve as an adequate foundation for a monetary theory', Hahn (1965, p. 131) states: 'It must distinguish between abstract exchange opportunities at some notionally called prices and actual transaction opportunities. The latter requires a precise statement of the methods of transactions open to an individual with their attendant costs'. In the execution exercises, even if 'middlemen' or 'money' are called in, they are *ad hoc* features (cf. Starr 1971, esp. pp. 3, 16–18).

(v) Decentralized execution and sequential trading
Next, we shall consider sequential trading, which means abandoning the neowalrasian 'simultaneous' multilateral barter and adhering instead to pair-wise exchange (bilateral barter), either direct or indirect also, in any case sequential. Ostroy and Starr refer to two sources of 'sequentiality' with respect to:

> the implicit logistical and informational assumptions of the theory of exchange. To begin, it is vital that trade be sequential, which involves more than the time-indexing of commodities. There are various sources of "sequentiality." One is the costs of making forward contracts in an otherwise highly organized market setting, which creates a need for markets to reopen over time. Another is the simple fact that in most instances individuals trade with each other one at a time. (Ostroy and Starr 1990, p. 56).

With respect to the first sense, unless we assume traders have no 'perfect foresight'[46] or that contracting in future exchange is not costless, sequentiality may be 'inessential' as shown by Radner (1972; also 1968) and Hahn (1971; 1973b). For such cases, models of 'sequential' exchange correspond to 'one-shot' exchange as in Arrow–Debreu where all choices are made at one instant of time (cf. Arrow 1968, p. 387; Clower 1977, pp. 233–4).

(On the existence of general equilibrium in a sequence economy with set-up transaction costs – and the consequent nonconvexity – see Heller and Starr 1976, based on Hahn 1971.)

Now we have to face the question of how sequential trading has been modeled, regarding the second source of 'sequentiality' considered by Ostroy and Starr. Merely presuming that traders meet sequentially in pairs is not enough to characterize the market arrangement. Aspects like the following matter: whether traders search or are assigned a predetermined list of potential trading partners; whether they trade only a pair of commodities at a meeting or they trade any size collections of commodities; whether trading occurs in a sequence of special commodity exchanges (all traders gather at a trading post to exchange two commodities bilaterally), or in a sequence of pair-wise meetings (pairs of traders meet to exchange all commodities bilaterally). One possibility is to assume that each trading post opens successively (Veendorp 1970a; Benassy 1975); another is to specify, parametrically, pair-wise encounters of individual traders (Ostroy 1973; Ostroy and Starr 1974; 1990); finally, we may let individual traders search for trading partners randomly according to some statistical distribution (e.g. Diamond 1982a; and others for monetary exchange, such as Diamond 1984a, Kiyotaki and Wright 1989, and Aiyagari and Wallace 1991).

Furthermore, we have to question which 'restrictions' to maintain. At the market level, the market clearing condition is maintained in order to focus attention on the logistics of exchange. But even on this dichotomized approach, this condition can be relaxed, and attempts to drop it were made (cf. Benassy 1975; Drèze 1975). As to individual trading rules, we have an important change. Without a central accounting scheme to enforce the budget constraint (as in the one-shot trading scheme of Walrasian ascendancy), a problem is thought to arise which is usually framed in terms of 'individual' incentive compatibility in competitive behavior in a 'finite' exchange economy. Under decentralized information and with trade occurring sequentially, the imposition of a sequence of budget balances is thought to be required in replacement of the single budget constraint in order to eschew the moral hazard problem (cf. Ostroy and Starr 1990, p. 13; Roberts and Postlewaite 1976; Hurwicz 1972, pp. 443–54, esp. p. 446; and 1973, pp. 27–9). This function consists in enforcing the budget constraint, namely by means of some sort of a 'record-keeping device' (Ostroy and Starr 1990, p. 11) to guarantee that trading plans are carried out at the competitive prices. This is imputed to avoidance of the moral hazard problem created by the presence of private information: by anticipating the effect of his offers to buy or sell on the formation of prices, a trader would have an incentive to misrepresent his offers, in order to alter prices to his benefit.[47]

All this concern is misplaced, it is a shadow of centralized execution which has no substance in the light of bilateral contracting; if two individuals transact, quid pro quo can be assumed to have been 'enforced' between each pair of trading partners. We could say 'greedily' enforced, to borrow Hurwicz's (1973, p. 25) expression, but this is not needed. In contrast to 'the Walrasian price taking paradigm',

> The Edgeworthian paradigm (1881) views economics as dealing with those aspects of social organization achieved by free contract between self-interested individuals or groups of individuals. Contract is the voluntary exchange of *quid pro quo*. What is the *quid* and what is the *quo* can vary greatly in character and concreteness from case to case, but purely one-sided arrangements – benevolence or force – are excluded. Self-interest need not be interpreted narrowly. What is required is Wicksteed's *non truism* condition (1933, Vol. I, pp. 170–83) – neither side to a contract should have the interest of the other at heart, although each may pursue the interests of third parties. (Whitaker 1987, p. 575).

Incentive compatibility in this context is another excrescence of the dichotomization between existence and execution, where notional plans precede actual transactions. Notice this ingenious clarification:

> The price consistency condition is merely the abstraction of the fact verified by casual empiricism that when one buys something one pays the seller for it. Payment for goods purchased seems a concept almost absent from general equilibrium theory. It is required there that the value of goods demanded equal the value of goods supplied, but there is no requirement that the supplier of goods be the recipient of goods supplied. (Starr 1972, p. 94).

In fact, enforcement of budget balance constraint at each bilateral trade is ensured in an informationally decentralized way through satisfaction of quid pro quo, which means that the value of commodities acquired equals the value of commodities delivered. But this is simply the definition of barter: if traders are observed to transact, then $x_{ij} \equiv y_{kl}$.

In our attempt to envision Walrasian general exchange as decentralized we abandoned the central market and replaced it with sequential trading occurring in a set of trading posts; at each special exchange, direct bilateral barter of each pair of commodities takes place. Under this trade arrangement trade occurs successively in each trading post; after all feasible trades at this trading post have been carried out, a new trading post opens and traders meet again for the exchange of a new pair of commodities. At a special trading post, each individual trader will conduct direct barter on a pair-wise, quid pro quo basis. The trading rule we referred to in the analysis of Veendorp (1970a) that at each trading post total sales equal total purchases of the two commodities for each other, is just a proxy for the condition of value quid pro quo, given equilibrium prices, and therefore it is a reasonable restriction, enforceable by traders on the basis of decentralized information.

Veendorp concluded that direct barter may not be feasible; planned trades fail full execution by means of direct barter, and rates of exchange may be seen in need of revision at some step of sequential trading. Furthermore, indirect barter is hardly conceivable in a trade arrangement made of successive trading posts and it requires the collection of information on excess demands of other traders, that exceeds the author's view of decentralized information, that of pure competition (this was tackled under rather overstretched expectational assumptions in Benassy 1975). The logistical complications of decentralized exchange were, however, hardly introduced, and it is not quite clear how to interpret his view of trading within each trading post. All we can think of is trading posts opening sequentially and at each one *all* individual traders conducting transactions 'simultaneously' through a 'specialized broker' before they move to another trading post. An attendant will make sure that all traders are present and that, over all traders, no more value goes one way than the other. If this is so, trade is conflated within each special exchange, and its logistics ignored.

If it is granted that this is a fair account of trading in Veendorp, then all the problems dealt with by Ostroy and Starr (1974; 1990) are entirely of a different sort. Their main concern is to model and inquire into the feasibility of individual trades, not to examine the consistency of trading in special exchanges with the maintained assumption of equilibrium prices.

In Ostroy and Starr there is no allusion to organized exchanges. In order to introduce logistical decentralization, they consider that the auctioneer 'retires from the scene to leave the individuals to trade on their own in pairs' (Ostroy and Starr 1990, p. 13). Here, each trader meets other traders, one at a time, sequentially. We have a succession of bilateral trades between pairs of traders,[48] that the authors presume to take place simultaneously.[49] A sequence of pair-wise meetings that allows each trader to contact everyone other 'once and only once' is called a round (ibid., p. 31).

Allocation of trading partners is parametrical. Ostroy and Starr choose to leave the problem of timing coincidence aside;[50] they acknowledge, however, that 'direct treatment of the timing decision would introduce greater complexity than we wish to treat in this model' (Ostroy and Starr 1990, p. 34), and they notice that the 'requirement [of explicit timing decisions of individual agents] enters essentially, however, in the analysis of sequence economies with transaction costs'.

Trading is potentially decentralized. According to the definition of informational decentralization, it will be less so (even though the authors do not acknowledge this clearly[51]) as long as in the course of meetings, in order for any trader to execute trades, he collects information on the excess demands of every other single trader; in spite of not being contemporaneous information, it may help each trader 'to make more precise estimates of the probable excess demands of future partners' (Ostroy and Starr 1974, p. 1097, n).

At each meeting information on net excess demands, based on equilibrium prices, is communicated and trade may take place, if the following restrictions are satisfied (cf. Ostroy and Starr 1990, p. 33). Beyond the conditions that (i) no trader can have at any step of barter 'a negative holding of any commodity' (no credit), and that (ii) trade is pair-wise ('goods delivered are received'), which implies that commodities are conserved until trading is completed (i.e. not consumed, nor disposed of), we may choose to add (iii) the quid pro quo trade restriction. This condition, as applied to pair-wise multi-commodity barter, restricts trading between two traders at each 'bilateral encounter' so that the total value of sales is equal to the total value of purchases, given equilibrium prices (cf. Ostroy 1973, p. 598). That prices are common knowledge is basic for understanding the imposition by traders of this quid pro quo condition on each other.

Thereafter, pair-wise trading rules are postulated, which define which trades each pair is allowed to perform and the information available to each of them at each step of barter – assumed decentralized at each pair-wise meeting. At any pair-wise meeting, and at any instant of the sequence of meetings, each trader is supposed to have information of 'currently unsatisfied excess demands and supplies' of the trading partner, the names of the trading partners, or, at the most, of (only) the two traders' previous trading history (cf. Ostroy and Starr 1974, p. 1097).

Under this roundabout barter arrangement, some conclusions are worth mentioning (Ostroy and Starr 1974; and 1990, esp. pp. 35–9). First, full execution of barter trading can be achieved in one round of meetings: there is a centralized assignment of a chain of trading partners for each trader to enter at, in the course of the sequence of meetings which allows full execution; besides other unpalatable features, it will require indirect barter (cf. Ostroy and Starr 1974, p. 1102). The authors also prove that, at given exchange rates, there is no informationally decentralized barter rule that will attain full execution in one round, hence their contention that it is impossible to decentralize exchange in a barter economy at equilibrium exchange rates. That is to say, 'within the class of all functions (rules) whose domain is what the traders know and whose range is their sets of feasible trades, there is none which satisfies the stated conditions' (Ostroy and Starr 1974, p. 1103); the conditions are those established in Theorem 2 (ibid., p. 1098), namely, (A): admissible trades, (D.3): informational decentralization, and (E): full execution in one round. Only given information on excess demands of other traders, other than the two meeting pair-wise, could each trader decide which trades to carry out that would be amenable for achieving execution of planned trades in one round. This non-decentralized solution would require indirect barter and relaxation of the quid pro quo rule. We should, however, grant the authors' point that 'in a world of complete information the requirements for enforcing overall budget balance are met, so quid pro quo is an avoidable constraint on the transaction process' (Ostroy and Starr 1990, p. 11).

Finally, the authors aim for a positive conclusion (Ostroy and Starr 1974,

p. 1108–11). In a crude form, this is that monetary exchange will allow for decentralized execution that is consistent with planned trades, thereby economizing on information about individuals' net excess demands. Another related result (Starr 1976, p. 1087) is that 'the use of money economizes on trading time'. But let us be more specific.

If allowance is made for repeated rounds of meetings among all traders, the authors show that convergence to full execution may be attainable in the limit as time tends to infinity. On the other hand, they consider two sets of situations in which full execution is attainable in one round of trades. One is the above-referred centralized trading rule (cf. Ostroy and Starr 1974, pp. 1098, 1102). The other relies on 'enough slack in initial endowments – either a trader whose endowments are sufficient to fulfill all others' excess demands ... , or a commodity such that the value of each trader's holdings of it is at least equal to the value of his planned purchases of all other commodities' (ibid., p. 1108). In the first case, a trader 'acts as a clearinghouse'.[52] The second case is inaccurately defined in the (1974) article: a commodity m works as a 'counting device to insure that the sum of additions to and subtractions from the value of one's holdings during the course of trade is zero' (ibid., p. 1111) – one commodity is chosen as the unit of account of a, let us say, 'central credit' payment system: '[the trading rule] narrows the choice of means of payment to commodity m without, however, imposing the restriction that m be in excess supply before it is given up' (ibid., p. 1109).

It is bizarre to call this commodity money, or to refer expressly to a medium of exchange when the accounting book (commodity m) is just used to cancel out trading accounts when quid pro quo fails to be satisfied (ibid., p. 1111). This slippage into 'telematic' money (cf. Ostroy and Starr 1990, p. 11) stretches the decentralization assumptions. It reveals that the authors fail to cope with execution as something distinct from consistency of planned trades, and so raises the question of what is being investigated.

We must pay attention, nonetheless, to how less confused – though erroneous – the later (1990) version of the subject is compared to the earlier (1974), which was obtained by means of a taxonomic distinction between a monetary and a bank credit economy. More precisely, the definition of a monetary economy is narrowed to the case where 'there is a zeroth good universally held in a quantity sufficient to finance all purchases' (Ostroy and Starr 1990, p. 35), and 'failure in quid pro quo is made up by trade in 0' (ibid., p. 38); in this case money is just enough to slacken the budget balance.[53] As to the second case, it is relabeled as a 'bank credit economy', 'with the credit instruments working as money', and where the 'bank' is allowed to violate the 'non-negativity requirement' – which is 'contrary to the idea of informational decentralization' (ibid., pp. 35–6).

Some general comments are in order. First, the functional confusion regarding the medium of exchange is not properly addressed. No clear definition of money (and of money versus credit) is provided, the outstanding feature seeming to be that of 'blue chips' or a record-keeping device (Ostroy and Starr 1990, pp. 9–10; cf. Alchian 1977).[54] This seems obvious for the case of the credit economy, it is even granted by the authors that it violates informational decentralization; whereas the case of slackness of the money commodity seems to imply that existence (and convergence) is not independent from execution, if the 'value' of the medium-of-exchange-commodity(ies) depends on the ease of trade enabled. This is well spelled out by Patinkin (1989, p. xxxiv), as referring to Ostroy and Starr (1988, Section 1.2; identical to 1990, Section 1.2), 'who point out that in order to determine the utility of such balances, the household must first have a general notion of the volume of transactions that these balances will have to perform; and this can be known only after the household has determined the outcome of the process of utility-maximization itself'.

This conclusion that existence is not independent of execution is here ascertained in the context of a monetary economy, as has been long recognized:

> In the usual existence problem the 'initial' position of the participants can be described independently of prices, i.e. in terms of the initial endowment of goods, technological knowledge, etc. The interesting point of a monetary economy is that we cannot do so. For it is one of the features of such an economy that contracts, as Keynes noted, are made in terms of money. (Hahn 1965, pp. 131–2).

But the reason lies in a separate, and previous aspect. The origin of the problem is not specifically the medium of exchange property of the money commodity, but the introduction of 'actual transaction opportunities' and 'actual relationships' (Hahn 1965, pp. 131, 133). Trading, and feasibility of trading, is the problem, not money as a facilitating device.[55]

Moreover, we may ask now what is the meaning in Ostroy and Starr's (1990, p. 34) exposition of execution, of the assumption that the total money endowment is sufficient to permit feasibility of trades. Since this problem is a value problem (as the authors indeed recognize), any aggregate quantity will do. It simply does not matter, we may assume any given total endowment of the money good. The relevant problem lies in that the total 'stock of a monetary commodity to be used as a medium of exchange ... must be distributed sufficiently broadly in sufficiently great quantity (*in value terms*) among the holders that all agents find that they can finance all desired purchases from endowment of the money commodity' (Ostroy and Starr 1990, p. 34). Whereas the problem regarding the aggregate stock of the money commodity may be mistaken (it is primarily a value problem), it is plausible to question whether quantity restrictions in money holdings will afflict individual traders in execution, when a notional equilibrium price set is presumed beforehand. Clearly, if existence were concomitant to execution (the consistency of trading opportunities as pertaining to the definition of equilibrium), the 'individual' sufficiency question would lose all meaning.

Overall, the problem in Ostroy and Starr's assessment of execution seems to derive from their trouble remembering the assumptions, namely informational decentralization. Still, it has to be acknowledged that their work is the most thorough, and reliable, source in this area. Be that as it may, our attempts at critical analysis are only meant to disentangle the arguments so that our reasoning can lead to finding some positive way out. One conclusion seems reasonable: dichotomization of the existence and execution has not yet provided the basis for the solution to the attempt to view execution as a decentralized affair. Existence of notional consistency of plans as metaphysically postulated in decentralized exchange, is possibly tying down understanding of execution. Consequently, existence and equilibrium may have to be brought down to earth, were they to become operative concepts in the explanation of the working of competitive markets. Without further elaboration at this point, the suggestion is clear that we will have to venture into a world where existence is not supposed.

(vi) Alternative attempts to formalize execution
Let us attempt a broad classification of decentralized logistical arrangements, where the organizing criterion is the facilitating device (brokerage or specialists, and money). I could glean the following types of formalizations in the literature: (i) organized exchange in trading posts; (ii) sequential bilateral barter according to rules, either with equilibrium prices as given or not; (iii) the presence of endogenous brokers in bilateral exchange; and finally (iv) the endogenous emergence of media of exchange.

The first type is organized exchange in *trading posts* (n $(n-1)/2$ exchanges), with trade facilitated by a set of (external) 'specialized brokers'. This is the case of Veendorp (1970a), Benassy (1975), and more recently Starr and Stinchcombe (1993; 1997).

The second type regards *sequential bilateral barter rules*, in two different contexts. One assumes *given and known equilibrium prices*, therefore requiring quid pro quo valued at equilibrium prices. This is the case of Ostroy and Starr (1974; 1990). I will presume that the conclusions of the analysis of Veendorp, and Ostroy and Starr are sufficiently clear from above, and will not elaborate.

Another context has been considered, in which *prices are not defined* (and thus, not known), exchange is not constrained by the requirement of quid pro quo valued at equilibrium prices, and in which each bilateral barter is utility non-decreasing. This is so in Feldman (1973). In Madden (1975) we have, additionally, that there are 'small' groups of traders and only the traders belonging to the groups are allowed to meet; groups are allowed to meet sequentially, and bilateral trades take place between the members of any two groups at a time. Madden deals both with problems of existence of a feasible trade, and of convergence of a bartering process, but his main concern is with efficiency in exchange.

The introduction, by assumption, of a money commodity in sequential bilateral barter will ease the coordination problem in Ostroy and Starr, by expediting the barter-cum-money exchange, given the slackening function of money. Feldman does not deal expressly with the logistics of barter, i.e., the 'conditions for the effectiveness of bilateral trade move sequences' (Feldman 1973, p. 471) – rather, an example is presented where, notwithstanding convexity assumptions, optimality is not established pair-wisely. He shows, however, that introducing the requirement that every trader is endowed with a given commodity ('money'[56]), guarantees that sequences of barter exchange (among all traders) attain optimality in allocation.

Madden gets to a similar result (1975, p. 589: Theorem 5). Another special conclusion in Madden (ibid., pp. 588, A.5, and 589, Theorem 4) is the following: if each group contains only one trader ('middleman'), the author shows that for optimality in exchange 'we require that all middlemen are connected irreducibly and all traders who are not middlemen meet at least one middleman'. Irreducible connection in this case means (cf. Rader 1968) we have a set of middlemen, such that they have common, uniquely defined support prices (rates of exchange allowing for utility non-decreasing trades), and that all pairs of middlemen are allowed to meet. Furthermore, it is shown in the general situation, that given sequences of rounds of barter – or more specifically, infinite sequences of predetermined cycles of bilateral barter among traders of each two groups – 'there exists a sequence of meetings of groups which exhausts the gains from trade' (Madden 1975, p. 592).

The final question arises whether these proofs of feasibility satisfy the restriction of informational decentralization. In the general case, where bilateral barter among the traders belonging to any two groups occurs in a sequence of meetings of any two groups, as well as for the two special cases of middlemen and medium of exchange, the logistical construction relies on an indefinite number of rounds, which is not a decentralized procedure (according to Ostroy and Starr's definition).

The third type considered is that of *endogenous brokers in bilateral trade*, based on the assumption of a fixed cost for each bilateral deal. Townsend (1978, p. 1) proposes a non-cooperative game by means of which a subset of agents acting as intermediaries 'economize on the fixed cost of exchange'. A more promising approach was attempted by Rubinstein and Wolinski (1987) where intermediation is a time-saving device in a market characterized by a matching process that is time-consuming (cf. Diamond 1982b; Mortensen 1982a). Here, middlemen are posited as a third type of agent, beyond sellers and buyers, and the model considers stationary numbers and trading opportunities. An indivisible good is traded, when a buyer and a seller have transacted they leave the market, but middlemen engage perpetually in search and transacting, though they cannot store more than one unit. The matching process between middlemen and their customers is modeled explicitly, and the extent of that activity is endogenously determined, as well as the transaction costs; the model is extended to study the implication of the middlemen assuming ownership of the good (dealer versus consignment – see Hackett 1992; 1993).

Finally, we have the explanation of the *endogenous emergence of media of exchange*, due to transaction costs. The emergence of a general medium of exchange commodity due to search costs is explained in Jones (1976) and Oh (1989),[57] in the line of Niehans (1969; 1971), and as hinted in Brunner and Meltzer (1971, pp. 787–8).[58] Another line of research in this direction has thrived more recently – based on Diamond's (1982; 1984) search models of trade – attempting to produce a theory of the origin of fiat money. This is the case of Kiyotaki and Wright (1993; 1991; 1989) and Aiyagari and Wallace (1991). On this I will not comment specifically; however, see Appendix E, below, on the foundation of the search models of trade, and Clower and Howitt (1997b, pp. 191 ff.) on the reasonableness of these models.

Information is decentralized, equilibrium prices are given and chosen to be 1 in terms of a numeraire, trading occurs bilaterally, and quid pro quo is satisfied by the pair-wise transaction of any two goods; besides, each individual is endowed with only one unit of a single good (which he exchanges in order to obtain the other good he ultimately demands). The central assumptions are, however, that traders 'do not know with whom they can or will make given exchanges', and that exchange involves a cost, which depends 'only on the pair of goods involved and the size of the trade' (Jones 1976, pp. 760–1); i.e. a proportional transaction cost is proposed, though differentiated for each pair of goods. Minimization of search costs or expected time (which is a random variable) means, given a constant rate of search, minimization of the number of contacts. Expectations about the willingness of a randomly contacted trader to supply or demand any particular good are constructed on the basis of previous contacting experience, and it is assumed that goods offered and demanded by any individual are independent. Aiming at a given ultimate demand, before the individual enters the market he 'plans a fixed sequence of trades which will effect this ultimate exchange' (ibid., p. 762). If the expectation is formed by individuals (according to their experience) that there is one commodity most commonly offered in trade, and this belief is common as to which commodity provides a sufficiently high probability of being offered in exchange against some subset of goods in the economy, this commodity will be used as a medium of exchange for the acquisition of such goods. Achievement of equilibrium – meaning that beliefs are correct – will be attained through a recursive meeting process during which the medium of exchange becomes increasingly common in exchange. And, according to the configuration of the probabilities of ease of trade in direct barter or intermediated (two-stage) trade between any two pairs of commodities, (unique) degrees of 'monetization' of this economy can be achieved.

Oh (1989) broadens the previous result by relaxing the assumption that each trader fixes his trading strategy before entering the market. He replaces this by a conditional trading strategy. An ordering of goods is postulated according to their probabilities of commonness in trading offers, and thereby 'individuals will not pass up the chance of getting a more saleable good by giving up a less saleable one' (Oh 1989, pp. 102–103). The conditional trading rule will enable traders to achieve the good ultimately desired in a smaller number of expected contacts than with the fixed trading rule. Differing from Jones, who bases evolution to equilibrium on an adaptive learning process, Oh (1989, p. 107) postulates rational expectations. As to the conclusion of the model, Oh adds that '[t]he conditional trading strategy generates a generally acceptable medium of exchange with partial monetization'.

Concluding this section, let us distill a few simple, and exploratory, conclusions. First, proofs of existence and convergence of feasibility given restrictions of informational decentralization are in a very poor state. Ostroy and Starr (1974; 1990) and Madden (1975), built upon Feldman (1973), seem to be the only general attempts. Second, this collection of articles points towards two basic (generally alternative) facilitating devices: brokers or middlemen, and a medium of exchange. Third, in order to show feasibility of bilateral barter in an informationally decentralized fashion, some means of *connection*[59] is summoned. This notion is used here in the broad sense of Clower (1994b, p. 3) that 'each marketor is economically contiguous to at least one other marketor, so the set of marketors – also the set of marketees – is economically connected'. Also of interest, is the reference to brokers in Stigler's (1957, pp. 258–9) discussion of 'complete knowledge' as one of Knight's assumptions of perfect competition, as well as the role attributed to 'intermediaries' in Hayek (1945, p. 526); or, in a broader perspective, as Hayek's (1948, p. 106) concise conclusion points out: 'Competition is essentially a process of the formation of opinion; by spreading information, it creates that unity and coherence of the economic system which we presuppose when we think of it as one market'. In any case, this means of connection may be a set of external brokers (as in Veendorp and Benassy), or 'middlemen' – as in Madden, where middlemen are posited, differently from Townsend, or Rubinstein and Wolinski, where they are endogenous; or, alternatively, a commodity with the property of medium of exchange – as in Ostroy and Starr, Feldman, Madden, Jones, and Oh. The final conclusion is, however, that a link between intermediation and monetary patterns of exchange is ultimately the interesting aspect to explain. This need to bring together the two salient trade-facilitating devices is expressed in Oh:

> even in a monetary economy there still exist substantial transaction costs given that individuals search for traders who have what they wish to consume. Thus, money solves only part of the problem of the existence of transaction costs. This fact may explain why trading posts have developed. In this sense, money, defined as a generally acceptable medium of exchange, and trading posts seem to be complementary aspects of individuals' attempts to minimize transaction costs. (Oh 1989, p. 117).

This point is clearly made in Clower's (1995b) *On the Origin of Monetary Exchange*. In the presence of set-up costs of information and transaction, the activity of a trader as a specialized middleman would be paid for by economizing on those costs by other traders. But to have explained that a middleman would specialize (e.g. in trading just two commodities) does not imply that the organization of trade would be 'monetary'. Even though no firm theoretical basis is easily provided to the historically supported conjecture that 'monetary exchange arises naturally from much the same forces of self-interest that induce individuals to make markets', a conclusion is warranted. If 'business firms and markets organized and operated by them lend coherence to exchange activities by establishing well-marked and easily accessible channels through which household and other transactors may trade', in an ongoing economy money works as the web through which economic activities are coordinated (Clower 1995b, p. 535).

4.3.4 The Obstacles of the Walrasian Program

Decentralization of exchange is a difficult matter and I am not proposing a solution. The intention is only to investigate the implications of possible alternative ways to deal with the subject; each one brings special problems, which have not yet found a satisfactory answer. The task is a simple armchair exercise to map out possible paths to follow. I intend only to locate the obstacles, indicate the bridges to be built, and so on. I envision two general directions to seek a possible way out, yet each one faces apparently insurmountable obstacles.

4.3.4.1 Equilibrium in a pure exchange economy
When discussing the meaning and usefulness of equilibrium notions I am confined to an exchange, stock economy, knowing however that it is meaningless to make sense of markets, of institutions for trade created to economize on costs of transaction. Especially, decentralized markets can only be adequately understood, and therefore formalized, for the case of ongoing, stock-flow economies where the notion of equilibrium can only be described

along the lines of Leijonhufvud and Clower (1973, p. 89), but for the fact that 'the values of all variables that are considered relevant for describing observable behavior [of an economic system] over time' are not to be related to 'the values of a corresponding set of theoretical variables that define the virtual (notional) behavior of the system along a postulated equilibrium path' but rather to the variables so defined that the mechanics of trade and its feasibility are not left unconsidered (cf. Veendorp 1970a, p. 6). Whether, and how, this can be formalized is not my problem now. I am not venturing into the world of ongoing trade arrangements, or 'the continuous market' in the words of Walras (Jaffé, ed. 1954, p. 380), not even of the Hicksian temporary equilibrium type – with sequential endowments, and discrete (re)contracting. That is, of the two functions that, according to Hahn (1970, pp. 5–6), the invisible hand is supposed to perform, first, that 'it should establish an equilibrium at every stage of the sequence', and, second, on the 'inducement of a coherent sequence of such equilibria', the second is totally ignored. All I am attempting at this point is to question the implication of the argument developed above on the meaning of equilibrium for a 'stock' exchange economy, with only one 'shower' of endowments. If we are to be confined within the Walrasian program, the question to ask is how the incorporation of logistics into the 'static' model of exchange has been attempted or circumvented, and whether the Walrasian program withstands such intrusion.

4.3.4.2 Framework for a solution

A first direction would be to reinforce rationality, that is, to build price decisions upon the rational behavior of individuals in order to replace the predetermination of prices: bargaining and trading would go together. The real problem is that once we give up the notion of planned trades and attempt a contemplation of the execution of trades, we cannot hold onto notionally determined individual net excess demands; i.e. dispositions to trade of every single commodity determined 'once for all' before trade starts. Trading opportunities are not predetermined, only the mechanisms of exchange will allow for their definition, and thus we lose the anchor of notional equilibrium (cf. Burstein, 1968, pp. 25–6[60]). The question to ask first is then: Is it possible to adapt or redefine the notion of general equilibrium (i.e. for the economy as a whole) to meet the degree of feasibility of decentralized trades?

A deeper problem surfaces, however, that may compromise this line of enquiry, and this is the effect of transaction costs on the generation of equilibrium behavior by individual traders. Rational behavior is incompatible with Lucas's view of economics – in line with Hahn (1973a, pp. 18–28, esp. pp. 25–8) – as 'studying decision rules that are steady states of some adaptive process, decision rules that are found to work over a range of situations and hence are no longer revised appreciably as more experience accumulates' (Lucas 1986, p. S402), unless some cost is present (information or transaction costs) that leads the individual trader to 'routinize' his behavioral patterns. But as has been shown, those costs are necessary to explain trading arrangements. Markets, created to economize on transaction costs, may well therefore be at the root of stories explaining the viability of convergence of adaptive processes to steady states.

Patterns of individual behavior, and market arrangements (the observable modes of interaction among individual traders) can both be seen as issuing from the same basic mechanism, economizing in information and transaction costs. Trivially, the existence of trading arrangements – or money – catalyzes the convergence of adaptive behavior to observable regularities; not so trivially, both may have the same economic reason.

Without transaction costs (implying trading arrangements) no recognizable patterns of trading could be expected. Direct barter (which, like any other decentralized trading mechanism, is characterized by quid pro quo, pair-wise exchange) is a serious contender as the prevailing trade mechanism in this setting, and no incentive whatsoever would be present for learning 'as more experience accumulates'. If we do not consider transaction costs, the individual can only be seen as going on searching and anonymously pairing up until he has gathered his preferred bundle. What sense can be made of learning and 'adaptive' processes to 'modes of behavior' that are 'steady states'? (cf. Lucas 1986, pp. S401–402). Yet, we could surmise that if some regularity of endowments prevailed, individuals would attempt to establish regular meeting patterns, but to raise this possibility is to beg the question! Why would 'manna' fall in regular patterns to start with?

Two doubts arise as a consequence. Once transaction costs enter the picture, a tradeoff will be present between the 'desired' consumption bundle and the continuation of meetings – in order to achieve the 'desired' (notional) bundle, or more appropriately, the feasible bundle. Here our troubles with the definition of equilibrium gain a concrete form and some practical interest.

More importantly, as seen, if transaction costs are lump-sum, intermediation is a reasonable outcome of 'rational' trading. Therefore, we may lack a good reason for proceeding with the analysis of barter in order to understand the working of the economy (cf. Veendorp 1970a, p. 22[61]), but this sounds a rather poor argument; in any case, to frame it more adequately we may ponder the other possible approach.

A second direction towards a solution to the Walrasian program would be to abandon altogether the postulate of rationality as used towards the determination of prices by a fictional agent; rationality here is of limited usefulness if it only allows for a notional consistency of plans. In Arrow–Debreu we start with plans, and we have formal theory of how they are 'coordinated' by prices; but to describe actual trades, we must append logistical glosses that seldom make sense. We might start the other way around. Do logistics of barter exchange, and then ask the reverse question, namely, about theory of behavior that corresponds to the assumed logistical facts. This has a parallel to 'the can-opener philosophy', to borrow the image Velupillai uses, as he refers to existence proofs in the course of his severe criticism of Katzner's unqualified defense of methodological individualism as the ground to erect general equilibrium. Velupillai writes succinctly:

> how to build a behavioral economics based on methodological individualism that does not rely on preferences at all. ... I have constructed agents as decision rules ... In the next step, to study and analyze the average behavior of a collection of agents – fashionably, but misleadingly, called aggregate behavior – one investigates the coupled outcomes of a collection of decision rules. It is as if several processes were activated in parallel ... Equilibrium, on this context, will be coherent outcomes. Since such an analysis is inherently constructive in the strict sense of computable analysis, existence proofs automatically carry information about the way coherence is achieved. (Velupillai 1991, pp. 28–9).

That is to say, if the execution of trades could be formalized in a decentralized 'setting', then investigation would proceed on whichever behavioral rules would be compatible with such a result.

As should now be clear, to formalize the logistics of barter under decentralized information as a basis for understanding 'coherence' in the theory of general economic interdependence has been a hard task, and appears to promise only uncertain payoffs. Its interest may even be questionable, unless for the purpose of making clear how crucial the mechanism of exchange is to make sense of markets. Barter is an encumbrance and 'solutions' apparently have been found that deal with that: these are markets and money. The real interest of studying the logistics of barter would be then accomplished once it has helped to find a satisfying way to describe the roles of intermediation and monetary exchange in the working of markets and the economy. I am not implying that we have come to this point, nor that dealing with the difficulties that the logistics of exchange pose is not worth a try, or several. All I am doing is basically repeating Veendorp's sensible admonition, in the course of his proposal to reconstruct the theory of barter exchange:

> Fortunately, the defense of an analysis of bartering does not depend on the desirability of such an ambitious attempt to demonstrate the intuitively obvious. Even if one accepts the familiar hypothesis that barter 'is so inefficient a method of transacting that its cost effectively rules it out of the realm of relevance' (Kuenne 1958, p. 2), a better understanding of the inefficiency of bartering may help in analyzing the operation of a money economy. The means of payment function of money has received scant attention in the literature; tracing the implications of the absence of a universally accepted medium of exchange is likely to increase one's appreciation of the essential function of a money commodity. (Veendorp 1970a, p. 22).

Despite this pessimistic stance, let us consider each path more closely, with a view to making the Walrasian program fit the facts of logistics.

(i) Bilateral bargaining and the notion of market/general equilibrium

Apparently, the logical outcome of the discussion in the last section is to proceed by dropping the separation between convergence and execution and, as a starting point, model exchange as involving direct bargaining and barter, both in a decentralized setting. According to the suggestions of Veendorp (1970a, p. 22) and Howitt (1973, p. 497), trade would take place before the Walrasian convergence is attained; i.e., bargaining and execution would be formalized under informational decentralization at each instant of barter. And a question could then be raised whether traders, by means of bargaining and possibly relying on trading agents, could approach and sustain equilibrium prices in exchange. Howitt's (1973, p. 494) conclusion is that in the Walrasian barter model 'the bargaining process cannot be decentralized'. The decentralization of bargaining as concomitant with decentralized execution of barter trading seems thus to be a first step – and a primary challenge – in order to formalize adjustment processes in decentralized exchange.

To put matters in perspective, a short detour may be helpful. The question is that the understanding of execution runs up against the ingrained notion of equilibrium in general equilibrium analysis. Apprehensions as to this have been expounded under various moods, fatalistic, somewhat dismissive or tentatively constructive.

If the general equilibrium model is to be explored under the logical implication of the behavioral assumptions of methodological individualism, a quite common view is that 'the economist has no choice but to pursue the relevant formalizations and inquire into the existence, uniqueness and stability of equilibrium in the model', as Katzner stated it, adding:

> as to the full general-equilibrium model ... satisfactory answers are available only in the case of existence. The problem is that, although sufficient conditions for uniqueness and stability are known, these conditions, contrary to the tenets of methodological individualism, are expressed as restrictions on aggregated, that is market, excess demand functions. Furthermore, it is not clear if it will ever be possible to give uniqueness and stability conditions that are stated with respect to the preferences or behavior of the individual agents. Therefore, if methodological individualism is to be maintained, even more resources and energies will have to be diverted to the mathematical analysis of general-equilibrium models (Katzner 1991, pp. 19–20).

In the same disembodied vein, and missing the crucial implication of logistics, Hahn raises the fundamental problem as regarding the notion of equilibrium:

> There is now also a somewhat subtler point to consider: the behaviour postulated for the auctioneer will implicitly define what we are to mean by an equilibrium: that state of affairs when the rules tell the auctioneer to leave prices where they are. But the auctioneer's pricing rules are not derived from any consideration of the rational actions of agents on which the theory is supposed to rest. Thus the

equilibrium notion becomes arbitrary and unfounded. If, on the other hand, we had a theory of price formation based on the rational calculations of rational agents then the equilibrium notion would be a natural corollary of such a theory. (Hahn 1987, p. 137)

The failure to provide behavioral microfoundations to the adjustment of price (or quantity) was formerly questioned by Koopmans (1957, p. 179) and Arrow (1959), and this led to various models of price adjustment based on maximizing behavior (cf. Hahn 1982, pp. 788–91), like for instance, Phelps and Winter (1970) in a competitive market, and Barro (1972) for monopoly. These constructions are flimsy for they lack a clear underpinning in market arrangements. Their logistics not being clearly defined, price adjustment mechanisms are liable to infeasibility in a decentralized way (see Section 4.4, below).

In any case, Hahn then adds:

> This line of reasoning leads one to a central objection to the auctioneer and indeed the tâtonnement: it sidesteps the important question of the co-ordinating power of the price mechanism. ... One might just about convince oneself that notwithstanding all these objections, the tâtonnement and its auctioneer are worthwhile, if it were the case that it provided one story which showed how equilibrium was brought about. Unfortunately, however, it does not do this for there are only a few special cases for which the auctioneer process leads the economy to an equilibrium. In many others it will not do so. Indeed, in so far as one holds the view that an equilibrium is the normal state of an economy one should not be tempted to understand this circumstance by means of a tâtonnement. (Hahn 1987, pp. 137–8; see also Hahn 1970, p. 3; and 1973a, pp. 7–11).

As seen above, however, a disturbing result is that 'in the aggregate, the hypothesis of rational behaviour has in general no implications; that is, for any set of aggregate excess demand functions, there is a choice of preference maps and of initial endowments, one for each individual in the economy, whose maximization implies the given excess demand functions' (Arrow 1987, p. 70, referring to the Sonnenschein–Mantel–Debreu result). Additional, usually strong assumptions are required for convergence, for instance that all individuals have the same preferences (utility function) but this conflicts with the desirable premise of methodological individualism: 'In particular, the homogeneity assumption seems to me to be especially dangerous. It denies the fundamental assumption of the economy, that it is built from trading arising from individual differences' (Arrow 1987, p. 71; cf. Kirman 1989, p. 138 [62]). But this is not very important anyhow, as the assumption of rational behavior is concerned. A shared belief is that '[i]ndeed, in many cases, provided that the factual assumptions are retained, the conclusions reached within the utility-maximization framework could be reached as readily from much weaker assumptions of 'reasonableness' in behavior' (Simon 1986, p. S212, citing Becker 1962; see also Arrow 1987, esp. pp. 69–70).

Hahn's argument above is inconclusive: equilibrium as asserted by tatonnement is of no use as a guide to understand 'the normal state of an economy', but he gives no suggestion to replace it. (Notice Walras's view on equilibrium as 'an ideal and not a real state', yet it is 'the normal state, in the sense that it is the state towards which things spontaneously tend under a régime of free competition in exchange and production' [Jaffé, ed. 1954, p. 224]). In a broader perspective, however, Hahn (1981, pp. 136–7) sheds some light on 'the correct path' toward 'new equilibrium notions', e.g. 'non-Walrasian equilibrium concepts'. More recently, Hahn (1989b, p. 106) has attempted to formalize 'the equilibrium of an economy as an economic state such that no agent has an incentive to deviate from the actions he is taking or from his policy of actions'; this notion of equilibrium would be dependent on the history of information communication and learning interaction among individuals, and would dispense with market clearing. Summing up, 'processes themselves will need to be invoked in the account of equilibrium' (Hahn 1994, p. 253; cf. Busetto 1995 [63]).

More constructively, Howitt (1973) emphasizes the role of the bargaining as intrinsic to the exchange process. In his criticism of the dichotomization of exchange and bargaining,[64] he touches a question of interest, that of giving non-convergence a tractable meaning:

> One qualification is in order here. It might be argued that however the bargaining process is defined it must come to an end before exchange occurs, because whenever two people are observed to engage in an exchange we have no choice but to assume that they agreed to exchange exactly the way they did. Thus their bargaining process must by definition have converged on the agreed exchange. In order for the non-convergence of bargaining to make sense we must have in mind *a more restrictive definition of equilibrium*. What is crucial is that in a market equilibrium the trades being engaged in by any one individual are the best that he could see himself as being able to engage in even if he were able instantaneously to bargain with everyone else in the economy. (Howitt 1973, p. 497, italics added).

'Equilibrium' becomes the outcome of the activity of bargaining and exchange by individuals facing 'perceived' opportunities. Even if we postulate that the trader knows prices of the sequence of transactions to come (how?), we cannot presume he knows the transactions he will consummate. Notional equilibrium can hardly have an implication, here. This problem has been mostly circumvented, as in models of convergence where there is no 'auctioneer', e.g. Fisher (1983). Referring to the model description of the adjustment of prices in disequilibrium when 'there is no central price-setter nor particular-market price-setters' in the 'excellent book by Franklin Fisher', Walker (1997a, pp. 29-34) conceives of disequilibrium transactions taking place between individual market participants, and concludes that '[i]t is impossible for an individual to know whether market equilibrium has been reached';[65] this is in line with our analysis of Veendorp's (1970a) paper in Section 4.3.3.1 (iii), above.

Because it is not within the reach of the individual trader under decentralized information to know in advance the chain of meetings, the ordering of the exchanges, and the actual exchanges to be entered at, feasibility is an unknown to the individual trader to start with (dealing with 'unaided' decentralized exchange, it is not up to the individual trader to know this; for instance, in Ostroy and Starr [1974; 1990] meetings are parametric, and in search models random). A possible 'idea' would be that the outcome of bargaining would be Walrasian 'if agents are allowed to trade arbitrarily many times and may not be prevented from realizing trades that are beneficial to others' (McLennan and Sonnenschein 1991, p. 1396; cf. Gale 1986a, pp. 787–8); but then what is the progress relative to Ostroy and Starr's case of non-decentralized execution?[66]

In *Sequential Bargaining as a Noncooperative Foundation for Walrasian Equilibrium*, McLennan and Sonnenschein really take the problem seriously, if only 'at an intuitive level' (1991, p. 1398). Facing the question whether allocations induced by steady state equilibria – as in Gale (1986a), also with sequences of 'entering and leaving' flows of individuals – are Walrasian, the authors recognize the need to have an 'initial' economy to compare: 'In order to even be able to talk whether an equilibrium is Walrasian it is necessary to have initial and final economies to compare' (McLennan and Sonnenschein 1991, p. 1420). What is an initial economy? The authors, as a starting point, just subsume it: 'Fix a Walrasian equilibrium of this economy' (ibid., p. 1395), which is given by their Theorem A (ibid., p. 1397). Then the authors proceed with artful reasoning:

> In the theory of general economic equilibrium prices are not displayed as variables chosen by individuals, and the relevance of the theory therefore depends on the belief that economic equilibrium correctly summarizes the noncooperative equilibria of an underlying game in which all endogenous variables are direct consequences of the choices of individuals. However, there are few principles to guide the modelling of the underlying game, and in fact our belief in the relevance of economic equilibrium rests on an intuition that this concept should characterize equilibrium outcomes for a large class of games. (McLennan and Sonnenschein 1991, p. 1398).

Borrowing sundry intuitive support,[67] their 'initial economy' is asserted as characterizing 'Walrasian outcomes by means of axioms that are, at an intuitive level, consequences of individual rationality in a world in which agents are not prevented from trading with each other repeatedly' (ibid., p. 1398).[68] In fact traders do not trade, here. Elsewhere in the article, after pointing out the problem that Gale's (1986a, p. 794) 'introduction of individuals' originates in the formulation of the pairing process – the existence of a continuum of i.i.d. random variables – the authors state, for the case of their continuum economy:

In our approach 'Walrasian' is a relation between initial and final measures on the space of consumer characteristics, and ... it is possible to discuss pairing probabilities and the evolution of the distribution of characteristics in the market without reference to any underlying pairing of individuals ... One might object that we allow pairing probabilities that cannot be justified by any pairing process. This is true in a narrow technical sense, but we believe that limit theorems for finite economies are the correct response. (McLennan and Sonnenschein 1991, p. 1403).

And when 'pair wise transactions' between 'individuals' are presumably allowed for (Gale 1986a, p. 791), bargaining is modeled under the 'as if' assumption that exchange rates are equilibrium (notional or Walrasian) prices; this is in fact so in bargaining models, such as in Gale (1986a; 1986b) where each instant of bargaining in random pair-wise meetings of individual traders is marked by the '(rational) expectations' of the outcome of future bargains, in the successive rounds towards convergence to the Walrasian consumption bundle (cf. Arrow 1994, p. 5). It is also Arrow's opinion that in these articles 'prices never appear as objective phenomena; they are only subjective, that is, expectations held in the agents' minds'. Given the full anticipation that only the Walrasian net trades will be accepted, each trader is willing to continue search and bargaining without any 'impatience' cost until the marginal rate of substitution between goods equals their (Walrasian) relative price (cf. Wilson 1987b, pp. 54–5). This artifice erases any distinction between 'target' and 'active' excess demands, and thus no trading can be said, in fact, to be present in the process of bargaining.

Be that as it may, the main result of McLennan and Sonnenschein's model is that for every market equilibrium, a Walrasian allocation exists such that an agent completes in finite time his preferred bundle and leaves the market (cf. Binmore, Osborne and Rubinstein 1992, pp. 208–209).

(ii) In the beginning ... logistics
If we needed to provide a demarcation from the former view, we would argue that this second proposed path derives from the difficulty of understanding 'rational behavior' when the actions of an individual are dependent upon the actions of others. As Hurwicz (1945, p. 506) put it, though in a different context:

There is no adequate solution of the problem of defining 'rational economic behavior' on the part of an individual when the very rationality of his actions depends on the probable behavior of other individuals ... [T]he individual's 'rational behavior' is determined *if* the pattern of behavior of 'others' can be assumed *a priori* known. But the behavior of 'others' cannot be known *a priori* if 'others,' too, are to behave rationally! Thus a logical *impasse* is reached. (Hurwicz 1945, p. 506).

Or, according to Hahn:

> There is also a canker at the heart of the theory. This arises from the logical necessity that a theory based on rational self-seeking actions ensures that its equilibrium notion is indeed that of a state in which no agent can improve himself by any action. But all General Equilibrium Theory has done is ensure this *provided market prices are independent of these actions*. (Hahn 1981, p. 130).

If we understand behavior here to refer not to maximization of utility given prices, but to (the solution to the problem of) exchange patterns[69] – patterns of bargaining and trading of whatever kind we might consider in a decentralized setting – then behavior is not independent of the market arrangement that we choose to postulate and the trading activities therein.[70] This is the question of feasibility of individual behavior to which logistical feasibility can be seen as an 'external' constraint that matters: 'Any choice can be exhibited as a maximization against constraints; what I have just been saying is that the constraints may be internal to the chooser, as well as external to him' (Hicks 1983, p. 371). In this regard, Arrow's (1994) comments on the adequacy of game theoretical analogies to deal with 'real-life phenomena', namely in the formalization of bargaining in general equilibrium analysis, conclude this way:

> What this example shows is that the *rules of the game* are *social*. The theory of games gets its name and much of its force from an analogy with social games. But these have definite rules which are constructed, indeed, by a partly social process. Who sets rules for real-life games?
> More generally, individual behavior is always mediated by social relations. These are as much a part of the description of reality as is individual behavior. (Arrow 1994, p. 5).

Of course, we are not entering the much harder subject of the emergence (or even the less pressing aim at 'optimality') of institutional arrangements for trade. According to our understanding of the feasibility question, the traders might just as well be assumed to be provided some sort of exchange mechanism, the rules of which they are supposed to obey.

The analysis of logistics in exchange could, therefore, be envisaged in two different senses. In a first sense, logistics can be addressed as a preliminary exercise towards the comprehension of the implications of certain specified market 'rules' on individual behavior, in line with doubts – such as those raised namely by Hurwicz, Hahn, Hicks and Arrow – about the independence of individual behavior from the behavior of *others* or, in general, *external* constraints. All that has been said about execution and feasibility of trades in section 4.3.3.1 (iv) applies at this point, but I would like to recall two notes. One is that feasibility of trades is defined independently of the presumption, or not, of predetermined equilibrium prices, and in this sense feasibility is not conceptually attached to the notional consistency of plans. Another is that feasibility relates to the aggregate coherence of any given set of trading rules and, therefore, if aggregate coherence can be shown to comply with decentralization criteria, the feasibility of execution will define the range of admissible behavior by the individual traders, or trader agents, as may be the case.

Some of the models we referred to in this chapter may provide some guidelines in this direction, but as may be clear, this perspective on the role of the study of the logistics of trade is absent from general equilibrium analyses. The basic reference is Ostroy and Starr on trading rules, although this type of exercise is hindered by the presupposition of existence. Also, exchange models that do not dichotomize may be of interest, like Feldman (1973), and Madden (1975) – although paying only cursory attention to logistics, relying on individual optimization as the foundation, and primarily addressing the question of optimality in allocation. In any case, tatonnement processes of neowalrasian extraction, as well as both the Edgeworth Process and the Hahn Process seem inadequate as a starting point, given their failures regarding informational decentralization (cf. e.g. Fisher 1983, Chapter 2; Weintraub 1985 and 1991; Clower 1995a; Walker 1997a). However, as pointed out in Chapter 2, above, Walras's attempt at understanding arbitrage in indirect trades, in the three-goods case in Lesson 11 of the *Eléments*, provides a good introduction; the analysis of pair-wise quid pro quo exchange as taking place in trading posts is potentially decentralized in all dimensions we defined, which regard information, the determination of prices and the execution of trades. No commodity money and no 'particular' trading post specialist is necessarily implied, and the modes of interaction are simply defined on the basis of assumptions regarding the 'location' where each good can be exchanged for any other can be made, and the rules of 'sequentiality' that individual traders must obey in indirect barter. This is an open question, which has remained unresolved since Walras first gave it a try (see Starr and Stinchcombe 1993). The obstacle that Walras met when attempting to generalize these decentralized trading rules beyond the three-goods case, was surpassed by means of a 'no-arbitrage' condition.

What for Walras was an obstacle, has eventually become a trap. The idea here is to raise the question whether it is of interest to face the obstacle and tackle the question of decentralized exchange as a do-it-yourself affair in the framework of a limited number of rules of interaction. Alternatively – and this is a second way of envisaging the logistical problem – we might raise the possibility that the obstacle be erased by the presence of institutions such as money or intermediaries, as derived from the opportunities open to 'agents' to create trade arrangements which are paid for by the reduction of informational or logistical set-up costs. In this case, the obstacle is surpassed, the feasibility problem surmised as enabled, and consequently the trap sidetracked. When set-up costs of transaction enter the field, and a certain trade organization is considered which is paid for by the transaction costs it economizes, we move a step forward in the direction of observed mechanisms of exchange. It should be noticed, however, that the theoretical complexity of this question is higher the further we move away from abstraction in the direction of real-world phenomena. The inclusion of such features requires that the rules of the trading 'game' be 'constructed' which appeal to 'a partly social process' (Arrow 1994, p. 5). In the same vein – and as seen above in the last paragraph of Section 3.2.2 – Fudenberg and Tirole (1987, p. 176) propose that models which consider the 'timing and information structure faced by firms' require 'constructing', and this obviously applies to the consideration of facilitating mechanisms, such as intermediaries or money in exchange. In the next chapter, we shall attempt to search for a few threads in order to sort these questions out, and the possibility is raised that the analysis of the workings of non-brokered markets may provide an appropriate basis towards the understanding of exchange in actual economies.

To sum up, following the line of thought as regards the definition of the features – and the implications – of the notion of feasibility of execution, this kind of exercise does not have to have a direct bearing on the concrete workings of markets. In the demonstration of feasibility of execution, as has been defined in Section 4.3.3.1 (iv), no claim is implied that the rules of the transaction game correspond in any sense to real-world features. Our concern here has centered only on the implication of interaction on individual behavior, and this is not inconsistent with Arrow's contention that 'individual behavior is always mediated by social relations. These are as much a part of the description of reality as is individual behavior' (Arrow 1994, p. 5).

4.4 DECENTRALIZED PRICING: *TOWARD A THEORY OF PRICE ADJUSTMENT*

By way of conclusion of this chapter, let us focus on Arrow's (1959) important contribution to the theory of price adjustment[71] in which the decentralization of the marketor function (cf. Clower 1994b, p. 3, n) is attempted; that is, price and quantity decisions are constructed as a result of maximizing behavior of traders.

Price adjustment to the equilibrium level is common to pure competition and monopoly, both need the function to be performed by some entity. In pure competition such 'entity' is usually referred to as 'the price mechanism', i.e. the function is attributed to the play of market forces, supply and demand. In monopoly it is assigned to the monopolist. But the problem this 'entity' faces is the same; since the marketor 'cannot be expected to know with certainty the exact shape and location of the supply and demand curves, it is necessary further to suppose that demand and supply conditions are *estimated* and that these estimates are used as a basis for setting current price' (Clower 1955, pp. 219–20).

The first question regards the standard adjustment of price in pure competition as conducted by the marketor.[72] If the marketor fails to choose the equilibrium sales–sales price combination, the market will be observed in disequilibrium by the marketor, and this leads to a new estimate of the sales curve. Further revisions of the sales curve can be thought as eventually leading to price adjustments such that 'current net (estimated) sales and current net demand are equal'. '[H]ence, market equilibrium price is defined by *two* conditions: that *estimated* net sales be zero, and that *realized* net sales be zero also' (ibid., p. 222). Uncertainty is present, as it is traditionally considered to exist in traditional price theory.

A different question is suggested by Arrow (1959), that of the uncertainty faced not by the central marketor but by the individual seller. His point is that when the individual supplier ascertains that his estimated sales – i.e. his optimal supply, given the prior market price – and realized sales do not match, he will come to the realization that his estimated individual demand curve is not horizontal (i.e. parametrical) and so he has to revise it in order to decide the new quantity to supply next (period). And the problem ensues as explained above, but for the fact that instead of one single marketor in the market, we have now a number of them, each one solving his particular adjustment problem by himself, without the help of a central marketor.

According to Arrow, in disequilibrium the individual seller becomes a monopolist, in the general sense that his estimate of the sales curve is downward-sloping. Moreover, since the seller is a profit maximizer, he realizes the possible gains from facing a sloping sales curve – which are (not possibly but certainly) attainable given that no costs are attached to the solution of uncertainty. This leads him to adjust his price. Given uncertainty, this should require successive revisions of the sales curve. Uncertainty surfaces in competitive pricing.[73] However, this is nothing special to pure competitors in disequilibrium, it is a feature of non-standard monopoly theory too (cf. Clower 1955), where the sales curve is not forcibly presumed to coincide with the real demand curve.

Arrow's article *Toward a Theory of Price Adjustment* opens this way:

> In this essay, it is argued that there exists a logical gap in the usual formulation of the theory of the perfectly competitive economy, namely, that there is no place for a rational decision with respect to prices as there is with respect to quantities. A suggestion is made for filling this gap. (Arrow 1959, p. 41).

Then as now, the standard 'textbook' economics suffers from the same drawback: the firms' problem is largely to choose output, and price setting or price adjustment to equilibrium positions are only dealt with in a complementary fashion. Price adjustment is introduced into the picture as a disequilibrium phenomenon; stability or convergence are at issue in order to provide a foundation for equilibrium states.

According to Arrow, for a monopolist – as well as for the perfect competitor turned into a monopolist in conditions of market disequilibrium – who faces uncertainty, we have to admit the possibility of a discrepancy between output and demand. This 'informs the monopolist of the extent to which he is in error and yields knowledge to estimate his demand curve; on the other hand, the discrepancy alters his stock of inventories, which may in turn affect his cost situation in the next period (Arrow, 1959, p. 45).[74] Price adjustment happens in response.

Arrow's construction seems at first sight to be quite general; he envisages different markets (goods market as well as labor market), and does not ignore market structures: 'the dynamics of prices may be affected by the structure of the market even in cases where there are sufficient numbers in the market to insure reasonably competitive behavior at equilibrium' (Arrow 1959, p. 47). In fact, however, the firms considered by Arrow are presumed to exist in a world of brokered markets.

> suppose we have a situation which conforms in all the aspects of homogeneity of output and multiplicity of firms to the usual concept of perfect competition, but in which the aggregate supply forthcoming at the 'market' price exceeds the demand at that price. Then the individual firm cannot sell all it wishes at the market price. ... Under conditions of disequilibrium, there is no reason to expect that there should be a single market price, and we may very well expect that each firm will charge a different price. (Arrow 1959, p. 469).

Arrow adds next:

> Let us consider in somewhat more detail the case in which demand exceeds supply. Assume that no firm can increase supply in a very short period. Then any individual entrepreneur knows that he can raise the price even if his competitors do not raise theirs, because they cannot satisfy any more of the demand than they do already. The entrepreneur is faced with a sloping demand curve and raises his price in accordance with the profit-maximizing tactics of a monopolist.

Despite all the reasonable steps of his thought experiment, one cannot avoid raising the possibility of contradictions in his story. The firms face a 'market' price; then, for some reason the aggregate supply forthcoming at the 'market' price exceeds the demand at that price. Next, each firm adjusts his price along a sloping demand curve as a monopolist would do.[75] How do firms first notice the discrepancy between supply and demand? Is disequilibrium perceived in the aggregate or as a localized phenomenon?

First, if it is a localized fact, one can assume that only some firms in the market observe the discrepancy between the quantity they choose to offer to the market, given the ruling market price, and the quantity the market is willing to take. Assuming that the firms are able to read this discrepancy as a disequilibrium, as a consequence, only those that recognize it adjust their prices, and to the degree it affects each firm – this 'special case' is hinted at by Arrow for a market 'where products are poorly standardized' (ibid., p. 48) but this is just an aside, not necessarily a fact.

This localized perception of disequilibrium requires that on the demand side, information is not perfect (costless and/or instantaneous diffusion of prices set by each firm to the buyers). Certain firms will perceive the discrepancy and others not, and price adjustment will differ among firms, only because buyers take time to notice or incur costs to get the information otherwise[76] – and this is the reason for the difficulty firms face in inferring their sales/demand curve. Even though he allows for 'a considerable dispersion of prices among different sellers of the same commodity' (ibid., pp. 46–7), Arrow seems to fail to grasp either the necessary informational background on the demand side (information costs on current prices in the market by buyers), or its consequence upon the inference problem faced by firms during the adjustment process.[77] Both sides of the market would have to show some sort of friction for this situation of localized perception of disequilibrium to eventuate. My contention is that Arrow is not thinking of such a market.

Second, and alternatively, we can imagine that disequilibrium is generally observed. We could think of it as being observed by all firms in 'the aggregate', so that each individual firm has information about the existence and degree of the market discrepancy. The question could be raised of who centralizes, processes and conveys this information back to the system, to the firms. For the information to be conveyed to suppliers, some agent would be needed to collect it, be it an auctioneer or a set of brokers trading in an organized market.

We could also conceive of disequilibrium being generally observed, not because this information is produced somewhere in the system and brought back to the firms, but because every firm tends to be equally (or proportionately) affected by the disequilibrium between supply and demand. Each firm notices the discrepancy between the quantity it chooses to supply and what the market is willing to take, and reads it as the reflex of an aggregate disequilibrium in the market. This is an orderly market where all the suppliers perceive a disequilibrium of the same sign (meaning either an excess supply or an excess demand) that, besides, is of approximate degree. In this situation we might expect the price responses among firms not to differ significantly. Consequently, in this case it is hard to agree with Arrow on the stress he puts on the amount of uncertainty during the process of adjustment as well as to agree with his conclusion that the 'adjustment process is apt to be very irregular' (Arrow 1959, p. 46).

Arrow's story pretends to be quite general but it has some loose links. None of the alternatives is satisfying. Arrow did not construct a market structure capable of tackling the questions he tries to answer. His model is not applicable to situations 'in which information would be expected to be relatively scarce' (Arrow 1959, p. 48), which our first case of localized perception of disequilibrium might fit. In the other case, in which the uncertainty is mostly resolved (either because central agents exist or because the market is very orderly), price adjustment by an individual firm can hardly be meant as a decision of the firm. During the adjustment process, a price signal is contemporaneously given to the individual trader, announced by brokers or a central agent; or, if disequilibrium is perceived in the aggregate because each firm realizes that the effect tends to be equally distributed among firms, adjustment may be expected to be quite smooth as well as quick – each firm's demand curve would provide sufficient information to infer the equilibrium price position. And price dispersion, if existent, would be of little implication on the price decisions of each firm: it could be assumed to be soon arbitraged out.

To sum up, Arrow does not fill the 'logical gap' in the usual formulations of the theory of the perfectly competitive economy that there is no place for a price decision as there is with respect to quantities. My conclusion is that he fails to appropriately raise the decision problem firms face in competitive non-brokered markets. But in these non-brokered markets such a gap cannot be left unfilled: the price is not produced externally to the firm, there is no 'going price' out there generated in a market in which the firm operates.

NOTES

1.   The 'market' plays a role in Smith's *The Wealth of Nations* but he is vague as to its organization. For instance: 'The town is a continual fair or market, to which the inhabitants of the country resort, in order to exchange their rude for manufactured produce. It is this commerce which supplies the inhabitants of the town both with the materials of their work, and the means of their subsistence. The quantity of the finished work which they sell to the inhabitants of the country, necessarily regulates the quantities of the materials and provisions which they buy' (Smith 1776, Bk. III, Chapter 1, § 4). See Coase (1977, pp. 320–21) on the institutional basis for the working of the price system in *The Wealth of Nations*.

   Market here just means interdependence, and the 'invisible hand' (Bk. IV, Chapter 2, § 9) the energy that drives exchange among interdependent individuals. Only cursory attention is paid to the mechanisms of exchange proper. Moreover, 'market' is taken for granted as the 'setting' where the market price is obtained. 'The market price of every particular commodity is regulated by the proportion between the quantity which is actually brought to market, and the demand of those who are willing to pay the natural price of the commodity.' (Bk. I, Chapter 7, § 8).

2.   This interesting image is adumbrated in Edgeworth (1881, p. 18) while establishing his concept of competition (or, better, the necessary and sufficient conditions for a competitive price): 'There is free communication throughout a *normal* competitive field. You might suppose the constituent individuals collected at a point, or connected by telephones – an ideal supposition, but sufficiently approximate to existence or tendency for the purposes of abstract science'.

3. This was not the question Coase proposed to answer. Coase's concern in *The Nature of the Firm* was '[i]nstead, a very general comparison of the benefits and costs of firms (in relation to markets)' (Williamson 1991, p. 7). See Coase (1988a, p. 63; 1992, p. 718) for his conceding the 'hardly surprising' shortfall that in the early thirties he could not have attempted a systematic incorporation of transaction costs into economic analysis.

4. These are costs of 'using the price mechanism. What the prices are have to be discovered. There are negotiations to be undertaken, contracts have to be drawn up, inspections have to be made to settle disputes, and so on' (Coase 1992, p. 715; see also 1937, pp. 21–2). As far as I could read, I could not dispel the doubt that these are not set-up costs. In Coase there is apparently no awareness of the fact that transaction costs only impinge upon the workings of coordination if they are set-up costs, i.e. costs that are lump-sum, since largely independent of the amount contracted or transacted; otherwise, they explain nothing. However, Coase (1937) leaves the matter undecided: for instance, referring to labor service contracts (ibid., pp. 21–2) he is better understood as dealing with set-up costs, though the opposite occurs in the case of, e.g., costs of organizing spatially (ibid., p. 25).

5. In order to explain intermediation, production is a doubtful accretion. There is no need to fuss about exchange versus production economies, and we should be content with Clower's view as quoted in Joan Robinson: 'An ongoing exchange economy with specialist traders *is* a production economy since there is no bar to any merchant capitalist acquiring labour services and other resources as a "buyer" and transforming them (repackaging, processing into new forms, etc.) into outputs that are unlike the original inputs and are "sold" accordingly as are commodities that undergo no such transformation. In short, a production unit *is* a particular type of middleman or trading specialist.' (J. Robinson 1977, p. 6).

6. Coase was aware in *The Nature of the Firm* that 'it is not possible to draw a hard and fast line which determines whether there is a firm or not. There may be more or less direction' (Coase 1988a, p. 55); on this basis, he rebuts a criticism by Klein, Crawford and Alchian (1978) who found that Coase's 'primary distinction between transactions within a firm and transactions made in the marketplace may be often too simplistic. Many long term contractual relationships (such as franchising) blur the line between the market and the firm' (ibid., p. 326).

   But Coase's theoretical point is that '[t]he existence of such mixed relationships does not mean, for me, that we should abandon the view that "the distinguishing mark of the firm is the supersession of the price mechanism", as I put it in "The Nature of the Firm" ' (Coase 1988a, p. 55–6).

7. Whether it is a decision or the result of an evolutionary weeding out process is not relevant at all.

8. Legal rules that 'may be made by those who organize the market, as is the case with most commodity exchanges', or otherwise that 'have to depend … on the legal system of the State', which applies '[w]hen these facilities are scattered and owned by a vast number of people with very different interests, as in the case with retailing and wholesaling' (Coase 1988b, p. 10). See also Coase (1992, p. 718) for the same distinctive role of 'private law' and the laws of the State.

9. Coase adds: 'The time has surely gone in which economists could analyze in great detail two individuals exchanging nuts for berries on the edge of the forest and then feel that their analysis of the process of exchange was complete, illuminating though this analysis may be in certain respects.' (Coase 1992, p. 718).

10. Adam Smith clearly recognized this problem with barter exchange, but his idea was different. He stated (1776, Bk. I, Chapter 4, § 1–2) that the use of a commonly accepted commodity, by making exchange less 'clogged and embarrassed in its operations', will permit an extension of the division of labor. In Smith, economies of scale in production can be better exploited if the market is extended by means of monetary exchange. This could be extended to the case of 'specialists in trade', as in Ostroy and Starr (1990, p. 29): 'Among the forms of specialization we expect to see in a low transaction cost economy is specialization in the transaction process itself. … Consistent with Smith's viewpoint, the distinct function of intermediary agents can be explained by scale economies in transaction costs'.

   Here, the reasoning is that set-up transaction costs (and economies of scale in exchange) lead to intermediation. The further idea that monetary intermediation may allow for a better exploitation of economies of scale in exchange is Smith's, but requires explanation. In any case, the two aspects need to be dealt with separately.

11. It seems hard to find any support for a technological advantage of the proportional type, other than on 'pure transfer costs'.

    Of 'trading costs' I can think of information costs (or those that make for goodwill, as in Alchian [1977]), but this brings us into a messier world than Hirshleifer meant (see his assumption of perfect information in 1980, p. 236). Hirshleifer's argument is valid under perfect information and let us be so confined. In any case, in order to explain the emergence of brokers or merchants (of the proportional commission type, let us say) we might need to indicate how they allow for lower information costs in the market. But, the further question arises of whether we can think of information costs that are not lump-sum, if only to some degree.

12. Beyond 'assuming some cyclical or other imbalances in productive, consumptive, or trading flows' (Hirshleifer 1973, p. 138).

13. Another instance where Hirshleifer seems to take markets for granted – and the difference between exchange and market is unclear – is his view of monetary exchange: 'As compared to barter, the system with a medium of exchange will have lower trading cost in proportion, but possibly larger trading cost in total due to the enormously greater volume of transactions' (Hirshleifer 1973, p. 144).

14. Except for positing 'technologically feasible' marketing activities at each date (t), 'fully integrated, ... under the control of a single firm' (Hahn 1971, p. 428), which I cannot distinguish from the case of multilateral exchange with the central market.

15. '[O]ne source of allocative failures in actual economies is the absence of a sufficiently large array of future and contingent commodities actively traded. A persistent objection to the class of models is that they require far too many active markets – many more than will be found in an actual economy. The reasons for these mismatches between theory and practice are not to be found in the theory; they reflect issues omitted from the model: the costs of operating markets themselves, and the difficulty or cost of verifying the state of the world.' (Starr 1997, p. 193).

16. 'In general equilibrium without transaction costs, the network of exchanges is indeterminate; there is no constraint on the gross trading volume', and '[t]he presence of transaction costs makes the exchange network determinate. In such a network, certain traders, in view of their lower transaction costs, probably emerge as middlemen, brokers or intermediaries. ... Transaction costs, therefore, are the key to an understanding of intermediaries and of the structure of the markets.' (Niehans 1987, pp. 321, 325).

17. 'Dynamic procedures, such as bid–ask markets, have received little attention although they have paramount importance in practice. ... Scant progress has been made in building theories with generality comparable to the Walrasian model of general equilibrium, even though the enigma of price formation in the Walrasian model is a prime motivation for studies of auctions.' (Wilson 1992, p. 271).

18. In Wilson (1987b, pp. 56–61) this model is summarized, and the deficiencies – or better 'challenging topics for research' – are clearly acknowledged. It is recognized that the result 'is implausible as a positive predictive theory' (ibid., p. 60), namely for experimental purposes. Beyond the referred limitations of the model, I would point out this: with a known initial distribution of valuations, and admitting common knowledge of completed transactions and transaction prices (which allows for probabilistic inference of outstanding valuations of the remaining traders), the model is far away from any representation of a *continuous* bid–ask market. Informational and computational problems would be compounded.

19. Hicks (1989, Chapter 3) constitutes producers as *the* market organizers, who historically replaced the wholesalers in both functions of stockholding and price formation. In any case, Hicks has a diverse view in *A Theory of Economic History*; although referring to an earlier historical stage of industrial evolution, Hicks considers the distinction between pure trader and producer not fundamental: 'It is a technological, not an economic distinction'(Hicks, 1969, p. 28).

    But this seems an unpromising old story that had wide currency in the 1940s. J. S. Mill in his *Principles* (1848, p. 246) makes a distinction between wholesale markets and other trades. Hicks, in *Capital and Growth* (1965, pp. 55–6) and in his (1976) article *Time in Economics*, presents an outline of what became the above argument. Joan Robinson (1977) recalls Kalecki's (1939) distinction between two systems of price formation, one dominated by supply and demand and one by costs plus profits, which Hicks had recently rediscovered. She writes: 'For manufactures, in modern times, the producers have taken over the merchanting function. They offer their commodities at an advertised price and produce for sale what the market will take.' (J. Robinson 1977, p. 18).

20. For the moment we are focusing on pure brokered markets, although we may allow for the possibility that brokers place limit orders for their own account (cf. Demsetz 1968; Osborne 1965, p. 88); the identification of some changes the presence of trade specialists or dealer-middlemen may bring, is attempted in note 23, below.

21. Dealers or merchant-middlemen are compensated by a profit margin, whereas broker compensation can take the forms of a revenue-sharing scheme (commission) and/or of a fee.

22. Another example would be for just the buyer to communicate orders to the seller, in the case of an order-signal as a decentralized control mechanism; this was studied by Kornai (1979), Kornai and Martos (1981, esp. pp. 42–3); on this topic, see Hurwicz (1973, pp. 10–11).

23. If we abandon our assumption of a pure brokered market and allow for the presence of dealer-middlemen – as not only facilitating, but also making a ready market by means of their own investment in inventories – several adaptations will have to be considered to our previous reasoning, which are anyway independent of the risk-taking function (whether this is the most significant function of specialist traders or not). First, since dealers are compensated by a profit margin on their trades, they have a bigger incentive to develop trading efforts. Second, they are in a better position to take advantage of speculation and arbitrage opportunities than buyers and sellers are (these are required to be intermediated by brokers in their orders to the market). Third, if brokers and dealers have different transaction costs, the signalling function of posted transaction prices is somewhat weakened: there will be a market spread between bid and asking prices but this is a less reliable guide to particular transactions involving different types of market operators. That is to say, if consideration is paid to the magnitude of transaction costs, which depend on the type of middlemen as well on the type of traders, there will be a market spread, but anyhow it will be only a reference for transaction prices; bargaining power will be relevant.

24. Cf. Hurwicz 1972, p. 428; 1973, p. 24. For a more rigorous definition of informational decentralization, see Hurwicz 1960, pp. 398–401. Although Hurwicz's contributions are important, in order to clarify the notion of decentralization, he basically focuses on the informational requirements for optimality in resource allocation, be it in the context of adjustment processes or of mechanism design. See also Ostroy and Starr 1974, esp. p. 1097; Ostroy and Starr 1990, esp. pp. 13, 33.

25. Or even infeasible, for if 'localized' information can be assumed reasonable for the individual trader in his decisions, in case centralization of information is considered, this is not sufficient: 'whole maps are to be conveyed' (Hurwicz 1973, p. 8).

26. '[W]hich means that no participant, including an enforcement agency if any, has any direct knowledge of others' preferences, endowments, technologies, etc.' (Hurwicz 1972, p. 448; see also p. 455, n; and Hurwicz 1994, p. 3).

27. We refer here to price mechanisms. Planning processes, be they 'price-guided' or 'non-price-models', have been analyzed (Calsamiglia 1977, pp. 265–6). For a general perspective on decentralized control mechanisms, see Kornai and Martos (1981, esp. pp. 36–9) and Martos (1990).

28. A third function is also usually thought necessary: enforcing the budget constraint, viz. by means of some sort of a 'record-keeping device' (Ostroy and Starr 1990, p. 11) to guarantee that trading plans are carried out at the competitive prices. On this, see Section 4.3.3.1 (v).

29. Smale uses Newton's method of solving non-linear equations (Arrow and Hahn 1971, p. 303). Smale (1976a) fostered work by Saari and Simon (1978) and Mas-Colell (1985).

30. See Martos (1990, p. 19) for a definition of orderly markets, and Kawasaki, McMillan, and Zimmermann (1982) for some empirical results.

31. Also, referring to the 'pure exchange Hahn process' and to its later developments, especially to Fisher (1983) 'disequilibrium' analysis, regarding both 'general monopolistic

equilibrium' and 'fix-price equilibria with quantity rationing', Busetto (1995) maintains that 'the limitations and difficulties of the non-*tâtonnement* models derive from the very fundamental features of the theory of General Equilibrium, and from the fact that within this theory the dynamic analysis of disequilibrium adjustment processes has been kept subordinate to static analysis.' (ibid., p. 90; also p. 109; cf. Walker 1997a, pp. 124 ff.).

32. For references on '[t]he problem of decomposing arbitrary excess demand function', see Mas-Colell (1985, p. 242), and, for a good survey, Shafer and Sonnenschein (1982).

33. The Walrasian tatonnement has widely been presumed paradigmatic as an informationally decentralized mechanism, i.e. 'involving lower processing (transaction) costs' (Hurwicz 1994, p. 4, n; also 1969, esp. pp. 515 ff.; Saari 1985b, esp. pp. 138–40). See also Arrow and Hurwicz (1960, p. 72) and Hurwicz (1973, p. 12) on the 'gradient process' and Hurwicz (1960, pp. 408 ff.) on the 'greed process' as informationally decentralized according to Hurwicz's definition; see, however, Calsamiglia (1977, p. 270) who considers the greed process 'for practical purposes ... as informationally infeasible'. For the definition of an informationally decentralized adjustment process in resource allocation, see Hurwicz (1960, pp. 398 ff.), and for a general but short summary, Hurwicz (1994, pp. 2–5).

34. For continuous time, Saari and Simon (1978) have most unsuccessfully questioned the possible reduction of the informational requirements of Smale's (1976a) 'globalized Newton method' that the price adjuster needs for a convergent mechanism. 'The globalized Newton method can be viewed as characterizing a story where instead of prices changing in response to supply and demand, they change in a fashion which always preserves the ratio of the aggregate demand for commodities. Thus this dynamic preserves the ratio $z/|z|$ [$z(p)$ denotes the aggregate excess demand function at the price p], and it is only the scale which changes. To the best of my knowledge, no one has examined whether this dynamic admits an economic justification.' (Saari 1985a, pp. 1118–19).

35. Examples have been devised for exchange economies with more than two commodities where there is no convergence (Scarf 1960; Gale 1963; Veendorp 1970b); and, as seen above, this result was broadened after a theorem of Sonnenschein (1972). In general, if equality of supply and demand is to be asserted as the limit of a price adjustment process, then this can only be shown for special sets of assumptions: for instance, that all goods are gross substitutes in continuous time, or the case of a 'representative' consumer.

36. In the same line, referring to adjustment processes in discrete time, Hahn recognizes that '[t]o obtain results now we must do more than restrict the form of the excess demand functions; restrictions must also be placed on the adjustment speeds', which 'is fundamentally a negative conclusion since we have no theory to help in this matter. Indeed, if the theory is to be taken as in some way descriptive we could not exclude mixed difference–differential equations for price adjustment and theory would yield few qualitative results' (Hahn 1982, pp. 768–9). For the same conclusion, even in the case of gross substitutes, see Arrow and Hahn 1971, p. 308.

   For a further comment on adjustment methods – like Newton's method, as used in Arrow and Hahn (1971, p. 303) and Smale (1976a) – that violate 'the supposed economy in information of decentralized economies', see Hahn 1987, p. 136.

37. Cf. Samuelson (1947, p. 261) referring both to '[e]xamples of functional equation systems', and to '*perfect stability* ... in the limit as time becomes infinite'.

   As to quasi-global stability as defined by a Lyapounov function, Arrow and Hahn (1971, p. 274) state that 'so far, while we can predict that after a sufficiently long lapse of time prices will be arbitrarily close to some equilibrium'. And also, raising doubts on the logical validity of ruling out trading at out-of-equilibrium prices, the authors grant that 'if [the auctioneer's rule is stable], trading will be permitted only "in the limit" (i.e., as t approaches infinity), for it is only in the limit that equilibrium and "called" prices coincide.' (ibid., p. 324).

38. General barter exchange is set in the framework of purely competitive assumptions, i.e., 'all traders should be well informed about the exchange rates that prevail on all commodity exchanges and should consider these exchange rates as given. However, no additional information on the part of individual traders concerning the preferences and endowments of the other traders should be required' (Veendorp 1970a, p. 2).

In the context of these informational assumptions of a 'purely competitive system', general equilibrium analysis handles two separate problems, one 'of deriving conditions for the existence of a set of equilibrium prices' and the other 'of deriving conditions for the convergence of a competitive price adjustment process, the adjustment being made by an auctioneer whose actions are meant to reflect market forces.' (ibid., p. 2).

39.   I use the odd designation of 'specialized broker' to distinguish from 'specialist'. In a partial equilibrium set up (dealing with a single commodity against 'money') they are equivalent, as they would be if referring to brokered markets of empirical extraction. This is not so in the trading post barter general model. (Walras, by the time of the first edition of the *Eléments*, refers elsewhere to calculators to whom 'order-books' are given, in his explanation of the mechanism of exchange; see Walker 1990b, p. 966.)

With exchange at given, and known, equilibrium prices this broker is dispensable. The accounting function he is supposed to perform is conveniently solved by the quid pro quo condition of each pair-wise trade. Anyhow, if trading at out-of-equilibrium prices is allowed, this trading post operator is called upon to perform the extra function of rationing (e.g. Benassy 1975; Drèze 1975); but this specialist cannot know who to ration.

40.   As seen above, if beliefs were maintained that prices are equilibrium prices, quid pro quo at these prices would be sufficient, and the market condition redundant; also, the trading rule would be identical to quid pro quo in the aggregate for trade at each trading post.

41.   Veendorp (1970a, p. 10) notes the importance of this distinction, between 'the problem of convergence of a bartering process from that of the existence of a feasible trade'.

42.   Veendorp's suggested solution to the problem of the inconsistency between existence and execution is to redefine existence as requiring feasible sequences of barter exchange. We agree with Veendorp, that in the case of direct barter economies 'it should be realized that the traditional conditions for the existence of an equilibrium solution are insufficiently restrictive. To be economically meaningful, the equilibrium solution of a direct barter economy should not only satisfy the usual non-negativity conditions for relative price and consumption levels, but feasibility conditions for direct barter as well' (Veendorp 1970a, p. 6). I agree, but not exactly to salvage existence. My argument derives only from an attempt at consistency regarding information assumptions in direct barter.

43.   Using the foregoing notation, we can express Walras's equation of exchange (Jaffé, ed. 1954, p. 87) the following way:

$$g_{ij} \times v_i = g_{kl} \times v_k, \quad \text{or:} \quad g_{ij} / g_{kl} = v_k / v_i = p_{ki} .$$

'Thus: *Prices, or ratios of values in exchange, are equal to the inverse ratios of the quantities exchanged*' (ibid.). Jaffé explains that '[t]his concept of value in exchange as a term in a ratio which is inversely proportional to the ratio of the quantities exchanged was adumbrated ... in Isnard' (ibid., p. 499). In the exchange of (only) two commodities, g_{ij} and g_{kl} correspond to excess supplies at the 'values in exchange' v_i and v_k, which are equilibrium values in exchange (since we are considering the exchange of given quantities of only two commodities between two individuals); the ratio v_k / v_i being designated by Walras as the '*relative* price' of commodity k (p_{ki}) (cf. Jaffé 1969, esp. p. 26).

The v's are either Walras's 'absolute' values (Jaffé 1969, p. 28) or 'valorie' (van Daal and Jolink 1993, p. 14), or expressed in an 'imaginary commodity' ('Cournot's *tertium comparationis*') (Jaffé, ed. 1954, p. 499). See Jaffé (1969, p. 28) for his reference to Walras's v's as 'semantic rigmarole about value in Parts I and II of the *Eléments*'.

44.   For instance, Arrow and Hurwicz's (1960) *Decentralization and Computation in Resource Allocation* deals with convergence (basically the 'gradient' method) as an element towards the demonstration of an optimal allocation of resources. Execution is not addressed; in fact, there is only one representative consumer, the helmsman. See also other articles by Hurwicz, in Arrow and Hurwicz (1977, esp. Part IV).

45.   Multilateral trade is assumed to be very costly, and this is the implicit rationale for alternative formalizations to resort to decentralized logistical arrangements based on sequential barter. Of interest here is Feldman (1973, p. 471), who raises the subject in a very unconvincing way since he substitutes 'endless series of bilateral trades' for the multilateral gathering, and thus provides in fact no rationale for his suggestion that information is costless in bilateral trade but 'prohibitively costly' in multilateral trade. The transaction cost argument hardly fits feasibility.

46. In the sense that traders differ in the probabilities they assign to the ocurrence of each state of nature, yet being assumed to form *common* expectations as to which price set will prevail in each such state (cf. Radner 1972).

47. On this question of 'individual' incentive compatibility in competitive behavior 'in a "nonatomistic" world of pure exchange', under the requirements of informational decentralization, see Hurwicz 1972, pp. 443–54, esp. p. 446; 1973, pp. 27–32. The author uses the 'term "atomistic" in the old fashioned sense, meaning that every participant is infinitesimal as compared with the total market. (In modern measure-theoretic language this case is called "nonatomic")' (Hurwicz 1972, p. 456, n). Thus, in Hurwicz 'nonatomistic' means 'finite'. Some posterior literature has disintegrated this finite economy and shown that, in the limit, as the economy becomes 'large' the incentive compatibility hindrance vanishes. However, as is observed below, this is an excrescence of centralized exchange.

48. 'We may learn from Niehans (1969) that even when exchange is restricted to pairs it need not be completely decentralized. The selection of a least cost bilateral trading network can be made by a central planner who solves a complicated programming problem.' (Ostroy 1973, p. 598, n).

49. It is harmless to presume, as Ostroy and Starr (1974, p. 1097) do, that several pair-wise meetings occur simultaneously; this is of no consequence, and useful only for notational purposes: see t, $t-1$, ... on decentralization assumptions.

50. Timing coincidence, more than coincidence of wants, is important for the explanation of market arrangements. Timing coordination is exogenously posited in Veendorp by conducting trade in organized exchanges with a timetable associated with any of them; organized exchanges do not mitigate the timing question unless a timetable for every exchange is postulated (or we allow 'organized exchanges' to be run by specialist middlemen and let them create a continuous ready market for other traders). On the other hand, timing coincidence is left to 'atomic' 'collisions' in the search models.

51. Ostroy and Starr's definition of a decentralized trading rule seems to suffer from a logical gap (cf. Ostroy and Starr 1974, p. 1097: rule D.3 – which however was dropped in the 1990 paper). Literally interpreted, it applies to each pair of traders in isolation and to an instant in the sequence: knowledge of contemporaneous excess demands of the other trader and of excess demands communicated between this pair of traders in previous meetings (1990, p. 33). On the other hand, centralization implies contemporaneous knowledge of every other trader's excess demand (1990, p. 33), or of their histories of excess demands as well (1974, p. 1074). The logical gap is due to the fact that traders meet sequentially: under rule D.3 they would be able to gather series of historical excess demand data in the course of meetings. If, at any meeting, information obtained at previous meetings with other traders is not called to memory this is a peculiarly defective 'memory'; if it is called to memory, then each trader is endowed with historical information on traders either the one he is actually meeting, though not contemporaneous; and if this is so, 'each trader would be able to make more precise estimates of the probable excess demands of future partners' (Ostroy and Starr 1974, p. 1097, n). Although everyone trades with everyone else, and this makes it difficult to set a range for decentralized information, this question had better not be disposed of, as in fact it was in the 1990 article. For a brief comment on 'restrictions on memory', see Hurwicz (1972, p. 455, n).

52. The possible fact that this trader may fail to have enough 'quantities of his own commodities' creates a further embarrassment (cf. Ostroy and Starr 1974, p. 1110).

53. 'In order for successful monetary trade to take place without violating (A.1), non-negativity, agents must have, at each trading instant, sufficient money to finance their current purchases. The money will come from endowment or the proceeds of past sales. We are interested then in characterizing economies with sufficient endowment of money so that illiquidity due to exhaustion of money holdings in the course of trade need not be a problem'. And it is added: 'we will characterize, at least at first, a monetary economy as one endowed with a sufficient stock of a monetary commodity to be used as medium of exchange. It must be distributed sufficiently broadly in sufficiently great quantity (*in value terms*) among the holders that all agents find that they can finance all desired purchases from endowment of the money commodity' (Ostroy and Starr 1990, p. 34, italics added).

54. 'An obvious record-keeping device is for the clearing-house to issue blue chips to each person in the amount of the excess of the value of the goods supplied compared to those received.' Adding, '[b]ecause prices are fixed at market-clearing values, each person can silently spend his chips on the available supplies when he returns to the auctioneer, knowing that all supplies will eventually be claimed by those who have a demand for them.' (Ostroy and Starr 1990, pp. 9–10).

   Notice Alchian's (1977) contention that monetary exchange cannot rest on a 'book-keeping, debt-recording function'.

55. This is why Colander (1994, p. 10) may be misguided in talking about money as 'imposing certain institutional constraints on individuals, which break the [Classical] dichotomy'. Constraints surely are present, but they belong in exchange. Arguments of this kind usually do not notice that it is the medium of exchange property of commodities in exchange that originates the constraint, not the institution of money itself. Money brings nothing new, except for helping alleviate constraints, and therefore 'money makes the economy more efficient'.

   This is altogether different from the proposed idea that 'money will be defined theoretically in terms of explicitly postulated restrictions on trading alternatives that assign a special role to certain commodities as payment media in organized markets' (Clower 1971, p. 109; see also 1967).

56. Madden (1975, p. 589) criticizes Feldman for this misnomer.

57. According to Oh, Jones's model does not explain the emergence of a generally accepted means of exchange, only one good will be money but not for all pairs of goods. In any case, Jones (1976, p. 758) defines a monetary economy this way: 'We shall say that an economy has a *monetary pattern of trade* if the exchanges which actually take place have the following two characteristics: (*a*) There is one good that enters into every exchange. (*b*) Any other good entering an exchange, if purchased is not sold, and if sold is not repurchased. The one exceptional good is termed the "medium of exchange" '.

   Alternatively, Oh (1989, p. 104) provides the following definition: 'A monetary economy is referred to as an economy that has a generally acceptable medium of exchange, rather than one in which every exchange is carried out through a medium of exchange'. This obtains meaning given that 'individuals use conditional trading strategies', and thus 'pure barter trade can exist as a conditional option in a monetary economy side by side with a generally acceptable medium of exchange' (ibid., p. 113).

58. In a broader context Brunner and Meltzer (1971, p. 788) state: 'Numerous sequences of transactions are open to [an individual]. His problem is to find the optimal sequence of transactions and the optimal investment in information while choosing an optimal bundle of goods or consumption plans'. Their first postulate on acquisition of information (ibid., p. 786) is akin to Jones's assumption that the cost of exchange depends on the pair of goods involved, and the second postulate on the marginal cost of acquiring information, is what drives the 'dynamic' result in Jones.

59. For another, and specific, definition of connected economy (as an assumption complementary to weak gross substitution), see Arrow and Hahn (1971, p. 227).

   Madden (1975, p. 588), dealing with the needed 'assumption on the smoothness of indifference surfaces', introduces the notion of connected 'groups' in order to provide a common supporting price set in trades between individuals (meeting pair-wisely) belonging to any pair of groups. This is a common feature, though, of topological proofs of existence; the innovation here is the application of the notion to groups, this allowing for the introduction of middlemen (as in Rader 1968).

60. Burstein (1968, pp. 25–6) discusses the meaning of disequilibrium, and states that, like in the physical sciences, disequilibrium 'can only be defined relative to a theoretical model'. Using the 'Harrodian' growth model as illustration, he succumbs to the obvious: 'It would seem that *equilibrium* in economics cannot have precise meaning outside of the notional state of universal pure competition in auction markets'.

61. Veendorp's hinted proposal to reconstruct barter exchange is: 'In the present context the relevant class of adjustment processes would seem to consist of these mechanisms that allow trading to take place before equilibrium is reached, that explicitly take into account transaction cost, and that restrict trades to those taking place at organized markets or commodity exchanges.' (Veendorp 1970a, p. 22).

62. Though confined to the exercise of convergence to the equilibrium price set, and despite the vagueness of the behavioral basis for the 'groups', Kirman's reflections on this subject are of interest: 'It is not mere chance that one assumption that leads to strong results as to uniqueness and stability is that society should behave as an individual. Yet we know that to obtain such behaviour individuals' behaviour must be very similar. If we are to progress further we may well be forced to theorise in terms of groups who have collectively coherent behaviour. Thus demand and expenditure functions if they are to be set against reality must be defined at some reasonably high level of aggregation. The idea that we should start at the level of the isolated individual is one which we may well have to abandon. There is no more misleading description of modern economics than the so-called microfoundations of macroeconomics which in fact describe the behaviour of the consumption and production sector by the behaviour of one individual or firm. If we aggregate over several individuals, such a model is unjustified. On the other hand if we do not deal with the aggregation problem then we should be honest from the outset and assert simply that *by assumption* we postulate that each sector of the economy behaves as one individual and not claim any spurious microjustification.' (Kirman 1989, p. 138; cf. Kirman 1992).

63. 'In all probability, the only possible route to follow in constructing a proper analysis of observable disequilibrium phenomena is directly focusing on the dynamics of agents' actual actions and separating disequilibrium analysis from the analysis of equilibrium positions in the General Equilibrium sense and their stability. This is a route thus far unexplored.' (Busetto 1995, p. 110).

64. Howitt criticizes the formalization of bargaining in monetary models depicting a sequence of temporary equilibria (like Grandmond's): 'Such an equilibrium analysis would dichotomize the process of exchange and the process of bargaining. ... Only after the bargaining process had reached completion would exchange take place.' (Howitt 1973, p. 496).

65. 'Those who are disappointed try another price, naturally always with the hope of buying or selling the amount that they offer to buy or sell when they quote their price. They know from past experience that sometimes they will be able to buy or sell all they wish, even if the market as a whole is not in equilibrium; and that sometimes they will not. They simply do not know with certainty what will happen at any particular new price.

    Fisher assumes that the participants in his 1983 model "realize that they are in disequilibrium" and "perceive and take advantage of arbitrage opportunities" and make a judgment as to when arbitrage opportunities have disappeared (Fisher 1983, p. 46; and see ibid., Chapter 4). Those assumptions were also made by all the neoclassical economists and by all modern theorists contemplating equilibrating processes. A problem arises in models, however, when it is assumed that traders must be aware of market equilibrium and market disequilibrium. It is impossible for an individual to know whether market equilibrium has been reached.' (Walker 1997a, p. 31).

66. This is incompletely and distortedly acknowledged in Gale (1986b, p. 808) who does not refer to the possibility of repeated (parametric) rounds in Ostroy and Starr (1974), only to imitate the procedure in his model. In Gale (1986b), meetings are random but he posits a sequence of dates where '[e]ach date here represents a complete round of the bargaining game' (ibid., p. 808). This would not be expected to comply with decentralized information assumptions, but there is no basic difference between either in this regard. Moreover, as in Ostroy and Starr, Gale introduces a 0th commodity to 'balance the budget' (ibid., p. 810), whatever that means.

67. From Aumann's (1964) core equivalence theorem, and from the fact 'that the equilibrium outcomes of fully elaborated extensive form games are Walrasian' (McLennan and Sonnenschein 1991, p. 1398) – but see Rubinstein and Wolinski (1985; 1990) for a contrary contention.

68. Alternatively, Rubinstein and Wolinsk (1985), by whom this literature was suggested, consider discounting directly, as a result of assuming that a delay in agreement in a current negotiation may prevent a trader from meeting comparable bargaining opportunities with other partners, and also the consequence of this, the risk that his partner abandons negotiation, which reflects a competitive pressure. But this time preference did not prove to be the determining assumption in order that frictionless bargaining and exchange should

result in a non-competitive allocation in their model (cf. Gale 1987 p. 24; Wilson 1987b, p. 53).

The reasons then are to be found elsewhere, namely in assumptions about the numbers of traders, the divisibility of the good, the possibility of repeated bargaining, and whether the numbers of buyers and sellers in the repeated bargaining game are stationary. Gale (1986a; b) increased the number of types of traders from two to 'many', and McLennan and Sonnenschein (1991) to a 'continuum economy'. Moreover, while in Rubinstein and Wolinski (1985) 'one' indivisible good is only traded once ('[a]fter two agents reach an agreement they leave the market' [ibid, p. 1135]), Gale considers divisible goods and multiple trading (he lets 'them trade as often and with as many partners as they like' (Gale 1986a, pp. 787–8)), which is taken up by McLennan and Sonnenschein (cf. Gale 1986a, pp. 802–803).

Furthermore, contrary to the latter two models, Rubinstein and Wolinski (1985) assume stationary numbers, i.e. a finite number of traders, which according to Binmore and Herrero (1988) is the crucial feature (cf. Gale 1986a, p. 803; Wilson 1987b, pp. 53–4). In a stationary equilibrium with a constant number of potential buyers and sellers, if numbers do not match (cf. Rubinstein and Wolinski 1985), the surplus would be divided proportionally to their numbers, and the result will not be Walrasian (but, if numbers are not stationary, the short side of the market is shown to appropriate all the surplus and the market clears, i.e., 'the classical Walrasian result is obtained' [cf. Binmore and Herrero 1988, esp. p. 17]).

However, in a stationary exchange economy (as in Rubinstein ansd Wolinski 1985), the characterization of a market-clearing price that equates the demands and supplies of the buyers and sellers who are in the market at each date – with equilibrium defined in terms of *stocks* – is not adequate to these models. With an indivisible good, as assumed in Rubinstein and Wolinski (1985), the market does not clear by definition, but this is irrelevant; yet, if the market is stationary the flows of buyers and sellers into the market must be equal and thus any price can be a flow equilibrium (unless stricter assumptions are postulated; see Gale 1987, esp. pp. 26–8).

In a stationary economy, where the flow of potential entrants in the market is constant, a stationary price equilibrium will be the one where the numbers of buyers and sellers that enter are equal, and therefore the *flow* market-clearing equilibrium price is the interesting equilibrium concept. In fact, Gale (1987; cf. 1986a, p. 803) argues that Rubinstein and Wolinski's (1985) 'result' derives mainly from their use of the 'wrong' definition of Walrasian equilibrium, since supply and demand should be treated as flows.

Furthermore, the effect of the information structure of agents on the possibility of non-competitive equilibria is addressed by Rubinstein and Wolinski (1990).

As an aside, notice that in Rubinstein and Wolinski (1985) (based on, and generalizing, the two players' bargaining case in Rubinstein [1982], in a line ascending from Edgeworth [1881]) a *strategic* approach to bargaining was attempted that might help provide a basis to the *axiomatic* literature in this area (cf. Diamond and Maskin 1979; Diamond 1981; 1982b; and Mortensen 1982a; b). For a good review of the literature leading to the formalization of bargaining in general equilibrium, see Binmore, Osborne and Rubinstein (1992, pp. 204 ff.).

69. When referring to maximizing behavior, I do not mean to meddle with the question of optimizing versus satisfying behavior, as in Herbert Simon. I only want to draw attention to the limitations of maximization when its results are plans, which feasibility is ignored.

70. Though only indirectly related to our discussion, Hahn raises interesting doubts on dealing with both preferences and conjectures as given: 'I would suggest that it is not obvious that one is justified in treating preferences as given and quite unjustified in treating conjectures as given. Certainly almost any feasible allocation can be a Walrasian equilibrium for some preferences and certainly we do not believe that we emerge from the womb with formed preferences or that the latter are independent of economic experiences. We treat preferences as exogenous for the very good reason that we have no good manageable theory of an economy in which they are treated as endogenous. In any case I would not be alarmed if conjectures, at least in the short period, are taken as formed by history' (Hahn 1978, pp. 2–3).

71. Beyond Arrow's, the most influential contributions to the theory of price adjustment are Phelps and Winter (1970) and Barro (1972). Other papers and theories should also require

consideration and analysis, like for instance Thore and Billström (1954), Thore, Billström and Johansson (1954), Gordon and Hynes (1970), Fisher (1970; 1972; 1973; 1983), Diamond (1971), Rothschild (1974), Hey (1974), Irvine (1981), Gottfries (1986; 1991), Bils (1989), Balvers and Cosimano (1990), Mirman, Samuelson and Urbano (1993). Comments on parts of this literature can be found in Hahn (1982, pp. 788–91) and Rothschild (1973).

72. Haavelmo (1958, p. 33) argues that 'traditional static demand-supply cross does not represent a complete model of actual behavior in a market. Consequently, we can give up the idea of achieving a sensible market theory just by arming the demanders and suppliers with, respectively, a demand and a supply curve – and then letting them loose on each other. If nonetheless we want to stick to the two curves as a practically feasible description of the behavior of demanders and suppliers, we will evidently need to introduce a third party into the game, some sort of *deus ex machina*. An example of such a third party, worth considering, would be an inventory-holding sector with, e.g. the rate of change of prices as its action parameter. Demanders and suppliers could then retain their classical roles as quantity adjustors with the inventory as a buffer between them'.

73. This seemingly intractable problem was simplified in Arrow and Hahn (1971). The question of information (on the demand side) was shunned by positing the simplifying assumption of an auctioneer 'that establishes unique and public terms on which goods may be traded'. And ingenuously it is added: 'and he adjusts these in the light of market observations by some particular rule' (Arrow and Hahn 1971, p. 424).

   Indeed, '[t]he fiction of an auctioneer is quite serious, since without it we would have the paradoxical problem that a perfect competitor changes prices that he is supposed to take as given.' (ibid., p. 322).

74. It is quite true that the new unexpected sales–price points will yield knowledge about the possibility of a shift in demand conditions, but this imparts no sure information about the magnitude of the 'error'. The estimation of the demand curve is a different affair altogether; even under the *ceteris paribus* assumption the learning process may be quite irregular or long-drawn-out (cf. Clower 1959).

75. Meanwhile Arrow criticizes the common view that there is one price in a competitive market and asserts that the law of one price only is valid under special conditions, which are not those in disequilibrium.

76. We might guess that his problem would not be present (or so pressing) if Arrow had not assumed output 'stickiness' in the 'very short run' (Arrow 1959, p. 46).

77. Arrow, coherently with the originally assumed market perfection conditions, does not envision this question at all. First, the competitive firm in disequilibrium is faced with a sloping demand curve, due to the supply rigidity in the very short-run: 'any individual entrepreneur knows that he can raise the price, even if his competitors do not raise theirs, because they cannot satisfy any more of the demand than they already do' (Arrow 1959, p. 46). And, second, granting the large uncertainty during the adjustment process, he adds that '[a]ny estimate of the demand curve to a single entrepreneur involves a guess as to both the supply conditions and the prices of other sellers, as well as some idea of the demand curve to the industry as a whole. Under competitive conditions none of these is likely to be known very well'. To hint at knowledge of the industry demand curve is absurd – as Arrow (1987, p. 71) himself recognizes for the situations of monopoly or imperfect competition where 'scientific analysis imputes scientific behaviour to its subjects' – but anyway, the question is that Arrow fails to recognize the implication of the informational problems faced by buyers in disequilibrium, supposedly with price dispersion.

5. An afterthought: How elusive is the construction of a general model of decentralized exchange?

In the Introduction, I attempted to clarify what I am dealing and not dealing with in this book, as well as to reinforce the actuality of the questions, doubts, and criticisms that have been raised by several authors, regarding the general equilibrium analysis as a foundation of the study of aggregate economic phenomena, both theoretically and empirically. Most doubts have not been interpreted as serious, and the criticisms have not permeated either the core of the subject, or the research practices in the profession. Most importantly, however, most authors who are contributing to the perfecting of the neowalrasian approach have not recognized the questions as problematical. Consequently, for want of realizing the issues, it is hardly surprising that the answers are not satisfactory. Throughout this book, I have attempted to pose some of the questions that have been raised in the literature, following a consistent thread of thought. The recognition of the lack of decentralization in models of exchange provided a sieve which helped clarify and organize such inquiry, and in doing so I could come up with some other questions, which eventually allowed all the material to be put together. This was done by means of contrasting the problem initially posed by Walras with the answers that have been thought to have provided the complete solution. No awareness exists though, that these answers do not deal with the problem Walras intended to deal with, and therefore that the neowalrasian reformulation of the problems cannot have an interesting answer, as long as we believe we are dealing with real-world phenomena. The Walrasian program – to show how the mechanism of free competition 'through the play of the raising and the lowering of prices' by traders who bid against each other leads to equilibrium – has become the road map. With this guidance, the neowalrasian diversion was evinced as a dead end, arrived at by way of the concentration on the problem of the existence, and of the dichotomization of this from the stability and execution exercises. As a result, both the subordination of these two exercises to predetermined existence, and (we could say without exaggeration) the neglect of the execution problem, eradicated the original program from which general equilibrium analysis grew. This reasoning is expanded in more detail in the introductory chapter, and thus, the conclusion proper is there. Accordingly, there is no point in repeating at this stage the critical query and the findings summed up in the Introduction and further reiterated in the opening of every chapter.

This chapter is an afterthought, raising some new questions, not so much in a critical perspective, but aiming instead at searching for feasible solutions to these questions, advanced by authors who have been concerned with them for some time now. Therefore, this final chapter discusses proposals for the construction of a general model of decentralized exchange pointed out in the literature with a view to resolving the set of critical questions that several authors have diagnosed, and to put this discussion in the conceptual framework assembled in this book in order to ask whether and how some of these proposals relate to the perspective delineated here.

The Walrasian program involves a difficult compromise. Attempting a generalizing perspective of the working of market economies requires abstraction. However, the incorporation of realistic features of exchange processes will require a choice of some particular features, although such features may be deemed representative of, or common to, the plethora of exchange mechanisms that empirical observation brings to our attention. Walras attempted this, as has been shown, but the obstacles he met when dealing with the formalization of the workings of competition in the market he took for his theoretical reference – the Paris Stock Exchange – led him towards simplifications which cleared complications and paved the way to fruitless abstraction. The neowalrasians realized how difficult the problem was, and pursued simplifications. Along the way, sight of the institutions of interaction was eventually lost, or rather, relegated to epiphenomena. Disembarrassed of the discipline that the focusing on actual market forces imposes on the setting of the theoretical questions, the Arrow–Debreu models have not accomplished more than an idealized representation of general interdependence, that is limited to a logic of choice surmising the provision of equilibrium prices. Attention was confined to a logic of choice of 'rational self-seeking actions' by 'agents' (decisions of quantities by potential buyers and sellers, or potential 'consumers' and 'suppliers' in the model of exchange-cum-production), and to a provision of a set of equilibrium prices. 'But all General Equilibrium Theory has done is ensure this *provided market prices are independent of these actions*' (Hahn, 1981, p. 130). The equilibrium state corresponds to a 'resting point' defined independently of 'market forces' or actions of agents. Therefore the notion of equilibrium is narrowed down to a disembodied harmony of those 'actions', by 'assuming that people's plans are coordinated from the beginning, by an unspecified mechanism' (Howitt, 1997, p. 133). This neowalrasian approach defines the standard configuration of the general equilibrium analysis (cf. Walker 1997a), and has won the profession's lead in micro theory – as well as in macro theory, as is the case of the new classicals.

Formal problems were met, the attempt of solutions to which have since defined the research agenda of the general equilibrium analysis, but at its core the dichotomized view of existence and stability remains ingrained, whereby equilibrium rests as a notional state (cf. Howitt 1996, pp. 75–6; Clower 1995a). Bargaining, trading, and actual adjustment processes became an oversight in standard micro theory, decentralized intermediation ignored, and money basically an endnote remitted to macro territory. Lapses were diagnosed and solved but relapses into the primitive problem and procedures have been the norm, as even some of the selfsame authors who contributed most to define the approach have admitted (cf. Arrow 1994, 1987; Hahn 1987, 1981, 1973, 1970). As we have shown, this is an instance of the neowalrasian code syndrome.

The solution to the problem of existence of general equilibrium in exchange has constricted the scope of the further exercises involving stability and execution. Since the questions themselves regarding these exercises had predefined bounds set by the existence problem, attention was narrowed to those aspects of actual exchange that were liable to purely mathematical and formal applications hinging on the existence problem. The consequence was the atrophy of the concern with (implications on general equilibrium analyses of studies about) the workings of decentralized exchange mechanisms in markets of empirical relevance, whether brokered or non-brokered markets.

Convergence to the equilibrium price set has been shown to be a hardly attainable result, under general assumptions. Bargaining has been dealt with within the neowalrasian code, and the solutions are incomplete and meagre, since basically they were not able to outdo Walras's accomplishments on positing the no-arbitrage condition. The treatment of the execution of exchange, on the basis of the previously asserted existence of equilibrium prices, has raised both a negative and a positive inference. It showed that the demonstration of the feasibility of exchange at given and known equilibrium prices is not possible under general assumptions of decentralized interaction, and, thus, that the questions of existence, convergence and execution are not separable. It also showed that the feasibility of execution is not independent of the facilitating mechanisms summoned to organize the exchange process, like intermediation or a money commodity. This is positive in the simple sense that, in order to explain the mechanisms of exchange in the general market, we may be on safer ground if a means of exchange or intermediation is incorporated in the analytical procedure as part of the foundations, even though possibly at the cost of blemishing the proof of pure existence. The inclusion of explicit institutional features and rules in the theoretical models will most certainly help prevent the overstretching of formal inquiry beyond the limits that empirical reasonableness might set.

With the Arrow–Debreu models, the structure of the general equilibrium analysis had gained its form but, meanwhile, plenty of market configurations have been studied, either descriptively or theoretically. It should be recognized, however, that we have not considered the most part of the developments in this area of theoretical research during the last decades.

Uncertainty, and information and transaction costs have close implications on the workings of markets, or on their not working. Just to name a few topics, the adverse selection and moral hazard problems, for instance, have led to fruitful applications, and the revelation principle proved instructive for example in the study of auctions. But the questions addressed have been originated by, and the results applied to, particular economic decisions or particular market organizations. Bargaining theory, on the other hand, has had an outstanding expansion, but, as we could observe in Section 4.3.3.1 (v), the applications to general exchange have been formally unpalatable and empirically poor. In fact, the large majority of this formidable body of more specific or applied research has barely been imported in general equilibrium analyses. In fact, the absence of actual trading in micro theory has been recently stressed by Kohn (1995), Clower and Howitt (1996) and Clower and Howitt (1997b).

Most of the contributions with implications on price theory or market analysis developed during the last two decades, have only been indirectly referred to when they have led to applications, or played a role in the reformulation of the perspectives or the development of models dealing with general exchange. Consequently, most contributions have been dismissed as lateral to our pursuit here, in spite of their importance to understanding the specific problems they focus on. Many important aspects of all endeavors are necessarily relegated to a secondary role, and the case here is that our main concern is the Walrasian program, the neowalrasian diversion; and eventually a tentative discussion of the proposals indicated in the literature as how to mitigate or resolve the hindrances to the general theory of decentralized exchange that the neowalrasian code has entailed. Many aspects that have not yet been attended to may be found to bear upon the advancement of the discussion. But this is altogether a different objective, to skim or to glean contributions, and build upon them; to provide an answer has not been the goal. My final concern is simply to uncover some tracks, recently opened or long abandoned, that might help reformulate the questions.

Of utmost interest in this regard, are the proposals expanded in Walker's (1997a) *Advances in General Equilibrium Theory*. Walker proposes that models built with a view to understanding the working of markets, should have as fundamental assumptions the institutional framework, namely, the definition of the intermediaries, and of the rules of interaction, as concerns information, bargaining and trading. Only by incorporating clear and empirically reasonable institutional features and rules in the assumptions, definitions, equations and mechanics of the model, would this be amenable to provide a representation of the workings of exchange in the market. Only on this basis, would it be possible to construct *complete models* that are *functioning systems*. The following quotations provide a summary perspective, in the aspects that most concern us here:

In order for a model to be a functioning system, it must be explicitly endowed with the structural and behavioural features that are necessary to generate economic behaviour. If the model is a functioning system, its workings can be investigated and the consequences of different variations of parameters can be compared. It can be converted into an empirical model and tested, precisely in order to discover whether it has identified the important features and interconnections of the economy and how their influence is exerted in the determination of economic magnitudes; and, if so, it can be used to predict the consequences of changes of conditions. If the characteristics of the model are not specified, it is incomplete and is therefore not a functioning system. (Walker 1997a, p. 6).

As an example of a model that misses the institutional elements that are required towards the construction of a complete model that is a functioning system, Walker (1997a) blames Hicks (1939/1946) for not having specified the behavioral features of the participants in his model that might comprehend his postulates, 'and thus could not justify them. It was in fact an error on his part to believe that it is possible to separate model-building from the treatment of institutions' (cf. ibid., p. 7). More specifically, Walker adds next:

Microeconomic foundations that are confined to specifying the properties of preference functions or of individual excess demand functions cannot possibly result in a model sufficiently detailed to be a functioning system. They cannot enable assertions to be made about its functioning nor therefore about such matters as existence, uniqueness, or stability. There are no special cases that are exceptions to this situation. Preference functions and microeconomic supply and demand functions need a defining, supporting, and enabling context. To come into existence and to be capable of playing a role, the individual supply and demand functions must be based on appropriate characteristics of the participants and the necessary market environment. Without a specification of the characteristics of the market in which the participants demand and supply commodities, nothing can be inferred about the behaviour of the model. ... If it is alleged that the markets are organized, it must be shown what the features are that result in that characteristic. It is not meaningful to state simply that a market is organized except in an established context, ... because there are different types of organized markets with different pricing procedures and different results. It must be specified how the information collection and dissemination process works. A complete model, namely one that functions, can successfully be constructed with microeconomic constituents, by which is meant the entire range of institutions, physical structures, procedures, rules, possessions, motives, preferences, etc., that are necessary to create a functioning system. (Walker 1997a, pp. 9–10).

Walker's attention centers on a variety of 'organized' markets of which he presents clear and detailed descriptions, in several respects. Regardless of this, however, Walker qualifies the above general statement this way:

Some economists recognize that an underlying functioning model is necessary to justify their equations, but believe that its existence is established simply by asserting that it is there without describing it. It has been seen ... how Hicks and Mas-Colell *et al.* [1995], for example, write as though the enunciation of the words 'private enterprise economy' is enough to create a model and thus provide the institutional and behavioural foundations necessary to justify their equations. It has been seen how Fisher [1972; 1983], instead of specifying what the institutions are in his model and seeing what would be the resulting behaviour, asserts that the 'institutions are such that' the behaviour he postulates is generated. Those theorists fail to recognize that their equations and mathematical statements must be validated by showing concretely that they have referents in general and marketplace institutions and other structural and behavioural features of markets. The equations otherwise have no connection with a model and the deductions made by manipulating them have no economic meaning. It is not the case that their equations are implicitly dependent on the structural and behavioural features of a model. Theorists should not say, as do Hicks, Fisher, and Mas-Colell *et al.*, that the features are there but are not discussed – to say that is to beg the question of what those features are and to avoid the difficult task of constructing a functioning model that could justify the use of various equations. (Walker 1997a, pp. 51–2).

A central conclusion of Walker's thorough perusal of original contributions and recent expositions of general equilibrium in specialized accounts or textbooks, is that it is theoretically futile to lay out systems of equations based on empirically unexplained or unfounded postulates incapable of dealing with the rules of participation and the modes of information exchange and conduct of transactions. Another conclusion is that most constructions in the path marked by the Arrow–Debreu models to our days – including some of the most salient contributors to theoretical production and textbook writers – have failed to recognize the conceptual flaws and the omissions of institutional structure of their constructions, and therefore their empirical sterility – which altogether renders their models or textbooks lacking, and in most cases actually failing.

This is only a short, and unavoidably light, summary of the thorough diagnosis of the state of the *Advances* of the general equilibrium approach, which only the acquaintance with the richness of the detail, and the clarity of the positions and proposals defended can supply. In any case, I would like to highlight the importance of Walker's book to this necessary reflection and discussion. Other scattered hints, at a reformulation of the general equilibrium analysis as it stands, have been referred to in Chapter 4, but none addresses the questions in both the logical and historiographical perspectives, as Donald Walker does.

Therefore, I would concentrate on only two proposed ways towards the understanding and formalization of the workings of an exchange economy. One is clearly posed by Walker (1997a). The perspective here, even though not as clear or positive, points in the direction of rebuilding a general theory, that is, to rekindle Walras's program. The definition of some contours of this perspective stem from our reflections in Section 4.3.4 on the way to face the obstacles to the Walrasian program, to integrate bargaining and execution in the same mechanism. We might start from 'unorganized' pair-wise exchange satisfying some reasonable set of decentralization criteria, and see next how the assumed patterns of information exchange, bargaining and transaction result in the organization of trade. The possibility that this may be enabled by means of intermediaries or a medium of exchange is only theoretically and empirically reasonable, and thus the goal would be to explain how unaided pair-wise quid pro quo exchange (bilateral 'barter') might lead to the emergence of trade arrangements, and define their role in the coordination of the exchange mechanism.

There is also the other possibility we raised, of beginning with logistics in isolation of the determination of prices, but its role may eventually be limited to an element, a preliminary exercise, of the proposed approach just indicated.

The demonstration of the feasibility of execution under postulated trading rules (without attending to the determination of transaction prices) that satisfy decentralization criteria may be seen as a tentative 'game' that may help set the bounds for the admissible rules of the primordial and larger game that we have prognosticated, which construction would involve decentralized bargaining and trading on a pair-wise quid pro quo basis, unaided by any facilitating arrangement like intermediaries or monetary exchange; the endogenous emergence of these trading arrangements would also be part of the larger game. It should be recalled that pair-wise exchange does not connote barter, it just means bilateral quid pro quo transactions, common to all kinds of free trade, be it direct barter, the purchase or sale of a good, a service, or an asset against money; that is, a 'commodity' – or a small set of commodities – that is the counterpart to the offer or demand of all other commodities, e.g. goods, services, other money commodities, or assets.

Walker's (1997a) proposal towards the reformulation of general equilibrium models, consists basically in defining the institutional framework and the rules of interaction among the participants in the market, and of constructing complete models thereon, which are functioning systems. According to Walker, models have to be designed upon working and factual assumptions, not upon *ad hoc* simplifying postulates. In this sense, Walker's perspective might be regarded as a search for empirically relevant models applied to particular situations; but the obverse of this might seem to be Walker's implicit recognition of the inadequacy or impossibility of seeking after a general theory of exchange, or markets. I gather that this cannot be inferred from his proposals, as is acknowledged, for instance, in his statements that 'equations ... must be validated by showing concretely that they have referents in *general* and marketplace institutions', and that '*general* equilibrium modelling will be free of ... contrived and unrealistic *special cases*' (Walker, 1997a, pp. 52, 144, italics added); in any case, in the following I will put this in context. Yet, we cannot eschew the possible dilemma that the construction of empirically relevant, complete and functioning models may raise when the aim is to further Walras's program, and henceforth attempt at a generalizing comprehension of exchange in competitive markets. In fact, the Walrasian program, as originally defined, is empirically relevant, although in a way that is not immediate.

Our proposals and Walker's are very similar in procedures, but some apparent differences need reflection. The questions arise: Can we proceed in either of the two ways and succeed in approaching a solution to the Walrasian program? Are they compatible, and if so, how?

The central idea posed in Walker's book, that of a complete and functioning model, is a general principle of model building and may guide and illuminate the construction of a general model of exchange. Not to recognize the role of this general principle might lead us towards a diverting concern with problems fostered by the impossibility of empirical confrontation of the predictions of models. In standard accounts of general equilibrium analysis, given the absence of empirical foundations for, or the absence of, concrete interpretation of the posited system of equations, reality brings no impediment to the formal development of models of general exchange, and furthermore, reality itself may become a story that presumedly mimics the model. If the model is not a functioning model, the possibility is open that either a distortion of the theoretical perspective, or an enclosure of the view of reality, may materialize. Metaphorically, it is possible that reality may turn into the fuzzy object of which a distorted mirror provides the visibly clear model-image.

However, if the question is how to build a model description of the general interaction in an exchange economy, the variety of actual types of markets necessitates the choice of a certain type as the reference for the model. As said above, Walker's focus is especially directed to 'organized' markets but the variety of 'organized' markets described and distinguished and, henceforth, the richness of the possibilities suggested could apparently become an embarrassment. For the purpose of the construction of a model of general exchange, which type of 'organized' market is most representative? Which institutional features regarding the competences of market organizers and rules of interaction better mimic (generalize) the workings of a market economy? And, supposing that some approximation is reasonable, would the model then pass the criteria of a 'complete' and 'functioning' model for the understanding of general exchange? To sum up, which choice of institutional configuration is most conducive to anchoring the Walrasian program so that it may become empirically relevant?

If the objective is to build a general model of exchange, the crucial step towards the formal treatment may be to choose the set-up, modes of interaction, market institutions and so on, as Walker proposes. But some issues come up that should be addressed. On which grounds is the concentration on agents, brokers or auctioneers – that has directed the theoretical perspective since Walras to present-day general equilibrium analysis in the neowalrasian approach – justified in order to build a model of general exchange? And why not look at non-brokered exchange patterns, such as firms as market-makers, wholesalers and retailers as information gatherers and processors, the 'agents' in charge of bargaining and information 'relays' between consumers and producers? We should add, if this option is chosen, how is money to be integrated in the exchange mechanism, wouldn't it be more coherent to deal with a monetary economy to start with? If we have chosen 'specialist' agents to conduct the operation of exchange, wouldn't it be coherent to opt for a 'specialized' commodity, as that accepted common means of exchange which, at the start, would allow traders to specialize?

Without a choice of a commodity used as the counterpart to payments and receipts of the specialist agent, there would be no opportunity for the specialist to exploit economies of scale in trading; without this common means of exchange for other goods, the specialist would be only a logistics processor, the services of which could be only explained by the reduction of the probability of a failure to find a counterpart for the transactions sought. If his inventories of goods are confined to those in which he specializes, meaning the money commodity and the others he is willing to exchange for that money commodity, then great economies are obtainable by the specialist, without compromising the primary function of reducing the probability of a mismatch.

On these grounds, for the analysis of ongoing exchange in market economies, I gather that the reasonable foundations should include these two related specialized features, one concerning the definition of agents in charge of the functioning of exchange, the other concerning the definition of a means through which the functioning of exchange takes place. As Hahn (1994, p. 254) puts it, 'looking at any modern economy the importance of shops, wholesalers, brokers, etc. can be seen with the naked eye. In my view then a modern theory of exchange must in the first instance be a theory of mediation. ... Mediators [are] endowed with a mediation technology ... [with] obvious increasing returns ... Fiat money is now a device to make mediation more efficient and, indeed, possible'.

The question arises, whether setting out with these two building blocks – intermediaries of the non-broker type and money exchange – warrants its acceptation as a general theory? Possibly not, if this is only postulated, and not explained in a functioning model. Walker proposes that a functioning model should include a definition of participants, agents, rules of price determination, bargaining and transaction; money being part of the game. For those modes of interaction to integrate a general model, they must be part of a whole, derived, not posited. The main tasks appear, thus, to be: first, to define the functioning of non-brokered markets in a simplified and 'generalizing' way; second, to propose a role for intermediation as well as money, as derived from basic behavioral features of market participants, in response to information and transaction costs they face; third to make both these facilitating mechanisms consistent with the 'stylized' formalization of the workings of the non-brokered markets of reference; and, finally, to emphasize trading relationships, and show how markets are made, run and tied together by decentralized 'specialists', or, to put it bluntly, by firms as market-makers (see Appendix F on 'Market-makers, and price and quantity adjustments', for a preliminary and partial mapping of some related ideas).

This set of questions and suggestions conjoins Walker's proposal of a 'functioning' model with our perspective of departing from unaided pair-wise exchange in order to derive the trading relationships in a decentralized set-up, and to analyze the mechanisms of interaction by means of which quantities exchanged and transaction prices are determined, and the logistics of trade is carried out; and, in the process, attempt at some general model of exchange. In case the distinctions or clarifications we made about the perspectives in Walker (1997a), and here, are deemed pertinent, the conclusion is clear that the directions pointed out here, in order to face and solve the Walrasian program, may look too ambitious a goal to be feasible. Problems of several orders are detectable in this direction; but a few attempts at attacking these questions in a constructive way have been pointed out (cf. Clower and Friedman 1986; Daniel Friedman 1989; Clower 1994a, 1995b, Clower and Howitt 1996, 1997a, 1997b; Howitt 1996; also of interest may be e.g. Okun 1981, Alchian 1969, 1977, Irvine 1981, Fisher 1983; gleanings from Hicks 1989 might also help). Nonetheless, I would agree with Walker's final optimistic call:

> When attention is directed away from purely competitive models and virtual models and they are relegated to a place of purely historical interest, general equilibrium modelling will be free of the pointless objectives, unfruitful methods, false problems and plethora of contrived and unrealistic special cases that have wasted the energies of so many highly capable minds, and it will become a field of study of great relevance. (Walker 1997a, pp. 143–4).

Be that as it may, my central finding is this. A central problem for economic theorists, since Adam Smith, has been to provide an intellectually satisfactory explanation of the working of observed trading mechanisms. As at the present time, that problem, though often addressed, has never been answered; until now indeed, the problem has more often been sidestepped than confronted directly. This may go a long way to explain why so many of the crucial questions still at issue not only remain unanswered but (as reflected in the queries raised throughout this book) have yet to be perceived as relevant by the bulk of the economics profession, whose thinking continues to be dominated by, and whose vision seems to be filtered through, the thick clouds of confusion produced by the neowalrasian diversion.

Appendix: Notes on the literature

A. The budget constraint

There is, in Walras, a restriction of 'zero value of (planned) net trade' for the individual trader, but this is quid pro quo (Say's Principle), not income-constrained utility maximization (cf. Jaffé, ed. 1954, p. 165). The concept of budget constraint is not in Walras. It appears to have been suggested by Pareto (1909), contrary to Stigler (1954, p. 211), who argued: 'When income was introduced into consumer theory by Slutsky and Hicks and Allen, their work was wholly in harmony with the line of development the theory of utility had been taking'. Hicks acknowledged primarily Pareto,[1] and Slutsky (1915), and all later users of the budget constraint concept apparently drew on the same source.

Walras developed his argument by explicitly introducing maximum utility in his equations of exchange but he presupposed consumer equilibrium (utility maximization) when dealing with the theory of exchange;[2] he did not formalize the equilibrium of the individual, as Pareto later did. The budget equation in Hicks (1939/1946, p. 305) bears a close resemblance to Pareto's 'budget of the individual' (1909/1927, p. 160; 1911, p. 90) and we might conjecture that constrained utility maximization entered standard price theory by way of Pareto. In *Mathematical Economics* (1911, p. 65; see fn.), Pareto clearly stated that equilibrium results from the contrast of tastes and 'constraints'[3] – in earlier writings, as in the *Manual*, Pareto refers to 'obstacles' (cf. Allen 1932, p. 210, n). In fact, this is how the problem of the individual is posed in Chapters IV ('Tastes') and V ('Obstacles' on production), and especially how economic equilibrium is defined in Chapter VI of the *Manual*.

In Hicks (1939/1946, p. 305), dealing with the equilibrium of the consumer, we have: 'provided [the individual] spends all his income, we must have $M = \sum_{r=1}^{r=n} p_r x_r$' (cf. Schultz 1935, pp. 434–6 for a detailed presentation; also Allen 1932, pp. 212–13). In Pareto, the matter is presented in two contexts, and in slightly different ways, on maximization of utility by the individual (1909/1927, p. 160), and in the mathematical Appendix when dealing with exchange (ibid., p. 412). First, when the budget of the individual is first introduced (ibid., p. 160), it is not defined as a condition as Hicks does – 'provided he spends all his income' (1939/1946, p. 305). Rather it is stated as an equality required by exchange: 'If there are more than two goods it is easy to see that the receipts must still be equal to the expenditure, because if this were not so, it would mean that the individual had received, or spent, some money in another way than the transformation of goods' (Pareto

1909/1927, p. 160). Notice in this regard, Pareto's insistence on his view that 'economic equilibrium is independent of the notions of ... utility, of value in exchange, or of ophelimity' and 'price' (ibid., pp. 393–4, n, 406), as well as his emphasis on 'quantities which observation gives' (ibid., pp. 411–12, 391, n, 394).

Dealing with exchange in the mathematical Appendix, when the budget plane of the individual is defined (ibid., p. 412), there is no reference to 'income' (cf. Schultz 1935, p. 437), yet Pareto states that the total value of an individual's holdings of commodities after exchange 'must also' be equal to the total value of initial holdings measured at exchange prices. From this equality of total values before and after exchange, Pareto derives the budget plane of the individual, relating net demands valued in numeraire units (i.e., d_x, d_y, ... valued in units of x) (Pareto, 1909/1927, p. 412): 'This equation has a special significance in political economy. It gives the budget plane of the receipts and expenditures of the individual under consideration. Whether the prices are constants or variables, the balance plane of the individual, for the exchanges [pour les échanges] d_x, d_y, ... , is always given by

$$d_x + p_y\, d_y + p_z\, d_z + \ldots = 0.'$$

The conditional character of the Hicksian budget equation is clearly anticipated. Using Pareto's notation, the parallel to Hicks's budget equation could be put thus:

$$x_0 + p_y y_0 + p_z z_0 + \ldots = x + p_y y + p_z z + \ldots \; .$$

The left hand side is just the numeraire value of the resources of the consumer ('an individual, who has a given sum of money M available for expenditure' (Hicks 1939/1946, p. 305); and the right is the value of expenditures. The assumption is that value supplied (via the 'auctioneer') is equal to value demanded: $V^S = V^D$. This is a planning constraint on the individual, which is the same as Say's Principle, that one can plan to acquire only by offering.

B. Hicks on trading at false prices

Trading at 'false prices' is considered in Hicks's *Value and Capital* (1939/1946, esp. Note to Chapter IX). Following Marshall's description of temporary partial equilibrium (two goods/fish market), Hicks considers that 'the process of fixing prices by trial and error ... need not have any appreciable effect upon the prices ultimately fixed' (ibid., p. 127).

Since traders cannot be expected to know just what the schedules of total supplies and demands will be, transaction prices during the course of trading will move up or down. Disposing of recontracting as an exceptional feature in markets, if trading at 'false prices' is considered, a problem ensues in regard to demand and supply analysis. Hicks discusses this problem, showing that change in price in the middle of trading has the same effect as a redistribution of wealth (income effects); 'but if [the buyer's] total expenditure on the commodity is small, the gain (or loss) must be small, and his demand for the commodity will be very little affected. Consequently the market will finish up very close to the equilibrium price' (ibid., pp. 128–9).

In the case of general interdependence, Hicks says that income effects create what he calls 'a certain degree of indeterminateness', and that as a result of false trading 'this indeterminateness is somewhat intensified'. And he adds (ibid., p. 129): 'But I think we may reasonably suppose that the transactions which take place at "very false" prices are limited in volume. If any intelligence is shown in price-fixing, they will be'.

Hicks adduces that gains to the buyers may be expected to be offset by losses to the sellers, and vice versa. Moreover, it is (oddly) added that the effect of false prices is limited to income effects by his assumption of markets being only open on 'Mondays'. Equilibrium prices are therefore used as indicators for production and consumption plans carried out for the rest of Hicks's 'week'.

Here some comments are in order. First, one must bear in mind Hicks's adherence to the assumption of perfect competition, including not only (i) agents' 'assessment of particular supply or demand conditions' (ibid., pp. 6–7) and (ii) 'perfect contemporaneous knowledge – that everyone knows the current prices in all those markets which concern him' (ibid., p. 123), but also (iii) 'an easy passage to temporary equilibrium': 'we need also to try to bring ourselves to suppose that price-changes are negligible during market hours on the Monday, when the market is open and dealers have to fix market price by higgling and bargaining, trial and error' (ibid., p. 123). Now, two comments.

First, why does Hicks bring in the misplaced fact of 'price-fixing'? The issue clearly lies outside the confines of his theoretical model. If he is conjoining 'perfection' with a radically different real world, to support that trading at false prices is limited in volume, that is bad economics. Whether or not his Note to Chapter VIII (ibid., pp. 110–11) on 'Conventional or Rigid Prices' could be interpreted in this context (as applying to any price-fixing, by the government or by firms alike) as § 6 on 'Price Rigidities' in Chapter XXI (ibid., p. 265) may lead one to guess that this is an instance of real world facts unrelated to his theoretical thread when dealing with temporary equilibrium, and would caution us against his possible mixed argument of theory and realistic description.

Hicks coins the expression *fixprice* market for his 'habit' (1988, p. 9) of looking upon diversified manufactures as a force which makes for stabilization (in contradistinction to speculative markets); he assumes a *fixprice* market as one in which prices are to some degree insulated from the pressures of supply and demand. In effect, Hicks analyzes income adjustments under the fixprice assumption in *Capital and Growth* (1965, Chapter 7, pp. 76 ff.), where it obtains a theoretical dimension, as he stresses in *The Crisis in Keynesian Economics* (1974, pp. 22–30).

Of course, Hicks might have intended to refer to price fixing in the sense of his weekly model. In that model, each price, once contracted, is fixed during the week it is contracted for, and trade takes place at prices defined on the past 'Monday'. A trade contracted for and due during a later week can be 'recontracted' by means of revision of prices only when next 'Monday' comes – in case price expectations or trading plans are inconsistent (ibid., pp. 133–4).

But his assumption that contracting takes place on 'Monday' is just a convenient way to separate contracting from trading, and to give his model a flavor of 'dynamics' (contracting occurs by means of a sequence of temporary equilibria). The fact that plans carried out by consumers and firms during the 'week' are based on equilibrium prices obtained on 'Monday' only has relevance because Hicks is working on the presupposition of 'perfect' markets. If he did not allow for an easy adjustment to equilibrium, how could information on 'equilibrium' market prices be so taken by traders? Hicks does not seem to be correct when he states that the effect of false prices is limited to income effects by his assumption of markets being open on 'Mondays', i.e., the separation between contracting and execution of plans. The reason seems to lie, differently, in the assumption of an easy passage to equilibrium.

Wherever Hicks's Note fits, as a real world interference, as it stands, it is an object lesson of bad economic theory. One wonders what the Hicksian model of the economy really is, it certainly is not the one discussed in his mathematical appendix. The problem is that the entire argument runs in terms of an implicit conception of the real world that Hicks does not share with his readers, so the entire argument has an otherworldly aspect.

C. Price-making mechanisms

Ralph Cassady (1967, pp. 8–14; 1974, pp. xix, 3) distinguishes three basic price-making schemes.

Cassidy considers, first, *take-it-or-leave-it administered pricing*, in which the price-maker (usually the seller) posts a price at which he is ready to transact, the other party being supposed either to accept or reject the offer without negotiation.

Second, he considers *private treaty pricing* through individual negotiation, in which a selling price is negotiated between individual seller and buyer for each transaction. The starting point of bargaining can be a 'specified' or list price that both parties know is open to negotiation, which will take place if the buyer is willing to treat that price as a take-it-or-leave-it proposition. Alternatively, when no price is 'specified', a quotation is made by one of the parties, usually an asking price enunciated by the seller, expectedly at a level that, attending though to current market conditions, leaves him with room for negotiation, without risking alienating the buyer. If a counteroffer is quoted by the buyer, bargaining between the seller and the individual buyer may then ensue, by means of which adjustments (downward adjustments of asking-price, and/or upward adjustments of offer-price) are discussed. The outcome of this will be mostly dependent on market conditions, knowledge of these by the two parties, and their tactical skills. This is all very loose and informal. However, according to Fudenberg and Tirole (1983, p. 239), the form and outcome of the bargaining 'game' may be very sensitive to the institutional 'setting' (e.g. the number of bargaining periods) and other parameters (e.g. valuations, the (a)symmetry of information and discount factors); notice also the authors' conclusion that 'general assertions about the effects of parameter changes on the bargaining process are suspect'. Be that as it may, the two traders will probably arrive at an agreement on the transaction price.

In a market so organized that pricing is conducted by private negotiation between seller and buyer, both seller competition in gaining or retaining custom and buyer competition in 'acquiring supplies' are present; but also each trader, when dealing with a potential transactor, will be attempting to obtain 'the most favorable terms' without compromising profitable dealings in the future, if he deems this favorable to his business with given buyers (cf. Cassady 1974, p. 97). Thus, both 'antagonistic' and 'cooperative' efforts are themselves made in the process of negotiated pricing. This is at the root of the fact that, although this price mechanism is best suited to those situations – 'product and market conditions' (ibid., p. 206) – where the setting of prices is required to conform to the particular circumstances of each transaction, it does require attention by traders to the market circumstances, which establishes a range of reasonableness in price quotations. As to the gathering of market information, sellers may observe market dealings, but their reliable, though indirect, information about the market may only be assessed through their private negotiations. Buyers, on the other hand, will benefit from sounding out several sellers on their quotations – not only for informational reasons, but also for the strategic interest of patronizing more than one seller.

Finally, the third scheme considered is *competitive bid pricing*, in two forms. One is *sealed-bid arrangements*, either by vendors who compete by underbidding (e.g. for a job), or by buyers who compete by outbidding other prospective bidders (e.g. for a given right or property) (cf. Cassady 1967, pp. 9–11; Hackett 1992; 1993).[4] The other is *auctioning*, which is a price-making method whereby competing buyers are led to outbid each other, so that the vendor may obtain a price tending to approach the highest demand price of bidders. The auction house usually operates as a broker-agent representing the vendor.[5] The role of the auctioneer in the ascending-bid auction is 'to recognize one bidder at each level, and to announce the amount of the bid, in order to establish a basis for increased bids' (Cassady 1967, p. 57); and in the descending-price auction, '[a]fter selecting the starting point, he calls out the prices at successively lower levels, recognizes the first and high bidder, and announces the amount of the successful bid and the name of the buyer' (ibid., p. 60). Auctions can be ascending-bid, descending price, or combine both in simultaneous bidding, but the purpose of each one is to drive prices to a high level, in a quick and expeditious manner (which is not synonymous with being economical).

Exchanges differ from auctions. A rudimentary form of exchange is just a meeting point for buyers and sellers to negotiate individual deals. But, as in the case of stock or commodity exchanges, it may also be a 'place' where competing buyers and competing sellers enter a multiple negotiation through appointed brokers, who deal with each other in order to accomplish transactions for their customers. According to Cassady, though, '[e]xchanges really are not a different type of price-making arrangement: the simple exchange involves merely private negotiation between individual buyers and sellers, while the more complex exchange is based on competitive bidding by both buyers and sellers' (Cassady 1967, p. 14). 'The stock market has been designated by some as a "double" auction because the exchange process is based on competition among sellers as well as among buyers' (ibid., p. 13).[6] But this seems poor reasoning since it is true of all markets.

A TWO-GOODS (ONE-MARKET) DOUBLE AUCTION IN A PURELY BROKERED MARKET

It could be of some interest to attempt a representation of the working of this double auction mechanism in a 'perfectly' organized market. For the sake of simplicity, let us be confined to a purely brokered market, and moreover to a two-goods, one-market case. The objective here is to make sense of Walras's description of the Paris Government Bond Market. I paraphrase from Walras (Jaffé, ed. 1954, pp. 84–6, 87 ff.) with the guidance of Howitt (1973, p. 490).

Let us assume a given price for a commodity. Those agents who have received orders to sell at this price or lower, will offer a certain amount for sale at such price. Conversely, those agents who have received orders to buy at this price or higher, will demand a certain amount for purchase at such price. If the amount proposed to purchase by an agent is matched by another agent's proposed amount to sell at the given price, a transaction takes place between these two brokers. Then, '[t]he terms of this trade are announced publicly, and the rest of the brokers attempt to carry out all the trades their clients wish to engage in at that rate of exchange' (Howitt 1973, p. 490).

Consider, next, that either seller or buyer agents do not find a counterpart for a proposed transaction in the market. Suppose this is a broker, formerly on the demand side, who was unable to carry out all his desired trades at the assumed price. He will recalculate his present outstanding orders to purchase at a higher price (dropping his orders to buy at the previous transaction price, and it is further assumed that no new orders have been placed meanwhile), and will announce a certain proposed amount to purchase at the new higher price. If he finds a matching offer (at this new higher bid there may be now proposed supply), trade is consummated, otherwise a revision of the demand price will have to be next considered, and bidding is continued until he is able to meet an agent with a counteroffer in the market.

If it were an agent formerly on the supply side, the opposite situation would occur: he would propose a trade at a lower price in order to find a matching 'counterbid'.

This is a depiction of a double auction, with the broker who found himself unable to fulfill his proposed transaction at the given price, acting as an auctioneer: if he is on the supply side, he is facing competitive buyers and underbidding; if on the demand side, he is facing competitive sellers and outbidding. Of course, it is not necessarily so simple. Even for a market in which only brokers are assumed to operate, and therefore no bargaining is present on their own account, there is the initial question of establishing the starting price. We must introduce some explicit or implicit form of bargaining proper, before the market settles to its first transaction; this is obtained in some securities markets (new US Treasury Bills, for instance) by means of '[s]tatic double auction, relying on sealed bids and offers' (Wilson 1992, p. 258). But bargaining has an explicit role in most organized exchanges.[7] For instance, in the case of those where trade is conducted by specialists, bargaining is crucial for the working of the market: by trading on his own account, and changing his quotes of ask or bid prices, the specialist allows for a continuous market.

D. Thick-markets

Thick-market, parametrical pricing, and price-taker are intertwined notions. Let us attempt a clarification.

As to the definition of a *thick-market*, let us consider that:

> to stay within the Marshallian tradition we must suppose that trading in every market area is sufficiently brisk, hence markets sufficiently *thick*, that the subjective price expectation assumptions defining competitive marketor behavior, viz.,
>
> $$\delta p^e_j \; / \; \delta q_j \equiv 0, \quad \text{and} \quad \delta w^e_j \; / \; \delta n_j \equiv 0,$$
>
> are not disconfirmed by experience. In short, marketors not only subjectively believe, but also objectively 'see' their markets as 'thick' or, more colorfully, as *experientially continuous*. (Clower 1994b, p. 378).

In fact, the author clarifies that '[f]ormally, the concept of "thickness" requires continuity (or "effective" continuity, somehow defined) of the marketor's sales function' (ibid., 384, n). Impressionistic descriptions in the literature suggest, however, that a thick-market is characterized by atomistic competition, high aggregate volume of trade, and high frequency of transactions, but there is no logical basis for any of this. As we will attempt to make clear, thickness is a general concept without specific reference to the characteristics or degree of market organization, brokered or non-brokered, competitive or monopolistic.

Notice that each marketor '*acts* competitively [Marshall, 1920, p. 341] in the sense that each plans its output (prospective sales) in the expectation that its probable sale price, p^e_j, is independent of its output: $\delta p^e_j \; / \; \delta q_j \equiv 0$', and that 'each marketor ... in fixing the planned input of factor services n_j and the associated bid price w^e_j, it *proceeds* on the competitive presumption that the probable wage rate required to attract and hold factors is independent of the planned quantity demanded: $\delta w^e_j \; / \; \delta n_j \equiv 0$' (Clower 1994b, p. 378, italics added).

The concept of thickness captures an essential aspect of *parametric pricing*, which being also a matter of perceived 'continuity', means that the estimated price function of the seller is independent of sales and output (cf. Bushaw and Clower 1957, p. 184). For instance, in adjustment (disequilibrium) situations, the firm may be adjusting price, a function of the discrepancy between sales and output or of unplanned inventory holdings, and still take its sales estimates or pricing decision as parametric – or perceive the market as thick, if its price function is perceived to be independent of planned sales at the new price.

Parametric pricing agrees with Pareto's view of free competition: 'Assume that all individuals follow [free competition] in their exchanges ... That means that each of them accepts the market prices although in reality the latter are *indirectly* modified by the exchanges made by these individuals' (Pareto 1909/1927, p. 431;[8] cf. 1911, p. 86; also see Allen 1932, p. 213 for a short, and slightly distorted mention of this); and '[a]ll the sellers (and buyers) of rentes [on the Paris Bourse] clearly modify the prices, but they modify them without previous design; it is not the purpose, but the effect of their actions' (ibid., p. 116). Pareto's view is that free competition 'corresponds to very numerous concrete facts' and 'includes a very large number of transactions among which are the majority or even all the transactions relating to household consumption' (ibid., p. 115–16).

It is interesting how this focus on the 'purpose' of actions of individuals apparently led to a change in perspective in the concept of free competition from Walras to Pareto. Pareto distinguishes two types of attitude of a trader in face of the market – Pareto uses the word 'contract'. Type I is the case of free competition: 'The determination of the market price does not depend on [the individual]'. Type II is the case of '[s]omeone who ... intends to modify the price'; in order to do this 'he compares mainly the positions which he reaches *via* different prices' (Pareto 1909/1927, pp. 114–15); also '[a]ssume that individual *1* does not accept the prices as he finds them in the market, but endeavors to modify them, with a view to achieving a certain end. This case includes the one which is commonly called monopoly' (ibid., p. 433); moreover, Pareto distinguishes 'between an individual's *power* to exercise a monopoly, and the *fact* that the individual does exercise it' (ibid., p. 438).

Parametric prices have, however, a different meaning when referring to prices as data in the calculations of agents (cf. Burstein 1968 [9]). A trader may be in a situation whereby the transaction he is entering leads to a change in price (through bargaining, or just a change of the posted price), and still take prices elsewhere in the market as given 'in the interim'. For this agent, other prices are given data, and in this sense prices are parameters.

The notion of *price-taker* is commonly associated with both parametric pricing, and price being a given (parameter), in contrast to the case of a monopolist: 'parametric pricing is associated only with selling under conditions of pure competition in the existing economic literature' (Bushaw and Clower 1957, pp. 184–5). The monopolist firm is supposed to be the only seller in the market, which produces two consequences: first, it faces a downward-sloping demand curve, and, second, it has no given price to follow and has to pick the best price. Contrary to the competitive firm, its price is not a given (parameter). This distinction between price-maker and price-taker seems liable to some confusion for two reasons.

First, even though the monopolist does not receive a price signal from the market place, as the competitive firm may be supposed to, similarly to the competitive firm, its sales estimates or pricing may be parametric. The whole revenue curve is fixed by 'impersonal forces'; thus 'there is no *a priori* reason why such behavior [parametric pricing] cannot occur in a one seller market since even in this case there may be fierce competition in a relevant sense among sellers in different but closely related markets' (Bushaw and Clower 1957, p. 185). To notice in this respect that, referring to Jevons's concept of competition, which 'was a part of his concept of a market', Stigler argues that '[t]he merging of the concepts of competition and the market was unfortunate. ... A market may be perfect and monopolistic and imperfect and competitive' (Stigler 1957, pp. 244–5; cf. Allen 1932, pp. 209–10, 214).

Second, in every market (atomistic or 'small numbers'), every seller can be said to have an asking price. Alchian and Allen's comments on how the 'price-searcher' 'sets' his price are of interest here. In a price-searcher market, as defined in contrast to a price-taker market, regarding the 'wealth-maximizing *output and price program*':

> Whether sellers are described as using their 'market power' to 'set' prices or merely searching for the best (wealth maximizing) price in the market is all a matter of semantics. ... *All* prices in all markets are administered in the sense that each person decides at what price he shall sell (in the light of market demand). (Alchian and Allen 1972, pp. 344–5).

Perhaps it is set and changed by someone or something else – but it is still the price at which the seller stands ready to deal with the willing buyer. Here, the relevant distinction is not between competitive and monopolistic pricing, but between brokered and decentralized markets. In organized brokered markets, transaction prices become a price signal 'contemporaneously' issued and rendered available to traders. Therefore, in organized brokered markets, the seller has information about a price to ask, so that his expectations are that he will be able to find a buyer at that price for a given quantity, at his discretion. He will experience his market as thick for a broad range of quantities proposed for sale. On the other hand, in decentralized markets, the seller will have no given price at which he could sustain the expectation to be able to dispose of (sell) any quantity he chooses to offer for sale; whatever his choice of an asking price, he has no guarantee that he will be able to contact willing buyers and sell the quantity offered for sale.

Two qualifications regarding this second reason should be made. One is that, even in the case of organized brokered markets:

> in which the buyers and sellers are both price-takers, it is not as a result of large numbers of participants but as a result of market institutions and rules. In them the price is changed by a market authority. He finds the equilibrium price and sets it as the one at which trade can occur ... [P]articipants in those markets are price-takers ... because ... their behaviour is a result of the mandatory pricing procedure in the market. (Walker 1997a, p. 16).

The other qualification is that:

> In the vast majority of perfectly competitive markets, the participants are not price-takers all the time; they often or always are the persons that change the price. Even in the markets on the New York Stock Exchange, the specialist may set the price at which the market opens in an effort to clear it, and may occasionally intervene to find a new price, but much of the time the traders change the price. ... Any participant is a price-taker only until he is not offered as much of the commodity as he demands or is not requested to sell as much as he would like. (ibid., pp. 16–17).

Summing up, the distinction between price-taker and price-maker may be unwarranted. First because the sales curve is estimated, or perceived by the seller; and independently of the shape of the 'real' demand curve, the seller may have no grounds (informational or experimental) to disconfirm that his is a thick-market. The standard (partial equilibrium) distinction between competitive and monopolistic (one-seller) markets provides no secure prediction regarding the estimation of the sales curve by the seller (standard theory deals *only* with 'perceived' revenue functions).

Second, because in the case of decentralized markets we are at odds to make sense of taker and maker. In the case where prices are the object of previous negotiation, or bilateral bargaining, the distinction is meaningless. There is also the other possibility that a price is posted by the trader, more commonly, an asking price by the seller; also in this case, the distinction basically misses the point. The reason is that such markets are better understood with sellers as quantity-takers: whatever the choice of price may be, with attention to market demand nonetheless, the seller has an asking price and will sell a minimal-size 'lot' at discretion to any single buyer. The market may be perceived as thick or thin, but the seller is a quantity-taker.

Furthermore, the case of a decentralized 'quantity-taker' market may be considered as thick if each trader 'plans its output (prospective sales) in the expectation that its probable sale price, p^e_j, is independent of its output' (Clower 1994b, p. 378). Which means that the quantity put up for sale is not expected to have an effect on the price at which that quantity is expected to be sold. We can make sense of this belief[10] by the seller as the best guess available to him in the case where a well defined relation between price and quantity/sales cannot be ascertained, given the difficulty of disentangling effects (viz. identification problem; lagged effects; informational costs; computational costs and feasibility). The expectation may be in error, and in general will be, unless the amount sold – or put up for sale – is 'infinitesimally' small. This relates to continuity of the demand curve (cf. Burstein 1968, Chapter 6, esp. pp. 134 ff.) whereas, as referred to above, 'the concept of "thickness" requires continuity (or "effective" continuity, somehow defined) of the marketor's sales function' (Clower 1994b, p. 384, n).

The upshot of this note is that in thick-markets expected transaction prices, regardless of being given or obtained by way of bargaining, are thought of by individual transactors, as being uninfluenced by the amount of planned sales.

E. Search models of trade

Search models of trade tackle a basic aspect of the proper formalization of decentralized exchange. Peter Diamond (1982a) is the first attempt to deal with barter in a search mechanism framework, later developed to monetary exchange by him (1984a) and others. Diamond built a model of trade-cum-production based on particular assumptions regarding decentralized logistics of trade, though he kept the question of the determination of equilibrium prices aside in order to concentrate on his problem: he posited prices as given, and let individual traders searching for prospective traders by themselves without any market arrangement to facilitate matches.[11]

Diamond raises the possibility of coordination problems: the technology of barter leads to increasing returns to scale in the aggregate. This trade externality has a positive feedback on production, making it optimal the production of higher inventories. Because of this trade externality, equilibrium is locally inefficient and, considering the positive feedback, the possibility of multiple steady state equilibria emerges. The author points towards the effect of the trade externality on business cycles: allowing for increasing returns, the volume of trade varies more than capital and inventory levels over the business cycle. Diamond claims that it is possible for a barter economy of self-employed individuals to have business cycles, when imperfections in trade coordination are considered. My objective here is to suggest inadequacies regarding the formalization of the trading technology which produces these results.

To start with, Diamond's (1982a) original barter model is summarized, and then the central assumptions underlying the matching technologies in this and related models are sorted out. Next, doubts and objections are raised about the adequacy of the assumptions chosen in Diamond's paper and extensions by him and others in order to formalize decentralized exchange in a search set-up. The first question relates directly to Diamond's (1982a) assumption that search opportunities are a function of the number of unmatched traders. This can only find support given that individuals employed in trade or in production cannot be told apart; only unmatched traders search but they can meet individuals employed either in trade or in production, and thus, the larger the proportion of the first in the population, the larger the probability of completing a transaction. This externality result in the model is due to the assumption of anonymity in trading. And this one is supported by presuming costless search: since no costs are considered explicitly in the trade searching process, there is no basis for the investment in information or the creation of any market arrangement to save on such trading costs. A second question regards the undue extrapolation of assumptions reasonable for a 'two-sided' market, like the labor market, to one where offer and demand go together, as in Diamond's (1982a) barter model. Here, increases in the number of individuals on the demand side, and on the offer side, exactly match. This is not so on 'two-sided' markets like the labor market, where transactions occur between two separate sets of traders exogenously defined, one on the demand side, the other on the offer side; in this case, an increase in numbers on one side increases the density of trading opportunities for an individual searching on the other side. Alternatively, in an interchangeable market, where a trader for the good who is on the offer side is also on the demand side, an increase in the number of individuals employed in trade does not bring about such an increase in density of trading opportunities for another potential trader. Finally, it is discussed whether later applications to monetary exchange by Peter Diamond and others, may suffer from the same drawback.

Summing up, the idea is defended that, without a clear definition of market arrangements, the analysis of decentralized logistics of exchange may lead to conclusions with only limited interest for the understanding of economies where exchange is institutionally organized in markets.

THE BASICS

If we preclude individual traders from exchanging directly with a central market authority, we will have to envision individual traders as in need of inferring exchange opportunities. And if costs of searching for prospective transactors are in any sense considered, the expeditious meeting of transactors cannot be taken for granted. We will have to have traders looking for trading partners, or, in an extreme case, we may have to start with individual traders carrying out exchange as a do-it-yourself activity.

Let us start by considering a market 'setting' where the central determination of market equilibrium prices creates an allocation inefficiency when the decentralization of exchange 'locations' is allowed for. Meyer *et al.* (1992) discuss the coordination problem that stems from central pricing when trade of a single good occurs at two separate places. Let us embark towards the South Seas and imagine two islets. The authors define a market for fish in two islands (the only element of decentralization they introduce), where exchange takes place separately on each island between its 'perfectly' competitive consumers and those fishermen who decide to sell there. Price in a numeraire commodity is set by auction.

Going on to suppose centralized market pricing by an 'auctioneer', the authors then state that the announcement of an equilibrium price would not be a sufficient condition for general market clearing, since fishermen would have no information about which island to supply,[12] so that it would be a matter of chance that either of the markets cleared at the announced price set. Thus, the conclusion is that 'traditional Walrasian models of general market clearing do not formalize and cannot analyze the allocation problem inherent in decentralized exchange' (Meyer *et al.* 1992, p. 295). (This relates to the traditionally held position that the auctioneer is not required to be endowed with knowledge of every individual's excess demands; to find equilibrium prices, only aggregate net excess demands for each commodity would be needed. The function of determining and announcing equilibrium prices would be centralized, even though information were decentralized.)

This problem of coordination of trade was raised by Peter Diamond, who proposed a search model with pair-wise exchanges between individual traders. Diamond's (1982a) barter model falls into this setting. This parable dispenses with the neowalrasian clearing-house but keeps central pricing. It assumes correct forecasts of future prices and rates of trading and production opportunities (since the author is interested in steady state equilibria, this assumption allows the author to restrain attention to the implications of trade coordination). In this island coconut market,[13] the matching of traders is left to a search process but the ruling unitary rate of exchange is obviously known at all times by all traders. Prospective traders with a 'coconut worth of purchasing power' search for another transactor with a coconut on hand, given the respected taboo that no individual can consume what he himself has produced. When two transactors in possession of one unit of the coconut-good meet, exchange takes place – by the artifice of sticking to a single good, and still forcing trade, price is one by assumption, and thereby the problem of the determination of the equilibrium price is assumed out. Pair-wise matching of traders obeys a random process, and trade is bilateral and costless.

After this brief look at the exchange mechanism, let us point out some salient features of the exchange/demand and production behavior. Individuals are either employed in exchange or in production. After an individual has decided to produce a unit, he will not consume the coconut – this is meant to represent the advantage of specialization in production or trade over self sufficiency, and this is a first taboo. He has a unit of purchasing power, and he will search for a trading partner; as soon as he finds one, trade occurs, and consumption takes place. In such a search model, demand is made to depend on the distribution of stocks of inventories of others (meaning the proportion of others that hold a coconut, and are therefore employed in trading), as well as expectations about future production and trade opportunities (cf. Diamond (1987b, p. 368).

Being freed from the trading activity, he strolls around the island looking for coconuts: finding a coconut tree, he will decide whether or not to reap a coconut, that is, whether the cost of climbing to pick up the fruit is compensated by the utility he will derive from the prospective consumption. The relevant feature here is that, the easier he expects it to be to find a match, the greater is his willingness to produce, i.e. the higher the cost which he is willing to incur (his 'reservation' disutility), and thereby the greater the output. Moreover, if an individual has unsold, produced output on hand, he cannot undertake a new project – this is an extreme assumption on the costs of inventory holding, and corresponds to a second taboo.

In this general equilibrium search model, trade is coordinated by a stochastic matching process. Production opportunities are also stochastic, but the decision to undertake the project is the control variable of the model: the decision to switch from searching for production to engaging in production is the driving force of the model.

Let us now present a summary account of some formal aspects regarding the trade technology. This consists of sequential transactions following a Poisson process. As to the motion equation that describes the trade technology, assuming that all production opportunities with costs below c^* are undertaken (this cut-off cost is the analogue of the reservation wage), the time derivative of the employment rate satisfies:

$$e = a\,(1{-}e)\,G(c^*) - e\,b(e)$$

where:

e	– proportion of the population employed in the trade activity,
a	– arrival rate of production opportunities,
c^*	– cut-off cost, meaning that all production opportunities with cost $c < c^*$ are undertaken,
$G(c^*)$	– cumulative probability distribution of the labor disutility cost of producing a unit of inventory,
$b(e)$	– arrival rate of trade opportunities, an increasing function in e.

Each of the $(1{-}e)$ unemployed in trade has the flow probability a of learning of an opportunity and accepts the fraction $G(c^*)$ of opportunities. Each of the e employed faces the probability b of having a successful trade meeting and being freed to seek a new opportunity. In a steady state, we have the equilibrium rate of unemployment by setting $e = 0$. It is shown that the steady state employment rate rises with c^*.

As to the decision variable in the model, which production opportunities to undertake, c^* is derived from the gain in expected lifetime utility when an individual becomes employed in trade, instead of being unemployed, that is, decides to produce a unit of the good. It is shown that in a steady state equilibrium, c^* is also positively related to e. It is this fact, that in a steady state equilibrium, in each of the equations (describing the optimal production decisions, and the constant rate of employment), e and c^* are positively related, which allows the possibility of multiple steady state equilibria. In this barter model, one equilibrium dominates the others; and since G does not necessarily have nice properties, there can be more equilibria than shown. Hence Diamond's surmising that, due to the externality in the trade technology, every steady state equilibrium attained with no government intervention is locally inefficient (cf. Diamond 1982a, pp. 893–4; 1984b, p. 5). Welfare improvements come from increasing c^*.[14]

Similarly, the presence of multiple steady-state rational equilibria implies the existence of multiple rational expectations paths from some initial positions. An example, built upon the barter model (Diamond 1982a), is provided in Diamond and Fudenberg (1989), which suggests a role expectations may have in aggregate demand management; the possibility of equilibria with 'endogenous business cycles' is raised and analyzed, also under the assumption of rational expectations, when trading externalities are present. In the same framework, an extension of this question is developed by Boldrin, Kiyotaki and Wright (1993), for the case of 'a large number of differentiated commodities and agents with idiosyncratic tastes' (ibid., p. 6); alternative trading technologies are studied, constant, decreasing, and increasing returns to scale. The results, however, are similar to the one-good case in Diamond and Fudenberg (1989), except for the welfare implications: the prediction of the standard model need not apply here, for the case of increasing returns to scale (cf. Boldrin *et al.* 1993, p. 746).

MATCHING ASSUMPTIONS

Coordination problems arise because this trade technology is expected to exhibit increasing returns to scale in the aggregate (cf. Diamond 1984b, pp. 2–6). The idea (more of an unproved, or biased, conjecture) pushed through is that if more people are attempting to trade (i.e. with increased inventories for trade[15]), each individual trader will find it easier to contact prospective transactors.[16] This creates a trade externality associated with higher inventories for trade, in the aggregate: when individuals add to the stock of inventories, the matching of trade partners is easier. Given this trade externality, a positive feedback on production arises because easier trade (i.e. a greater stock of inventories for trade by others) increases the expected profitability of producing for inventory.

The externality is introduced by making the rate of arrival of potential trading partners (b) a function of the fraction of the population employed in the trading process (e): $b(e)$; the number of trade meetings is a function of the stock of individuals with purchasing power on hand, times a rate of arrival of potencial trading partners, a stationary Poisson parameter $b(e)$. Individuals think of *b* as a parameter, which means that they do not recognize the relationship between *b* and the aggregate stock of inventories. And the positive feedback is forced into the barter model (1982a) due to the consideration of a variable cost of production (or of a disutility of effort in production), and of making the 'reservation' disutility a function of $b'(e)$ (with $b' > 0$) (cf. Diamond 1982a, pp. 885–6).

Thus the parable goes, that the trading externality can originate an inefficient production level, since a decreased number of buyers in the search process reduces the probability of a sale and, as a consequence, production activity is discouraged: this feedback on production can lead to multiple equilibria. '[T]his externality involves a positive feedback: increased production for inventory makes trades easier and easier trade makes production for inventory more profitable and therefore justifies its increase. This positive feedback with an externality implies the possibility of multiple equilibria' (Diamond 1984b, p. 5; see also Diamond 1987b, p. 368).

It should be noticed at this point, that similar results have been achieved in search models applied to the labor market under corresponding assumptions, namely, the presence of two externalities (cf. Howitt 1988, p. 157). One is the external economy of scale introduced by Diamond: 'Specifically, the greater the recruiting effort by firms, the more quickly will the average unemployed worker find a job'. And the other, 'a common property externality' (cf. Diamond 1982b; Mortensen 1982a; Howitt 1988, p. 157; Howitt and McAfee 1988, p. 90): 'Each firm takes as given the stochastic process driving unemployment in its sector. Therefore, it fails to take into account the effect of its current recruiting activities in depleting the stock of unemployed workers and hence in raising future costs of hiring. This external effect is what produced the nonlinearity'.[17] This second externality corresponds in Diamond (1982a; 1984a) to considering the rate of arrival of prospective contractors as a parameter by any searcher. The relevance of this parallelism will be apparent below.

In fact, for a better comprehension of search models of trade we need to provide some history about how these models entered the literature, and clear a few concepts upon which some doubts and objections will be raised.

The literature on search had its beginnings with applications to 'two-sided' markets in a partial equilibrium set-up, of which the labor market has been the most studied. Presenting the notion of 'two-sided matching markets', Roth and Sotomayor explain that '[t]he term "two-sided" refers to the fact that agents in such markets belong, from the outset, to one of two disjoint sets – for example, firms and workers. This contrasts with commodity markets, in which the market price may determine whether an agent is a buyer or a seller' (Roth and Sotomayor 1990, p. 1). (This may be all confused: either in one or the other type of markets the behavior is similar if we are talking of decentralized/non-brokered exchange. Transaction costs in general prevent any individual from the possibility of choice of being a buyer or a seller; why this tendency of viewing the economic world through the lenses of brokered markets?) Examples of two-sided search models, as applied to the labor market, are Diamond (1981; 1982b), Mortensen (1982a; 1982b), Pissarides (1984), and Howitt and McAfee (1987) (cf. Mortensen 1990, p. 132), and, having as a possible example 'waterfront summer rentals', Diamond and Maskin (1979; 1981).

In Diamond (1981, esp. pp. 799–802), the labor market is modeled as following a Poisson process with fixed parameters, and the arrival rates of job offers and break-ups are 'independent of the unemployment and vacancy rates', even though the author acknowledges that one can expect the rate at which workers know of job opportunities to increase with unemployment. Also assuming a fixed coefficients technology, Diamond (1982b) considers the implications of unequal numbers of jobs and vacancies;[18] here, however, two types of trading technologies are analyzed, linear and non-linear technologies.

Two basic trading technologies had been considered in the literature: the linear and the quadratic. For instance, in Diamond and Maskin (1979, pp. 283, 300) where '[i]ndividuals can continue to search after joining a partnership', these are so defined:

1. In the quadratic technology, 'an additional searcher raises the meeting probabilities of all his potential partners', which creates an externality. In this case 'the individual's probability of meeting someone at all raises linearly with the number of potential partners. The aggregate number of meetings ... increases with the square of the number of searchers'.
2. In the linear case, 'an individual's probability of meeting *someone at all* is independent of the number of potential partners'. It is named linear 'since the aggregate number of matches increases linearly with the number of searchers'. In this model, 'searchers exert no externalities on others'. (It should not however go unnoticed the authors' remark [ibid., p. 283] that '[w]ith a high density of potential partners, the quadratic technology seems a poor approximation'. Hence the consideration of the linear technology in their model.)

In Diamond's (1981; 1982b) search models of the labor market similar definitions are chosen.[19]

Mortensen (1982a) considers both the linear and quadratic technologies, and in his (1982b) synthesis, only the linear one. In Mortensen's models, however, the assumptions underlying the definitions of the linear and quadratic technologies are different from Diamond and Maskin's (1979), namely: 'First, no search by matched agents is allowed. Second, the aggregate rate at which matches form is endogenously determined by the search intensities chosen by individual unmatched agents. The breach of contract issue is ignored given the first assumption' (Mortensen 1982a, p. 234). Here the definitions are the following:

1. As to the linear technology, '[i]f the probability that a match will form in a short time interval is independent of the number of unmatched agents, ... no unmatched agent searches intensively enough given any fixed division of the value of the match' (ibid., p. 235). An externality arises since, if the intensity of search by an unmatched individual increases, he will expectedly be able to form a match with '*some individual of the opposite type*' quicker.

2. In the quadratic technology, 'the probability that a match will form in a short interval is proportional to the number of unmatched pairs'. As to the question of the externality, the case now is so put: 'Although the externality discussed still exists, more intensive search by all other agents reduces the number of agents of the opposite type that each individual can expect to find in the future. As a consequence of this second externality alone, unmatched agents search too intensively. Interestingly, the effects of the two externalities in combination cancel, given an appropriate bargaining outcome' (ibid., p. 235; for an analytical presentation, see p. 237).

As may be clear,[20] two basic assumptions impinge on the definition of the trading technologies. First, whether only unmatched traders search. In this respect, Diamond and Maskin (1979) is the only case seen here where all individuals are engaged in search at all times. This is explicitly addressed by the authors and may be reasonable when the possibility of breach of contract or of recontracting are at issue. Second, whether the probability of a match is dependent only on the numbers of unmatched traders, or otherwise depends on the number of matched traders. Both Mortenson (1982a; 1982b) and Diamond (1982a; 1984a) define trading technologies based on the latter assumption. In Diamond (1982a) the case is that, in the course of search, any unmatched trader may meet either a willing transactor, or an individual employed in production. The search process is not congruent with the meeting process: only unmatched traders search for a trading partner, but the meeting process involves all individuals in the island. Since an individual employed in trade may either meet a potential trader or not, unmatched as well as matched traders participate in the meeting process. The doubt is whether this is an adequate assumption when applied to barter or monetary exchange.

DOUBTS AND OBJECTIONS

In order to make sense of the search models as applied to barter exchange, a clarification is due and a possible confusion needs to be avoided. Starting with the clarification, we need, first, to distinguish between the effect of an increase in the number of potential trading partners on search opportunities, and the 'strategic interdependence' (how does this differ from non-strategic interdependence?) in the choice of search intensity of unmatched traders (cf. Mortensen (1982a, pp. 234–5). In 'two-sided' markets of the 'mating game' type,[21] dealing with symmetric bargaining,[22] the solution of the repeated bilateral matching game is a Nash equilibrium[23] in search intensities (each agent's strategy is a choice of search intensity). In the exchange models of the Diamond (1982a; 1984a) type, there is not such an *ex ante* choice of search intensity. Here search obeys a Poisson process, where the rate of arrival of trading opportunities is taken by individuals as parametric. This rate may be posited as *constant* (Kiyotaki and Wright 1991; 1993),[24] leading to a constant returns to scale meeting technology, which is consistent with the linear technology, as defined by Diamond and Maskin (1979); or *increasing*: the rate of arrival is assumed as a function of the fraction of unmatched traders, where 'individuals think of b [the rate of arrival] as a parameter and do not recognize the relationship between b and the aggregate stock of inventories' (Diamond 1984a, p. 10).

Peter Diamond (1982a) assumes that search opportunities increase with the increase in the number of unmatched traders: the arrival rate of potential trading partners (b) is a function of the fraction of the population employed in the trading process (e): ($b(e)$), with $b' > 0$. Since an individual employed in trade may either meet a potential trader or not, the larger the proportion of individuals searching, the easier the completion of a match for any of them. This creates an externality, and with it, increasing returns in the trading technology. This is the result of complete absence of trading arrangements – *ex ante* a trader employed in exchange (holding a coconut) cannot be told apart from another trader hunting for coconuts. I gather that to rely on complete anonymity in exchange is not the adequate formalization of exchange. If we were to assume that islanders can be spotted as traders, an increase in the number of traders would just mean an enlargement of the market, not a higher density in trading opportunities; and consequently, an increase in the number of traders would imply a proportional increase in the total number of meetings. Such a trading technology creates no externality and does not present increasing returns to scale.[25] In this case, a higher number of individuals employed in trading would correspond to more trade meetings, but not to an increased *rate* of trade meetings.

Regarding the point that Diamond's formalization of the trading process may only be reasonable in the complete absence of trading arrangements (an appealing possibility, and sufficient for the matter, would be the custom to meet for trade at a clearing somewhere in the forest), has an underlying assumption to support it. Costs are only considered on the supply side (production): not only the production cost itself, but also time preference, which is explicitly considered in the production decision function (cf. Diamond 1982a, p. 885). No direct cost is attached to the demand side, strolling along the island with a coconut in hand searching for another trader is not costly: if time spent in this search process were costly in some meaningful way (for instance considering time preference in exchange explicitly, not only through the production decision), an incentive would arise for some investment in information – only a step from the inclusion in the model of a trade specialist of the commission agent type (cf. Hicks 1976).[26] There is, however, an ineffectual allusion to transaction costs: the indivisibility assumption – trade of coconuts, one for one – is thought of as a proxy of transaction costs, for '[t]echnically, lumpiness of transaction can play the same role as transaction costs by ruling out small entries into markets' (Diamond 1987a, p. 82).

There is also potential confusion between a two-sided non-interchangeable market (a 'bilateral' market like the labor market,[27] or, in general, 'the mating game'), and a market where demand and supply go together (e.g. 'one good' barter model). In the former case, there are two separate and fixed sets of traders, one of individuals on the demand side, another on the supply side. In the barter models, we have only one set of individuals on both sides (either on the demand or on the supply side) since every trade is both a sale and purchase for both traders.

In the former case, an increase in the number of people on the offer side expectedly makes it easier for any employer to find a match, which means an increase in the density of traders on the other side of the market. This is the case for non-linear meeting technologies characterized by Poisson processes with fixed parameters, as shown for the labor market, or in Diamond and Maskin (1979; 1981); and in this two-sided market, the externality could possibly be present; likewise, in Mortensen's models, where the interdependence between the two sides of the market gives rise to the definition of search intensities as a strategy in a bargaining game. As referred to above, these models lead to a different prediction. With constant/linear arrival rates (λ) (where linear means that the probability of a meeting is independent of the number of *unmatched* traders), the model generates an externality: 'The existence and nature of the externality present in this formulation of the mating game is revealed by the fact that the value of play to an agent of either type increases with the search intensity of the other in equilibrium' (Mortensen 1982b, p. 974). This is because, in the presence of two non-interchangeable groups of types 1 and 2, the chances of entering a match depend not only on the initiative of the individual of one type to contact but also on the probability that an unmatched individual of the other type contacts him; here numbers on each side (and therefore their search intensity) affect the probability of a match, and even with constant rates of arrival, an externality is generated.[28]

In the case of barter, however, an increase in the number of people on the offer side exactly mirrors the increase in the number of people on the demand side – they are the same people. There is no increase of the density of trading opportunities faced by any trader, and consequently there is no externality in the trading technology. Therefore, a linear matching technology – 'the possibility that a match will form in a short time interval is independent of the number of unmatched agents' (Mortensen 1982a, p. 235) – which in a two-sided market may originate strong externalities, need not do so in the case of exchange with interchangeable agents (simultaneously on the demand and offer side) where only unmatched traders participate in the meeting process. Hosios (1990, p. 290) creates a variation of Diamond (1982a) which makes it analogous to a labor market model, with 'blue' and 'green' traders and coconuts; this transposition simply creates a two-sided market, which the barter model in fact is not. Thus, the conclusion is that the modeling transposition from the labor to the barter models is unwarranted, contrary to Diamond's (1984b, p. 5) wishful thinking.

FIAT MONEY MODEL

Now, let us question how the introduction of fiat money alters the conclusions advanced so far – models of credit in search (Diamond 1987a; 1988; 1990) will not be analyzed. Diamond (1984a) introduces a given amount of fiat money, which at any moment in time, is purchasing power in the hands of an equal number of prospective buyers. Having completed a bargain, this money holder abandons exchange and starts searching for production opportunities. The same decision must be taken, whether to go on searching for production or to engage in a production project. This is equally a function of the cut-off level of disutility c^*, as in the barter model. Having decided to produce a unit of the good, the individual becomes a seller, and begins searching for a fiat money holder, until a bargain is struck, and so the story goes on. To sum up, individuals go through a three-step process: they produce for inventory, sell inventory for money, and then search for a supplier from whom to buy; after consuming, the process restarts.

The presence of money seems a hindrance in this model because two transactions are now required in exchange, instead of one. Its consideration is justified on the grounds of a cash-in-advance constraint, and it is suggested that the model 'is a sensible starting place for thinking about the liquidity role of money' (Diamond 1984b, p. 43). And the objective is to enquire whether and how (fiat) money plays a role in the coordination of trade, as well as to allow for a basis to the study of monetary policy in a framework where there is a transactions role for money.[29]

The inclusion of money doesn't affect the main assumptions driving the exchange technology, namely: increasing returns in trade creating an externality, and the positive feedback on production due to its effect on the level of the choice variable ($c < c^*$). Money substitutes two transactions for one; but individuals are not stuck as belonging to a given type in a 'two-sided' market, they just follow a roundabout kind of exchange. There seems to be a difference, though. If some sort of market arrangement were present, the increase in numbers of unmatched traders in case of barter, would lead to an increase in the number of trade meetings, not an increase in the rate of trade opportunities, as seen above. Here, however, the possibility arises that the number of offers by sellers (coconut holders) and the number of demands by buyers (money holders), per interval of time, could be out of line with the equilibrium steady-state aggregate number of matches.

In the barter model, with more individuals employed in trade, in case traders would be spotted as traders, the density of trade opportunities would not increase. In the money model, and with a higher amount of tickets to start with, an increase in the number of sellers due to the choice of a higher cut-off cost c^* (the control variable) has exactly the same effect on the steady-state equilibrium as in the barter model: the rates of arrival of trading opportunities by sellers and buyers would adjust so as to allow for consistency of 'individual experiences' with 'the aggregate experience', that is, for 'micro-macro consistency' (Diamond 1984a, p. 4).[30] Individual buyers and sellers would certainly still perceive those rates of arrival as parameters, but the model implies that they adjust to allow for consistency in trading opportunities. Therefore, my idea is that, if some sort of trading arrangement were present, by means of which individuals employed in trade (coconut holders and money holders) could be spotted as such, the money model presents the same pattern of behavior as regards density of trading opportunities as that perceived by individuals employed in exchange.

The appeal to increasing returns to scale in trade in interchangeable (non-two-sided) exchange models is doubtful, and Diamond himself sees the need to justify it (cf. Diamond 1984a, p. 5; and Diamond and Maskin 1979, p. 283). The only problem is this: that the author seems unaware that complete anonymity of functions is not a reasonable assumption in order to lay proper foundations for the study of exchange in markets – even though he could not avoid slipping when referring to 'retail trade facilities' (1984a, p. 3), which is a misplaced concreteness of sorts.

F. Market-makers, and price and quantity adjustments

I am not going to explain the presence of a trade specialist from first principles, starting with individuals on a foggy island searching for trading partners. I am going to jump over the difficulties posed by the coincidence of timing and wants in barter trading, and presume them 'abated' at the start by the presence of specialist traders. These will be our market-makers, operating in an ongoing exchange environment where media of exchange either exist, or are 'made' by means of credit facilities by these trade specialists. All the problems raised in the body of the book are deemed resolved. The concentration will be directed towards understanding price versus quantity as the variables of choice by a (decentralized) market-maker.

The first goal is to characterize a market-maker. One side of the question considers which functions turn a seller or a supplier into a market-maker; the other is logically interrelated and examines the characteristics of demand that favor such market arrangement. Transaction costs will be considered next, and how the seller can reduce costs of information and shopping on the demand side by incurring selling-costs. Finally, an attempt will be made at the scope for adjustment of price and quantity of the 'ongoing' market-maker.

THE FUNCTIONS OF THE MARKET-MAKER

It has been hinted above that the basic functions played by the trade specialist are stockholding and price formation, and that in substance these belong together (cf. Demsetz 1968; Hirshleifer 1973; see also Hicks 1989[31]).

First, and attempting to make it general, every seller can be said to have an *asking price*. Perhaps it is set and changed by someone or something else – but it is still the price at which the seller stands ready to deal with the willing buyer (cf. Demsetz 1968). Alchian and Allen's comments on how the 'price-searcher' 'sets' his price are of interest here (a price-searcher market as defined in contrast to a price-taker market, regarding the 'wealth-maximizing *output and price program*'):

> Whether sellers are described as using their 'market power' to 'set' prices or merely searching for the best (wealth maximizing) price in the market is all a matter of semantics. ... *All* prices in all markets are administered in the sense that each person decides at what price he shall sell (in the light of market demand) (Alchian and Allen 1972, pp. 344–5).

Second, using stocks of inventories as a 'shock absorber' may be thought of as a possible feature of any trade specialist, but it is quite a different thing to make the trade specialist's capacity to trade dependent on the holding of stocks.[32] However as a simplifying assumption,[33] we will stick to inventories from here on; in fact, the quantity controls the seller can rely on are of two kinds, a stock of inventories or a backlog of orders. Besides, stockholding is anyway a poor instrument for making effective the price that was 'set'.

Alchian and Allen establish a relationship between stockholding and pricing quite neatly:

> it will pay sellers to maintain an inventory of buffer stocks and predictable prices for consumers to meet the transient fluctuations in daily market demands rather than to try to produce to order instantly as buyers are faced with transient, unpredictable price changes. Inventories stabilize prices and make the *momentary* supply schedule a horizontal line at the selling price, out to the limit of the existing inventory. (Alchian and Allen 1972, p. 338).

Third, if the trade specialist is said to provide a 'ready market' for prospective buyers, i.e. to offer a good for sale and post an asking price, the next function we may consider is that of providing information, as well as incurring 'the main "selling costs" of putting his good into his customers' hands' (Friedman 1989, p. 391[34]). That is to say, the trade specialist deals with the marketing function, the organization of the logistics of trade. This is central to understanding the workings of competition in a non-brokered market. Competition among sellers cannot be perceived as ruled by the blind forces of the market place (this does not happen in any case), clearly it can only be assessed as carried out with more or less ability by market-makers. The situation is that readiness to sell, and the organization of the logistics of trade both now come under the responsibility of the seller/market-maker.

Goods and services are offered for sale to buyers who, before the purchase, are supposed to have had access to information about the good, by some means, in a more or less purposive or costly way. Information on price, quality, location, availability of inventory or risk of stockouts, payment arrangements, quality of service, or whichever aspects concern the buyers; as for instance, in the case of a differentiated good, the buyer may have to appraise it, and possibly to learn to use it.

If this is so, scope exists for advertisement and salesmanship (cf. Hicks 1989, pp. 24–5[35]). And buyers may also depend on various services that increase the information, convenience, reliability, or dependability of the good or service. Firms incur costs with a view to 'cement customer relations by many methods. They may appeal to customers on the basis of quality, transportation arrangements, credit terms, and speed and reliability of delivery' (Okun 1981, p. 150). These are meaningful to suppliers of services that are not easily evaluated by shopping, and sellers of differentiated items where the price tag offers only limited information to prospective buyers. But information problems are also pervasive in the case of homogeneous goods. '[T]he amount of dispersion of asking prices of sellers ... is ubiquitous even for homogeneous goods ...That they do not wholly vanish (in a given market) is due simply to the fact that no combination of advertising media reaches all potential buyers within the available time' (Stigler 1961, pp. 213, 223). Okun stresses also 'the importance of dependability and reliability to *professional* buyers, even to those procuring physically *homogeneous* products'; some industries of this type have established 'a rather unusual two-price, two-market system' (Okun 1981, p. 151; cf. Friedman 1989 [36]).

SET-UP COSTS

Now let us take a closer look at the demand side of the picture. Customers incur search costs and transaction costs each time they search and trade (cf. Alchian 1969;[37] Hirshleifer 1973). These costs have a lump-sum component, that is to say, are largely independent of the size of the transaction. To the extent that these are set-up costs, customers are better off not collecting all the information which might be relevant to their shopping decisions: information about the variety and quality of all the goods which compete for the satisfaction of a customer's need, and information about price and service by their suppliers.

Now we may ask: Can the supplier help alleviate these information costs? Can he do it more efficiently than the customer alone would be able to gather that information?

Customers' search for products, the identification of the sellers and their prices and conditions, is costly. Sellers can help. They can advertise in order to bring that information onto the customers' horizon and thereby reduce their set-up costs, either by replacing search and shopping altogether[38] or by funneling it into a smaller set of alternatives. Sellers may advertise their presence in the market, their good(s) or varieties and, in some situations, their prices and conditions. With regard to prices, however, as Stigler (1961, p. 216) has suggested, an alternative to advertising is 'the development of specialized traders whose chief service, indeed, is implicitly to provide a meeting place for potential buyers and sellers' (as an example, mention is made of dealers in used cars). And as far as both prices and conditions are concerned, market-makers may replace advertising for a less conspicuous activity, that of 'price stability as an information economizing device' (Alchian 1969, pp. 50; also 37–9, 49). As Okun puts it, firms may pledge continuity of past offers and foster the customer's belief that he can rely on past information as a guide to present and future offerings: 'The firm wants to promote a reliance on intertemporal comparison shopping'.[39] Or at greater length:

Customers are valuable to sellers because of their potential for repeat business ... The firm comes to recognize its ability to discourage customers from shopping elsewhere by convincing them of the continuity of the firm's policy on pricing, services, and the like. It knows that its customers have indicated by their previous purchases that they regarded the firm's offers as satisfactory. It can encourage them to return to buy, or at least to shop, by pledging continuity of that offer, ensuring them that past experience will be a reliable guide to present and future offerings ... Customers are attracted by continuity because it helps to minimize shopping costs. They know the terms of the previous supplier's offer without shopping if they can count on its continuance; but they must shop to determine the offer of unfamiliar sellers. That information is available, but it can be obtained only at a cost ... If the status quo is satisfactory, the expected value of the information about alternatives is low. (Okun 1981, pp. 141–2).

Alchian has stressed the importance of recognition and assessment costs as inducing the provision of services by the seller, as for instance the assurance of quality by 'specialist, expert middlemen of high reputability' (Alchian 1977, pp. 111, 122; cf. Clower and Howitt 1997b, pp. 194 ff.). Moreover, an obverse informational economy will be generated that will contribute to the cementing of customer relations: by means of continuity, the seller will be able to gather information on the buyer – on his dependability, could we say – and this will make it feasible (less costly) for him to offer convenient payment arrangements, or trade credit, in a regular fashion (cf. Clower and Howitt 1996, Sections 2.1 and 2.3 [40]).

This implicit commitment, to avoid disappointing the customer, is a feature of our market-maker's behavior that is radically different from sticky prices brought about by menu-costs. Menu-costs relate to the administrative costs of altering offers about price and conditions, and providing customers with that information.[41] Menu-costs generate price stickiness, not as an informational device but quite the opposite, as an interruption in the regular (and efficient) flow of information the market would otherwise display.

Distinctly, the customer market appeals to a process of acquisition and diffusion of information (which can hardly be made sense of in a static context). That pledge needs to be repeated in order to keep recurrent purchases and feed the flow of customers. The search diffusion process may drive customers away but it may also bring some shoppers in. Customers are attracted by continuity (of offers) because they save on set-up costs of information gathering. They create attachments to sellers, which encourage recurrent purchases. Nevertheless, as attachments are built and information about the broad market becomes obsolete, information may require updating.[42]

Some fortuitous (though costly) search may interrupt or break attachments, or an intermittent assessment of the competitors' advertisements may bring relevant information thereto. These take place so that the customer can check whether he is doing the right thing by sticking to his supplier. But he may experience a surprise: in that case, he may have to look for some broader picture of the marketplace by continuing his information gathering for a while. Let us simplify by considering that, on aggregate, this gives origin to a diffusion process of uncertain consequences, spread over time. (The more the seller responds, the quicker the information of the customer wears out, and the greater his need to update it increases. All this leads towards continuity and the status quo.)

As we saw, the firm invests in several ways to further a clientele. A clientele constitutes capital to the seller, and its rate of obsolescence mirrors, in great measure, the liveliness of competition in the market; this meaning that an interruption or a failure of these investments on maintaining a clientele may seriously undermine the seller's position in the market, despite other strengths of the seller – technical or otherwise – being untouched. This is a picture of the seller as competing to keep his pool of customers and to attract new shoppers away from other sellers. The seller is attempting not to disappoint repeat customers, as well as to encourage the disaffected or disappointed shoppers of others to stick with him.

However, the same forces that allow for this continuity increase the payoff of an 'entrepreneur' who ventures an incursion into the competitors' field. A small start may gather momentum by means of the diffusion process, although at the cost of high uncertainty. Settled sellers may take time to notice raiders but when they recognize them, it may be too late to recover lost ground. This raider is a market-maker. In an uncertain world, he out-competes the settled sellers. Since the signals these receive are mostly particular to their individual business, some time elapses before they realize some innovation has occurred in the market(place). The same forces that have worked to sustain settled suppliers are called for to explain the process by which new suppliers get settled. Both the settled seller and the raider are market-makers; the relevant features are simply made clearer for the case of the latter. Both have appealed to a clientele and devised ways to sustain a continued flow of customers, but for neither of them is that guaranteed. In either of them a clientele has to be created, in a continued way.

We have introduced the market-maker, presented economic incentives for his emergence, and discussed his functions in general, but little has been said about his decisions or behavior, as far as adjustments of price and quantity are concerned. This is attempted in the next section, in the course of a story constructed on evolutionary lines whereby, by playing his functions, the seller adapts to this environment (no special attention will be paid to the broader questions of his actions with a view to transform it for his benefit).

THE SCOPE FOR PRICE AND QUANTITY ADJUSTMENTS

Using as a departing point, Arrow's (1959) question of the scope for decision on price versus quantity, let us now handle the forces that underlie price adjustment in a non-brokered market. Our market has no device to produce a central price signal. Sellers are left to their own perception of their market and there is no price signal (currently available in the market). The seller is not a price-taker but, in Alchian and Allen's terminology, he is a price-searcher:

> the price to the price-searcher is not determined for him as if by some impersonal market mechanism. Instead he must search out the optimal (wealth-maximizing) price. And, not knowing the demand schedule exactly, he will have to resort to retrial-and-error search processes. No demand-and-supply intersection principle determines his price, although the demand (and ... the costs of production) plays a crucial role in determining his prices. (Alchian and Allen 1972, p. 118).

Before the question is addressed of which signals a market-maker might observe on a regular basis, so as to direct his price and output decisions, we had better attempt to identify those choices already available to him (that are previous to our thought experiment).

We have an ongoing market and concentrate our attention on a supplier in that market; he is representative as far as observable signals and decision processes are concerned. The supplier's characteristics will be taken as given, both decisions and market responses have interplayed in shaping our market-maker as an ongoing concern. To begin with, it is assumed that the supplier has made some earlier decision regarding technology and capacity in his material, human and organizational components. He has been incurring selling costs (viz. advertising, salesmanship) and possibly investing in research and development, in order to consolidate a clientele. He has evolved through time, and today has a given *capacity* that is used to bring a good to the market and get it sold. We assume that the costs of altering capacity (increasing or decreasing) are far too great for it to be a short-run consideration; this is Marshall's short-run.[43] As a consequence, the supplier uses given capital, and incurs fixed costs.

Fixed costs are important here. Under the assumption of a given capacity, their total amount can be known *ex ante,* and thus 'present' fixed costs anticipate incoming ones fairly well. As a consequence, a distinction is called for. Total fixed costs, and the variations of fixed costs per unit of output, impinge on pricing quite differently. The fact that the *variations* of fixed costs per unit of output can only 'play little part' in price adjustment[44] has no bearing whatsoever on the *level* at which the price shall be (cf. Marshall 1920, pp. 376–7, 458–9[45]). The seller will post an asking price that is expected to permit its viability, and if fixed costs are not expected to be recovered, this will be quite improbable.

Thus, the supplier has a given technology and capacity; and, for the ensuing construction, costs are assumed to be only partially adjustable (cf. Marshall 1920, pp. 374–7; Wiles 1961, esp. p. 8; also Clark 1923, pp. 72 ff., 90 ff.). Capacity is here defined as the rate of output above which marginal cost gradually starts increasing, so that output ultimately faces a cost barrier. The definition is independent of the shape and slope of marginal costs at rates of output below or at the capacity level; in any case a clear upward turn may be expected. Capacity is not an objective limit, physical or otherwise. It is a cost barrier: the seller can only extend his rate of supply in the short-run to a limited degree, and at the expense of rising marginal costs. This is a consequence of both limited substitutability (law of diminishing returns), and of high transaction costs in order to adjust (some) factors of production in the short-run. Planned capacity is thus the level of output above which 'partial adaptation' is expected to lead to a marked increase in marginal cost. (Of the vast literature on cost and supply curves, a noteworthy reference is Joel Dean [1976], where his statistical studies of short and long-run cost curves are compiled, and a generalization is attempted in the Introduction.) The question of the shape of the long-run cost curve is sidestepped here for the two reasons: one is that in order to discuss quantity and price adjustment in the short-run we need not presume (precise) static equilibrium; and the other is that the effect of variations in capacity on long-run costs may be presumed harder to anticipate than the effect of short-run partial adaptation, so that the firm may be thought of as carrying out short-run adaptations, under the belief that these do not affect long-run average costs (cf. Andrews and Brunner 1975, p. 26).

To begin our thought experiment, let us assume that in the near past the environment has been quite smooth – in the sense that, sales having evolved according to some tendency, the seller has managed to adjust. For instance, he has adjusted the level of operations, or price, so that he could maintain positive holdings of inventories at virtually all points in time (cf. Clower and Leijonhufvud 1975, p. 184).

Again, the market-maker has no precise current guidance on the price to post; as we have seen, he is a price-searcher. Nonetheless, under the circumstances, price can be expected to inhere in a certain range. I raise a twofold hypothesis. The first one is that a range of *survival prices* exists: this is a range of prices that could have been posted during the foregoing period (characterized by a stable environment), and that would have permitted the seller to survive. As regards the future, it is a range within which a price may be posted and survival expected. The second hypothesis is that this price range is in the neighborhood of what we may call – despite the confused connotations – *normal* or *full-cost*, along the lines discussed by Andrews and Brunner (1975, pp. 25–8), Andrews (1949, Chapter 5), and Wiles (1961, Chapter 5). Notice that full-cost here is not a decision rule – nor in any sense a norm, as standard cost is for accounting purposes. Let us quote from Alchian:

> These constructed rules of behavior should be distinguished from 'rules' which, in effect, do no more than define the objective being sought. Confusion between

objectives which motivate one and rules of behavior are commonplace. For example, 'full-cost' pricing is a 'rule' that one cannot really follow. He can try to, but whether he succeeds or fails in his objective of survival is not controllable by following the 'rule of full-cost pricing.' If he fails in this objective, he must, of necessity, fail to have followed the 'rule.' The situation is parallel to trying to control the speed of a car by simply setting by hand the indicator on the speedometer. (Alchian 1950, p. 218, n).

The role of the 'full-cost' hypothesis is very weak. Its main use here is that it allows the circumvention of the question of defining any precise asking price as a starting point of analysis, and therefore eschewing discussion of the static equilibrium of the 'firm'. We only need to make the not-unreasonable assumption that the observed posted price is within this set (cf. Wiles 1961 [46]).

The market-maker aims at survival and uses rules of decision (cf. Alchian 1950 [47]) that have conformed to that goal.[48] The objective of survival drives current decisions insofar as their repercussion is expected to extend into the future; and in the case uncertainty, and the resulting response by the firm of valuing continuity of offers (cf. Okun 1981), is allowed for, current decisions might even restrict the range of possible decisions in the future (in a way that is not present in brokered exchange).

So the hypotheses are that current decisions of the seller are influenced by its anticipation of survival potential; and besides, that the price rule must have led its asking price to lie within a range in the neighborhood of full-cost.

Now, the seller has survived for some period of time characterized by a smooth environment, and we assume that the seller anticipates the period ahead to be as smooth as the foregoing period – whatever its duration has been; the only relevant aspect is that the seller has adjusted to the environment in such a way that he has no motives today to change his rules of action, since they have proved viable until now. We should notice that survival can only be ascertained *ex post*. Survival is an *ex post* fact, and decision rules towards that goal are only good given environmental stability (cf. Alchian 1950, esp. pp. 213, 219).

This survival range does not set limits on observable prices, though; we do not constrain our market-maker to survive. He may be representative as far as signals observed and decision processes are concerned, but fail to survive due to cost or demand factors not adequately dealt with. There are no such things as survival decision rules. Although set in another context, Winter's view is relevant:

> Let us suppose, tentatively, that what corresponds to a genotype in the theory of the firm is a *rule of action* or *strategy*. What the environment operates on, and rewards and punishes, is not the rule but the actions evoked from the rule by variables in the environment itself. This is a major objection to any claim that economic natural selection tends to produce situations in which the surviving *rules* are optimizing ones. (Winter 1975, p. 97).

Survival is only defined *ex post*; and, although the seller's decision rules are meant to have a survival goal, they do not guarantee survival (cf. Alchian 1950).

At any point in time, asking prices could be observed within a broader range. It is now presumed that the upper bound is only governed by 'particular' demand and this will, in general, be dominated by competitive forces (cf. Andrews and Brunner 1975, p. 24). (Entry considerations, especially cross-entry or vertical integration, may play a role but these are beyond my concern, since they would call forth long-run considerations involving expectations of competitors whether a certain price level by the seller is temporary or permanent, of expectations of prices in the competitors' field, as well as of anticipation of responses by competitors.) Conversely, the lower bound has a cost anchor; we can assume that the producer has no incentive to post an asking price below the marginal cost level of current output (cf. Marshall 1920, pp. 374–5). The supplier is assumed to be capable of approximating current marginal costs, which is not too unreasonable since a large fraction of these costs – except for 'the user cost of machinery, and also the risk that fast running entails of bottlenecks and breakdowns' (Wiles 1961, p. 51) – can be computed without the need to maintain expectations about future performance.

Now, let us assume our seller's supply at a certain rate, somehow adjusted to the current rate of sales; besides, the price rule for the *level* of price has proved viable. (Viable rules – as to the decision variables we are concerned with, price and rate of supply – are those that permit the firm to sustain the anticipation of survival.)

We observe the asking price and let time flow. What rate of sales can be expected? Expected sales volume obeys some distribution affected by a rate of departures and a rate of arrivals, which are due to a diffusion process. The technology of information gathering by customers involves search (either triggered by surprise, or initiated on a random fashion be it fortuitous or intermittent) as well as advertising or other selling costs (these reduce the amount of search and thereby change the rate of arrivals); conversely, the rate of departures depends also on these activities by competitors. However, the basic element in this process is that the expected rate of 'stickers' (Hicks 1954) is large because, in a smooth environment, information depreciates slowly. Sellers help reduce the information costs of customers by means of adjusting prices and conditions only parsimoniously, this allowing customers to maintain the belief that information collected in the recent past will be valid in the near future. Inertia is to be expected in the circumstances.

Moreover, the seller has not perfect information about current prices by competitors or about their selling costs (and all they stand for). The seller has limited information about the current state of demand in his broader, or in the aggregate, market; and it takes him some time to recognize new cost advantages of actual competitors as well as the presence of new sources of competition (cf. Andrews 1964[49]). In a decentralized market, the seller faces a complex inference problem (an additional complication is that several factors affecting the parameters of the current distributions are only possibly known with delay and/or at a high cost).

We might possibly conceive of the seller as sustaining the belief that he faces a stochastic revenue function that is downward-sloping (cf. Wiles 1961[50]). The relevant question in the circumstances is, whether it compensates the seller to experiment with the market in order to know better or whether experiments might be conducive to produce information that could be reliably extrapolated into the future (cf. Rothschild 1973[51]). To begin with, the adjustment of prices will interfere with the customers' constructed beliefs about the market conditions and may set off a wave of search activity of uncertain results; a rise in price might expectedly increase the rate of departures, and a reduction in price would expectedly increase the rate of 'stickers,' although at a risk of 'unsettling' the customers. But these evolutions will be spread over some future period of time, so that two conclusions ensue. First, experiments to estimate demand would require that the price be kept constant for a period of time for the full effects to be observable; and, second, no standstill in competition can be assumed in the meantime. Experiments presumably take more time than that over which the *ceteris paribus* assumption can be supported.

In order to carry the argument forward, let us assume that the seller does not expect experiments with the market to produce a well defined relation between price and quantity demanded; or, if such is envisioned, that the expected net gain of the experiments is of uncertain sign. (This is not at all a trivial assumption, and for completeness it needs further discussion. In any case, our presumption is that the argument would not be radically affected, otherwise. For a possible case where the monopolist's demand curve is uncertain and where 'a price setter would not experiment while a quantity setter would, and the firm would prefer to be the former', see Mirman, Samuelson and Urbano [1993, p. 557]).

So, given his asking price, the seller's only expectation about the rate of sales is that it will oscillate erratically around his 'existing goodwill' (cf. Andrews and Brunner 1975, p. 25). The seller has created a ready market and will sell what the market will take. Thus, given the seller's current asking price, the relation between price and quantity demanded defines a sales curve: 'for naturally the setting and sticking to a price creates an infinitely elastic *sales* curve while it lasts. The sales curve is of course by no means a demand curve' (Wiles 1961, p. 47). Wiles is close to the point but this is a little metaphysical. Contrarily, Alchian and Allen (1972) are closer to concreteness: they give a material reason for a 'momentary horizontal supply schedule', as well as a limit, and this is existing inventory.

Now let us allow for a surprise. The seller begins realizing that the rate of sales must be increasing since inventories are being depleted faster than expected, and this tendency becomes more clear as time passes. Our construction implies that the firm will wait and see. The problem is for how long, and to what extent?

First, sales will be satisfied drawing on inventories, and no change in price will be considered yet. An interesting proposition is made by Alchian and Allen:

> prices in price-searchers' markets are not 'less adaptive' to changed market conditions than are prices in price-takers' markets. Because of inventory availability, price-searchers will provide amounts wanted by demanders during transient fluctuations without having to change price. This stability is not a reflection of price rigidity or power of seller to control price. It reflects instead the greater ability to provide price predictability by use of price-searchers' inventories. (Alchian and Allen 1972, p. 338).

This buffer may be short-lived. Most significantly, however, this change in inventories *signals* some adjustment is required. Before long, in order to maintain an appropriate level of inventories, the supplier may have to adjust *quantity offered* and/or its *asking price*.

Under the actual circumstances, the producer can be expected to have been operating at a level of supply around capacity (given that we have allowed for the producer to adjust to the previously 'stable' environment). If this is so, an apparently sustained higher rate of sales can be satisfied by increasing supplies in order to restore and sustain the stock of inventories. The rate of supplies is geared to the level of inventories. The degree to which this margin extends is limited by capacity. That is to say, depending on the rate of increase of marginal costs, these will eventually attain the level of the asking price, so that extending output above such level is not satisfactory (unless for rather temporary episodes, given the eventual benefits accrued to the seller from continuity of offers).

Thus, the producer will try to accommodate that apparently-increased rate of sales, by adjusting the rate of output in order to keep inventory levels at an appropriate level. The case may be, however, that marginal costs are pushed up so far that the extension of supply above that level is not sustainable, given present capacity and despite all partial adjustments envisioned and implemented (for a list of possible measures to extend output under partial adjustment, see Wiles 1961, pp. 51–2).[52] Before the seller is assured that the new tendency in sales is not temporary and reaches the decision of investing in increased capacity (which we assume is not feasible for the short-run), he may raise the possibility of increasing its posted price, with a view to stabilizing the level of inventories at an appropriate level. Now the operation of the quantity control of the trade specialist would have to be worked out, possibly along the lines drawn up by F. Owen Irvine (1981); see also Thore, Billström and Johansson (1954), and Thore and Billström (1954). Irvine (1981) builds a model where the price adjustment policy is a 'short-run inventory-based pricing policy'. He follows a suggestion from Clower and Leijonhufvud (1975, p. 184; as in Irvine 1981, pp. 247–8) that middlemen firms would play a critical role in coordinating trade: such firms would vary their prices 'with a view to maintaining average quantities traded at levels that will ensure positive holding of traded commodities at virtually every point in time'.

The converse observation of an increased unsold stock of inventories, will bring about an adjustment process of similar characteristics but in the opposite direction. It seems harder to tackle, however, as far as the decision to adjust price is concerned; this question of devising a reasonable control mechanism for price reductions requires further examination. In what concerns an increase in price, marginal costs would provide a justification, but for a price reduction, the role of marginal costs is harder to justify. In any case, even for price increases, the upward bend of the short-run marginal cost curve may be of limited implication for pricing by the individual seller in a competitive market, since it may not affect competitors (cf. Andrews and Brunner 1975, pp. 27–8), but this is beyond the scope of this exploratory note – the anticipation of responses by competitors, and the possible increase of capacity would have to enter the picture. For the moment, let us stick to inventories as the only relevant variable of control, and let us end this note by quoting from Clower's *The Fingers of the Invisible Hand*, where the relation between price adjustment and inventories is discussed:

Over short intervals of time, there is no need for quantities purchased to equal quantities sold. Differences between commodity inflows and outflows to any shop can be buffered in the short run by variations in inventories. If the shopkeeper attempts to increase sales volume by offering lower prices to customers, he will sooner or later run out of stocks or find himself forced to pay a higher price to his suppliers. Conversely, if he attempts to increase his inventory by offering higher prices to suppliers, he will sooner or later be swamped with unsold stocks or he will be forced to offer lower prices to buyers. ...
The adjustment of prices by shopkeepers in response to variations in inventories might be less prompt and smooth than the preceding remarks suggest. No shopkeeper can discriminate in the short run between variations in net sales that are transient and changes in net sales that are permanent, much less link particular variations with particular causes. An ongoing economy is subject to many random and inexplicable shocks. The representative shopkeeper's ultimate actions should be much the same regardless of the source of such variations. If, on average, inventories are declining, he will sooner or later raise both his selling price and buying price. If inventories are increasing, he will sooner or later lower both his selling and buying price. We should not expect unanticipated variations in inventories to be accompanied by immediate price changes. Lacking knowledge about the factors responsible for variations in inventories, we should expect the

typical shopkeeper to follow a policy of wait and see – which is to say price changes will lag behind changes in inventories and will take place sporadically and by finite jumps. ...

In a common sense way, we may thus say that prices are governed by 'demand and supply'; but to say (or to insinuate) that current prices and price movements correspond at all closely to currently observed conditions ... would be a mistake. (Clower 1994a, pp. 10–12).

NOTES

1. 'Our present task [in this book] may therefore be expressed in historical terms as follows. We have to reconsider the value theory of Pareto [and Walras] and then to apply this improved value theory to those dynamic problems of capital'. It is Hicks's opinion that 'Walras ... confined himself, in the main, to setting out the problem' in mathematical terms. 'It was Pareto (*Manuel d' économie politique*, 1909) who began to take things farther', i.e. 'Pareto's improvements in value theory' (Hicks 1939/1946, pp. 2–3).
2. 'If we suppose maximum satisfaction to have been attained ...' (Jaffé, ed. 1954, p. 165).
3. Also, '[i]f there are as many equations of constraint as there are variables, everything in the system is determined' (Pareto 1911, p. 65).
4. The distinctive features of sealed bidding comparatively with auctions are quite smudged: they are the time interval between reception of bids and assignment of the right, and, more importantly, the period of time that bidders can count on to devise their strategies before they file sealed bids (Cassady 1967, pp. 12–13).
5. However, auction firms often operate also as merchants, through acquisition of title to the property before reselling; or as 'merchant-middlemen', where beyond the transmission of title, there is also physical acquisition of the property (cf. Cassady 1967, pp. 9–11).

   Hackett (1992), referring to Stern and El-Ansary (1982), distinguishes two main types of intermediaries, dealers and brokers. Merchants or dealers acquire title to the intermediated goods, and obtain compensation by reselling them on their own account for a profit ('residual surplus'). On the other hand, there are brokers, who are agents of the buyer or seller in the intermediation, they do not acquire title to the property of the intermediated goods, and are compensated with a revenue-sharing commission. (Consignment agents are identical to brokers, and are compensated by a commission [Hackett 1993].) Hackett searches for reasons to opt between the two contracts. He builds a model that considers demand variance, as well as the responsiveness of demand to sales efforts by the intermediary; given the compensation forms, the two schemes generate different incentives for the intermediary to exert sales efforts. See Hackett (1992, p. 300) for references to the literature on intermediary structures, especially concerning financial intermediation.
6. Walker (1990a, pp. 660–63) is very critical of the application of the notion of auction to this unfamiliar market scheme.
7. In case an agent-buyer is bidding against a group of competitive suppliers, will there be any room and incentive on the part of each prospective agent-seller to bargain, or not? If there is, how to explain how it works?

   In the case where specialists or dealer-brokers operate, these in fact, by quoting ask or bid prices on their own account, are clearly bargaining in the ongoing double auction mechanism; in the New York Stock Exchange, for instance, bargaining is a continuous feature of the operation of specialists as market-makers. In any case, in the NYSE, orders are of various types which contribute to the continuity of the operation of the market. The two main types of orders in the NYSE are unrestricted market orders (to be 'bid or offered on arrival at the trading post until executed'), or limit orders (to be 'executed at or better than the specified price ... upon them, or not at all'); other types of orders are placed in organized markets, but these are quantitatively less important (cf. Osborne 1965, p. 90; see also Demsetz 1968, esp. p. 40).

8. Here Pareto adds this footnote: 'As we have already remarked, this condition must never be forgotten. Its omission would make the proposition, of which it is an essential part, false. We often repeat certain things because they are constantly neglected, forgotten, and ignored by some persons who write about economic theory.' (Pareto 1909/1927, p. 431, n).

9. Burstein (1968, p. 25) writes: 'what I should view as the central ground, namely the distinction between the *objective* constraint posed by the vector **p** in idealized competitive markets and the *subjective* evaluation by "monopolists" of their sales possibilities now and in the future'. Every seller may be thought of as meeting an objective vector of prices of relevance elsewhere in the economy, as well as facing a subjective sales curve. Notice also that Burstein (1968, p. 135) refers to producers, both in states of competition and monopoly, as being 'governed by the feasible-sales region ..., a subjective notion leading to all-round monopoly pricing'.

   Notice also: 'Professor Hicks *does* point out "false trading" leads to shifts in asset positions, parametric for $f(p)$, but the real problem is much more serious. In a *disequilibrium* economy *à la* Clower, or in a world of all-round monopoly, traders treat parameters of probability distributions of recognizable *quantities* as parameters for their decision-process.' (Burstein 1968, p. 25).

10. As seen in the beginning of this note, in a thick-market 'the subjective price expectation assumptions defining competitive marketor behavior ... are not disconfirmed by experience. In short, marketors not only subjectively believe, but also objectively "see" their markets as "thick" or, more colorfully, as *experientially continuous.*' (Clower 1994b, p. 378).

11. In Diamond's search models of trade, exchange could be characterized as a situation of logistical decentralization, where, however, it is allowed for knowledge by each trader of the set of relevant equilibrium prices contemporaneously prevailing elsewhere in the economy. According to Section 4.3.1 above, this means that: (i) the information on endowments and preferences of individuals is private; also, net excess demands are private information, and communication of information on net excess demands is limited to the parties trading (limited to bilateral meetings between prospective traders); (ii) equilibrium prices are predetermined, and costlessly available to all traders; no bargaining takes place, nor do trade specialists play any role in the determination of rates of exchange; (iii) the execution of trades is left to pair-wise meetings between traders.

12. 'Without a centralized allocation authority, prices alone provide no information to any specific supplier concerning which island to supply.' (Meyer *et al.* 1992, p. 295).

13. This is a spatial fiction, without any analytical implications, that helps, however, provide intuition for the problem. See, however, Diamond (1984a, p. 3), where a reference is made to 'geographic dispersion of buyers and sellers' and 'increased use of retail trade facilities', totally at odds with this pinpoint economy.

14. A generalization of the basic model (Diamond 1984b, pp. 18–20) incorporates a distribution of utilities in consumption by individuals, and introduces a second decision, the cut-off level of utility (y^*) that leads an individual to consume; it is shown that the optimal cut-off level is $y^* = c^*$. A greater willingness to carry out trade corresponds to a decrease in y^*. This results in a lower stock of inventories with trade becoming more difficult: 'Thus the external economy comes from being less eager to trade'. The conclusion is that in a steady-state equilibrium, welfare improvements come from increasing c^* and y^* together, with people more willing to produce and less willing to trade. The author claims (ibid., p. 20) that '[t]he foregoing analysis yields a result that runs counter to the presumed advantages of increasing aggregate demand'.

15. In an economy where a trader is prevented from accumulating inventories, an increase in inventories is equivalent to an increase in the number of individuals employed in the trade activity.

16. This external economy of scale is elsewhere thought of as 'implicit in the notion that trading is more costly the thinner the market' (Howitt 1988, p. 148; see also Howitt and McAfee 1987, p. 90). Also: 'Increasing returns to scale are very plausible at low levels of activity. They also become plausible at higher levels once one recognizes the geographic dispersion of buyers and sellers and thus the gain from increased transaction locations as the density of traders grow. In a business cycle context, with a fixed infrastructure of trading capacity, there is increased short run profitability from increased use of retail trade facilities.' (Diamond 1984a, p. 3).

17. This is an external diseconomy: 'more recruiting by firms will reduce the pool of unemployed from which the firms recruit, thereby reducing the incentive to recruit' (Howitt and McAfee 1988, p. 90). However, the welfare conclusions differ. This, and other models using the same framework of analysis, perform more in consonance with standard Keynesian or neoclassical models. An inefficiency is present, as is common in this set-up, but they reveal almost similar output price predictions (cf. Howitt 1988, p. 261; and Howitt and McAfee 1988, p. 159).

    Also, '[o]ver time, an additional worker raises the unemployment rate and lowers the vacancy rate. The former makes it easier for jobs to find workers, the latter makes it harder for workers to find jobs.' (Diamond 1982b, p. 226).

18. Differently from Diamond (1981), Diamond and Maskin (1979; 1981), and Mortensen (1982a; 1982b), in all of which the numbers of jobs and workers in the market are considered equal.

19. For a detailed presentation of the assumptions underlying a linear matching technology, see Diamond (1982b, p. 223): 'The first assumption of the linear technology is that the matching of unemployed and vacancies depends only on the numbers of unemployed and vacancies. That is, filled jobs do not affect the ability of the unemployed and the vacancies to come together. Second, both the unemployed and the vacancies are assumed to be seeking each other, with the number of matches equal to the sum of those coming from meetings initiated by workers and those initiated by jobs. The third assumption is that any searching worker makes contact with jobs at a rate independent of the number of vacant jobs (which is assumed to be strictly positive). The same condition holds for searching vacancies'.

    As an example of non-linear search, the author considers the case (ibid., p. 225) 'that the number of filled jobs will affect the ease with which workers can find vacancies'.

20. It is not clear whether Rubinstein (1987, pp. 215–16, 221) considers Diamond (1981) and Diamond and Maskin (1979) as characterized by the same matching technology as Mortensen (1982a; 1982b). The same seems to apply to Diamond (1982b, p. 223, n): 'The linear technology has been analyzed by Diamond and Maskin (1979, 1981) and Mortensen' (Diamond 1982a; 1982b).

21. See Mortensen (1982a; 1982b) and Howitt and McAfee (1987, esp. pp. 94–5). Diamond (1982b, p. 224) can be interpreted in the same fashion.

22. Symmetric bargaining means that no agent or commodity type plays any special role (cf. Boldrin *et al.* 1993, p. 726); and that the trade surplus is 'split evenly' between the parties contracting (cf. Diamond 1982b, p. 219).

23. In these articles 'it is assumed that a meeting is concluded with an instantaneous agreement which divides the associated surplus in an arbitrary predetermined way (when the surplus is assumed to be divided equally, the division rule is, in fact, Nash's axiomatic bargaining solution)' (Rubinstein and Wolinski 1985, p. 1133; also p. 1149).

24. Kiyotaki and Wright (1993, p. 65, n) assume a constant-returns-to-scale meeting technology by choosing a constant arrival rate of trading opportunities: 'The assumption that the arrival rate ... is constant (and independent of the number of traders) is equivalent to the assumption of a constant-returns-to-scale (CRS) meeting technology. That is, a CRS meeting technology implies that the total number of meetings per unit of time is proportional to the number of traders, and so the arrival rate for a representative trader (which is just the number of meetings divided by the number of traders) is a fixed constant' (see also p.75, n); Boldrin, Kiyotaki and Wright (1993, p. 7) also make the same assumption.

25. A model by Albin and Foley (1992) simulates two-goods decentralized exchange with informational or search costs, where bilateral bargaining takes place sequentially at non-Walrasian prices, and 'boundedly rational' rules of interaction are used by traders. The authors associate their study with Diamond (1984b), and extend 'technology specification' to Diamond's assumption of 'correct forecasts of future prices and rates of trading opportunities' (Albin and Foley 1992, p. 49; quoting from Diamond 1984b, pp. 1–3). This is the main focus of the study: traders use a 'limited computational' algorithm with local interaction (parametric neighborhood size is assumed) in order to define communication and search intensities for ensuing rounds of trading. 'It is interesting to conjecture that, with

the local formulation we use, the unit cost of coordination does not rise with the size of the economy. In other words, for an economy of N agents sensitive to the costs of computation and organized in neighborhoods of radius r, the efficiency outcome is essentially ruled by the radius parameter and is independent of N' (Albin and Foley 1992, p. 50). Diamond's model could be seen as relying on 'fully rational strategies' of individual traders who 'maintain a model of the state of the N-agent economy' (ibid.), save for the fact that agents do not anticipate the externality effect.

26. 'The most obvious example, of direct dealings between non-merchants, surviving into otherwise sophisticated economies, is the market in dwelling-houses. We rarely find house-merchants holding stocks of dwelling-houses ...; but there remains a problem of communication, which is dealt with in another way. This is by the appearance of house-agents, a particular kind of commission agent, who has the function of bringing buyer and seller together, and consequently of advising them of the price at which they should trade. He charges a commission to cover the cost of his services ... In a complete theory of markets, the commission agent would have to find a place.' (Hicks 1976, p. 299). (On a search model applied to such a case, see Diamond and Maskin 1979; 1981.) This line of research has been pursued on another strand of search models, which generate endogenously the emergence of middlemen, or of a common medium of exchange, based on search/transaction costs.

27. 'Diamond's contributions suggest a possible explanation for the phenomena of persistent large-scale unemployment. However, they are cast in terms of models that are hard to relate to every day labor-market phenomena' (Howitt and McAfee 1988, p. 89). In footnote 2, the authors specify the simplifications, one of which is of interest here: '(e) after each act of production search begins anew with no possibility of recalling the previous trading partner, in contrast to long-term bilateral relationships of real-world labor markets'.

28. 'The probability that a particular agent of type i enters a match during a short time interval equals the probability that the agent makes a successful contact during the interval, $\lambda_i \, dt$, plus the probability that he is contacted by some agent of the opposite type during the interval, $\lambda_j \, dt \, n_j / n_i$, where n_1 and n_2 represents the numbers of the two types of agents. Given any pair of search intensities (λ_1, λ_2), the random time to match for any agent of type i is characterized by the "hazard" rate

$$h_i(\lambda_1, \lambda_2) = (1 / n_i) [n_1 \, \lambda_1 + n_2 \, \lambda_2], \quad i = 1, 2.'$$ (Mortensen 1982b, p. 973).

29. The proposition will not be addressed here that, if the fictional Walrasian auctioneer is not present, and frictions are introduced in the execution of trades, it is possible to have macro unemployment problems in an economy with correctly perceived, flexible prices and wages. Our goal is more limited, and the consequences of money in the coordination of trade will not be tackled, either in the positive, or in the efficiency perspectives. In fact, this is dependent on assumptions regarding namely, the technologies of trade, the consideration of search costs, the number of goods considered, and the characterization of the preferences of individuals.

30. Micro–macro consistency requires (Diamond 1984a, p. 4):

$$be = sm = f(e, m)$$

where e – number of individuals with inventories
  m – number of individuals with money
  b – rate of arrival of buyers experienced by sellers
  s – rate of arrival of sellers experienced by buyers
  $f(e, m)$ – rate of completion of transactions describing the aggregate transactions technology, which is assumed to be non-stochastic.

31. Because I will be quoting from Hicks (1989) on the pricing of manufactures, let us introduce his producers as market organizers. Hicks brings out a market organization based on the producers as the market-makers in his *A Market Theory of Money*. In the case of those goods for which the conditions do not apply that favor the emergence of what he calls speculative markets, Hicks proposes a production system with primary producers,

manufactures and consumers and two sorts of intermediaries in between, primary and secondary trades. Regarding the latter, he conceives of an economy where 'the product, as soon as it was completed, would be sold to secondary merchants (wholesalers) at a price which was mainly determined by trading among the wholesalers themselves' (ibid., p. 20). Then Hicks raises the possibility that on occasions, decisions to introduce new products had been made; when this happens '[o]ur entrepreneur has to devise a new product, make arrangements for manufacturing it, and also make arrangements to get it sold'.

And Hicks goes on: 'For since the product is specialized, no other manufacturer producing anything exactly like it, any merchant to whom he sells it directly must be dependent on him for supply. The merchant must thus be acting, in this part of his business, as a manufacturer's agent. So we have here manufacturing and selling come in substance under the same control.

There were two functions which we were attributing to our secondary merchants and their markets: stockholding and price-formation. As we saw, they are nearly allied; so it is here. The selling department is able to set a selling price and make it effective by holding stocks. That is to say, it can do its own buffering; and can do it relatively easily, since producing and stockholding have been brought so close together. So the price that is set can be chosen, as a matter of policy.' (ibid., p. 24).

32. This is an illusion, except in a two-way market for a good handled by numerous secondary sellers – e.g. auto parts, grain.

33. Cases exist also where either the period of time that the inventories are held, or the time taken to satisfy orders, are negligible. These cases should not be discarded, not only on logical but also on empirical grounds; for instance, most services seem to fall in this category.

34. Our market-maker can be so defined as in Daniel Friedman (1989, p. 381): 'Markets can be usefully distinguished by asking two questions: (a) who sets prices? (b) who handles the logistics of exchange? By a *producers' market*, I mean a market for which the brief answer to each question is "the producers of the good"; that is, each producer publicly announces his current price and incurs the main "selling costs" of putting his good into his customers' hands'.

35. Hicks (1989, pp. 24–5) emphasizes this aspect in a setting where producers are constructed as having taken over the merchanting function: since the producer is now 'selling, at least at the end of the chain, to a consumer who is not an expert', 'it is now the producer himself who has to take responsibility for the quality, and usefulness of what he is offering'. And Hicks goes on: 'That is why at this point there is a function for advertisement, which is basically a promise about the character of the thing being sold. It is a promise like that which is given by the retailer, when he opens his shop. In each case it is given by a professional to a non-expert, so it quite ordinarily needs to do more than just give information. The attention of the customer has to be attracted, by a smart shop-front in the one case, by pretty pictures and suchlike in the other. But he has then to be persuaded on the strength of the information given to him, including a promise, explicit or implicit, that the information is correct'.

36. Daniel Friedman also recognizes that this may matter even for the homogeneous good case ('technically the simplest and cleanest'): 'A producer who can deliver the goods and receive payment at a time, place and manner that is convenient to the customer will attract more orders. But this service is costly to provide, since it requires such things as friendly sales representatives, local sales outlets, toll-free telephone lines, lunch invitations, flexible credit terms, etc.' (Friedman 1989, p. 382).

37. Alchian stresses the role of information and transaction costs throughout his work. 'We can now identify a "perfect" market – one in which all potential bids and offers are known at zero cost to every other person, and in which contract enforcement costs are zero. Characteristics of every good need to be known perfectly at zero cost. A "perfect" market would imply a "perfect" world in which all costs of production, even of "exchanges", were zero. It is curious that while we economists never formalize our analysis on the basis of an analytical ideal of a perfect world (in the sense of costless production) we have postulated costless *information* as a formal ideal for analysis. Why?' (Alchian 1969, p. 42, n).

Also of interest: 'Because most of the formal economic models of competition, exchange, and equilibrium have ignored ignorance and lack of costless full and perfect information, many institutions of our economic system, institutions that are productive in creating knowledge more cheaply than otherwise, have been erroneously treated as parasitic appendages. The explanation of use of money, expertise with dealing in a good as a middleman specialist with a trademark or brandname, reputability or goodwill, along with advertising of one's wares (and even unemployment) is often misunderstood. All these can be derived from the same information cost factors that give rise to use of an intermediary medium of exchange.' (Alchian 1977, p. 123).

38. This may be a critical effect. For instance, Daniel Friedman (1989) on 'producers' markets' may have failed in this respect. Let us see how. By producers' markets Daniel Friedman means that 'each producer publicly announces his current price and incurs the main "selling costs" of putting his good into his customers' hands'. The producer sets prices and handles the logistics of exchange. Also 'the selling costs incurred by producers are primarily regarded as a means of reducing the cost to customers of searching for the best price and attribute mix' (ibid., pp. 381–2). In his set-up, customers are meant to search for prices, but selling costs by firms provide customers with sufficient information to generate an 'efficient' price searching by customers. Since the diffusion process of information has enabled convergence to a single price in equilibrium, search does not occur.

The question is that the demand characteristics that may be conducive to generate such type of market organization are only implicitly formalized; price uncertainty vanishes in equilibrium, and thus Friedman's model 'has essentially assumed away search costs' (ibid., p. 383, n). This model is therefore lacking a seemingly basic element to explain the role of the producers as the market-makers. In any case, the author shows that in his *non-cooperative* model of producers' markets for a *homogeneous* good, 'sticky, asymmetric price responses can arise in the absence of search costs or collusion.' (ibid., p. 383).

39. The upshot is well put forward by Hicks: 'The price is one aspect of the offer that is made; there are some characteristics of other aspects which are shared by it. The chief is that it must not be changed arbitrarily, at a moment's notice. Arbitrary changes "unsettle" the consumer. He may be taking time to decide to buy; so if, when he finally decides, he finds the price has risen against him, his confidence is lost, and the seller's reputation is damaged. And it can happen that there is a similar obstacle to price-reductions; they cast suspicion on the quality of the product, they suggest that something is wrong. Thus the diversified market had a tendency to be what I have called a *fixprice* market, meaning not that prices do not change, but that there is a force which makes for stabilization, operated not by independent speculators, but by the producer himself.' (Hicks 1989, p. 25).

40. 'Most transactions in a monetary economy are not spot but credit transactions involving explicit contracts in which one side promises to deliver goods or services'. Clower and Howitt (1996, p. 25) add: 'This is perhaps most evident in trades involving labor services, where some degree of future commitment is almost always involved on both sides. But it also involves markets for consumer goods, where retail organizations implicitly offer their customers future delivery on demand, and in markets for industrial goods, where long-term supply relationships are crucial to the smooth operation of manufacturing processes'.

41. The inclusion of menu-costs, as of any transactions costs, enriches the standard model of price adjustment and may generate interesting predictions. Yet, menu-costs lack any logical basis in the market, apart from the strict 'direct administrative costs to the producer (seller)' (Barro 1972, p. 21). And empirically it has not been easy to justify. Estimates of such costs, even by users, suggest that they are too slight to be of significance. Overall, menu-costs may be less promising than those who use them tend to suppose.

42. Okun, on concentrating his attention on the demand side, loses some sight of the competitive drive of producers; he overlooks the role of selling costs in breaking attachments of customers to individual sellers, at least fortuitously. Okun pays only cursory attention to the possibility of customers to initiate some shopping around at intermittent points in time, in the belief that some price moves may have happened meanwhile.

43. 'The supply of specialized skill and ability, of suitable machinery and other capital, and of the appropriate organization has not time to be fully adapted to demand; but the producers have to adjust their supply to the demand as best as they can with the appliances already at their disposal' (Marshall 1920, p. 376).

44. 'Overhead costs ... are assumed by definition constant under partial adjustment, and to have merely to be borne by more or fewer units of output. But since output is never known in advance, as it is determined by the market, these variations in fixed costs or overheads per unit of output, although well known, play little part in price determination.' (Wiles 1961, p. 51).

45. '[A]lthough nothing but prime cost enters *necessarily and directly* into the supply price for short periods, it is yet true that supplementary costs also exert some influence indirectly. ... [A] controlling influence over the relatively quick movements of supply price during short periods is exercised by causes in the background which range over a long period; and the fear of "spoiling the market" often makes those causes act more promptly then they otherwise would. ... In long periods on the other hand all investments of capital and effort in providing the material plant and the organization of a business, and in acquiring trade knowledge and specialized ability, have time to be adjusted to the incomes which are expected to be earned by them: and the estimates of those incomes therefore directly govern supply, and are the true long-period normal supply price of the commodity produced. ... Thus that investment of capital in a trade, on which the price of the commodity produced by it depends in the long run, is governed by estimates on the one hand of the outgoings required to build up and to work a representative firm, and on the other of the incomings, spread over a long period of time, to be got by such a price.' (Marshall 1920, pp. 376–7).

46. An avowedly not very reasonable 'solution' to the problem is raised by Wiles, but he drops it in favor of the full-cost *principle*: 'How, then, would profit maximization look in this sector? The firm would set a price which would result in an output such that (price – a.c.) × output was maximized. By *logical necessity* at this price and output true m.r. = true m.c. (partial adjustment), where "true" refers to the (wisely) chosen length of "run." Just because practical thought is not conducted in marginal terms we may not conclude that analytical thought is precluded from applying them.

    Moreover all the lines would be thick bands, ... owing to uncertainty, and profits would be maximized *ex ante* by a price and output combination anywhere within the lozenge-shaped continuum [at the top of the figure]. The upper lozenge gives, to be exact, an upper and a lower limit to the profit-maximizing price, and accordingly to the exact price chosen a range of probable outputs. Of course one of these prices and one of these outputs gives the *maximum-maximorum* of profits, but uncertainty prevents us from knowing which it is. Nor, if we did happen to hit on precisely that price, would we necessarily find ourselves asked to sell just that output.' (Wiles 1961, p. 59).

47. For an assessment of this point, as well as to clarify concepts, let us quote from Alchian: 'The pursuit of profits, and not some hypothetical undefinable situation, is the relevant objective whose *fulfilment* is rewarded with survival. Unfortunately, even this proximate objective is too high. Neither perfect knowledge of the past nor complete awareness of the current state of the arts gives sufficient foresight to indicate profitable action. Even for this more restricted objective, the pervasive effects of uncertainty prevent the ascertainment of actions which are supposed to be optimal in achieving profits. Now the consequence of this is that modes of behavior replace optimum equilibrium conditions as guiding rules of action.' (Alchian 1950, p. 218).

48. Adam Smith's view of competition 'as rivalry, as a process' was, according to Coase (1977, p. 318) 'quite robust' and this he documents at length. Of interest to us here is the following; contrasting the price of monopoly with the price of free competition, Smith writes: 'The natural price, or the price of free competition, on the contrary, is the lowest which can be taken, not upon every occasion indeed, but for any considerable time altogether. ... [The price of free competition] is the lowest which the sellers can commonly afford to take, and at the same time continue their business.' (A. Smith 1776, Bk. I, Chapter 7, § 27).

49. We may consider entry to be open in the sense of Andrews (1964) – cross-entry competition as he names it, which is quite reasonable in the case of a market composed of multi-product suppliers.

50. The following reflection by Wiles seems appropriate, even though he has it all mixed up: 'the genuine marginal revenue, which is marginal to the demand curve, is not known. Moreover even if they were known the true m.r. and demand curves would not be thin lines; for there is a great deal of tolerance among buyers of heterogeneous products to small

differences in price, so that each output can in fact be disposed of at all prices within a range. The demand curve, then, is not a line but a band; but in any case no one knows where the band runs' (Wiles 1961, p. 47).

For one, the last sentence is trivially inconsequent; where the band runs does not matter if 'each output can in fact be disposed of at all prices within a range'. All that matters is that current output can be expected to be disposed of at the current price.

51.   Considering a market in which consumers get price quotes for purely informational purposes and continually search for bargains, the supplier may find the determination of the demand function an impossible task. Rothschild and Yaari analyzed a model in which suppliers face a dilemma. The answer to 'What price to charge to increase knowledge about the demand function?' is likely to be different to the answer to 'What price to charge to maximize expected profits?'. Their conclusion is that it does not pay for the firms to be curious and the optimal strategy does not entail knowing their demand function with certainty. Following the optimal strategy, the firm will, in the course of its history, with positive probability charge the wrong price infinitely often and the correct price only a finite number of times. If there are many firms, price variability will persist (cf. description of results of Rothschild and Yaari, in Rothschild 1973, pp. 1299–1301).

52.   We might presume that some of these adjustments had not been fully anticipated and only discovered under the pressure of the actual circumstances, so that the notion of *ex ante* marginal costs will have to be slightly discounted as a precise guide for decision.

References

Aiyagari, S. Rao and Neil Wallace (1991), 'Existence of Steady States with Positive Consumption in the Kiyotaki–Wright Model', *Review of Economic Studies*, **58**, October, 901–16.

Albin, Peter and Duncan K. Foley (1992), 'Decentralized, Dispersed Exchange without an Auctioneer. A Simulation Study', *Journal of Economic Behavior and Organization*, **18**, 27–51.

Alchian, Armen A. (1950), 'Uncertainty, Evolution, and Economic Theory', *Journal of Political Economy*, **58** (3), June, 211–21.

Alchian, Armen A. (1969), 'Information Costs, Pricing and Resource Unemployment', *Western Economic Journal*, **7**; as reprinted in *Selected Works by Armen A. Alchian. Economic Forces at Work*, Indianapolis: Liberty Press, 1977, 37–71.

Alchian, Armen A. (1977), 'Why Money?', *Journal of Money, Credit, and Banking*, **9** (1), Part 2, February; as reprinted in *Economic Forces at Work. Selected Works by Armen A. Alchian*, Indianapolis: Liberty Press, 1977, 111–23.

Alchian, Armen A. and William R. Allen (1972), *University Economics*, 3rd edn, Belmont, California: Wadsworth Publishing Co.

Allen, R. G. D. (1932), 'The Foundations of a Mathematical Theory of Exchange', *Economica* (o.s.), **12**, 197–226.

Anderson, Robert M. and William R. Zame (1997), 'Edgeworth's Conjecture with Infinitely Many Commodities: L^1', *Econometrica*, **65** (2), March, 225-73.

Andrews, P. W. S. (1949), *Manufacturing Business*, London: Macmillan.

Andrews, P. W. S. (1964), *On Competition in Economic Theory*, London: Macmillan.

Andrews, P. W. S. and Elizabeth Brunner (1975), 'Competitive Prices, Normal Costs and Industrial Stability' in *Studies in Pricing*, London: Macmillan, 18–34.

Archibald, G. C. (1961), 'Chamberlin *versus* Chicago', *Review of Economic Studies*, **24**, 2–28.

Archibald, G. C. (1967), 'Monopolistic Competition and Returns to Scale', *Economic Journal*, **77**, June, 405–12.

Archibald, G. C. (1987), 'Monopolistic Competition', in John Eatwell *et al.* (eds), *The New Palgrave*, vol. 3, London: Macmillan, 531–35.

Archibald, G. C. and R. G. Lipsey (1958), 'Value and Monetary Theory: Temporary *versus* Full Equilibrium', in R. W. Clower (ed.), *Monetary Theory*, 1969, 149–61; from 'Monetary and Value Theory: a Critique of Lange and Patinkin', *Review of Economic Studies*, **26**, 1958, 1–22.

Arrow, Kenneth J. (1959), 'Toward a Theory of Price Adjustment', in M. Abramovitz *et al.* (eds), *The Allocation of Economic Resources. Essays in Honor of Bernard Francis Haley*, Stanford, California: Stanford University Press, 41–51.

Arrow, Kenneth J. (1968), 'Economic Equilibrium', *International Encyclopedia of the Social Sciences*, **4**, London: Macmillan, 376–89.

Arrow, Kenneth J. (1969), 'The Organization of Economic Activity. Issues Pertinent to the Choice of Market versus Nonmarket Allocation', in Joint Economic Committee, U.S. Congress, *The Analysis and Evaluation of Public Expenditures: The PPB System*, Washington, D.C.: G.P.O., vol. 1, 47–66.

Arrow, Kenneth J. (1987), 'Economic Theory and the Hypothesis of Rationality', in John Eatwell *et al.* (eds), *The New Palgrave*, vol. 2, London: Macmillan, 69–75.

Arrow, Kenneth J. (1994), 'Methodological Individualism and Social Knowledge', *American Economic Review*, **84** (2), May, 1–9.

Arrow, Kenneth J. and G. Debreu (1954), 'Existence of an Equilibrium for a Competitive Economy', *Econometrica*, **22** (3), July, 265–90.

Arrow, Kenneth J. and Frank H. Hahn (1971), *General Competitive Analysis*, New York: North-Holland.

Arrow, Kenneth J. and Leonid Hurwicz (1960), 'Decentralization and Computation in Resource Allocation', in R. W. Pfouts (ed.), *Essays in Economics and Econometrics*, Chapell Hill: University of North Carolina Press; as reprinted in K. Arrow and L. Hurwicz (eds), *Studies in Resource Allocation Processes*, 1977, 41–95.

Arrow, Kenneth J. and Leonid Hurwicz (eds) (1977), *Studies in Resource Allocation Processes*, Cambridge: Cambridge University Press.

Arrow, Kenneth J., Samuel Karlin, and Herbert Scarf (eds) (1958), *Studies in the Mathematical Theory of Inventories and Production*, Stanford, California: Stanford University Press.

Aumann, R. (1964), 'Markets with a Continuum of Traders', *Econometrica*, **32** (1–2), January–April, 39–50.

Bala, Venkatesh and Nicholas M. Kiefer (1994), 'On the Existence of Universally Convergent Mechanisms', *Journal of Economic Dynamics and Control*, **18** (2), 299–316.

Balvers, Ronald J. and Thomas F. Cosimano (1990), 'Actively Learning about Demand and the Dynamics of Price Adjustment', *Economic Journal*, **100**, September, 882–98.

Barro, Robert J. (1972), 'A Theory of Monopolistic Price Adjustment', *Review of Economic Studies*, **39**, 17–26.

Becker, G. S. (1962), 'Irrational Behavior and Economic Theory', *Journal of Political Economy*, **70**, 1–13.

Benassy, Jean-Pascal (1975), 'Disequilibrium Exchange in Barter and Monetary Economics', *Economic Inquiry*, **13** (2), June, 131–56.

Bils, Mark (1989), 'Pricing in a Customer Market', *Quarterly Journal of Economics*, **104** (4), November, 699–718.

Binmore, K. G. and M. J. Herrero (1988), 'Matching and Bargaining in Dynamic Markets', *Review of Economic Studies*, **55** (1), January, 17–31.

Binmore, K. G., M. J. Osborne and Ariel Rubinstein (1992), 'Noncooperative Models of Bargaining', in R. J. Aumann and S. Hart (eds), *Handbook of Game Theory*, vol. 1, Amsterdam: Elsevier Science Publishers, 179–225.

Boldrin, Michele, Nobuhiro Kiyotaki and Randall Wright (1993), 'A Dynamic Equilibrium Model of Search, Production, and Search', *Journal of Economic Dynamics and Control*, **17**, 723–58.

Bridel, Pascal (1997), *Money and General Equilibrium Theory. From Walras to Pareto (1870–1923)*, Cheltenham: Edward Elgar

Brunner, Karl and Allan H. Meltzer (1971), 'The Uses of Money: Money in the Theory of an Exchange Economy', *American Economic Review*, **61**, December, 784–805.

Bulow, J., J. Geanakoplos and P. Klemperer (1985), 'Multimarket Oligopoly: Strategic Substitutes and Complements', *Journal of Political Economy*, **93**, 488–511.

Burstein, M. (1968), *Economic Theory. Equilibrium and Change*, London: John Wiley.

Busetto, Francesca (1995), 'Why the Non-*Tâtonnement* Line of Research Died Out', *Economic Notes*, **24** (1), 89–114.

Bushaw, D. W. and R. W. Clower (1957), *Introduction to Mathematical Economics*, Homewood, Illinois: Richard D. Irwin.

Calsamiglia, Xavier (1977) 'Decentralized Resource Allocation and Increasing Returns', *Journal of Economic Theory*, **14** (2), April, 263–83.

Calsamiglia, Xavier and Alan Kirman (1993), 'A Unique Informationally Efficient and Decentralized Mechanism with Fair Outcomes', *Econometrica*, **61** (5), September, 1147–72.

Cason, Timothy N. and Daniel Friedman (1997), 'Price Formation in Single Call Markets', *Econometrica*, **65** (2), March, 311–45.

Cassady, Ralph Jr. (1967), *Auctions and Auctioneering*, Berkeley: University of California Press.

Cassady, Ralph Jr. (1974), *Exchange by Private Treaty*, Bureau of Business Research. Graduate School of Business, The University of Texas at Austin.

Cassel, G. (1918/1932), *The Theory of Social Economy*, 2nd edn, translated by S. L. Barron, New York: Harcourt, Brace and Co.

Chamberlin, Edward H. (1933), *The Theory of Monopolistic Competition. A Reorientation of the Theory of Value*, Cambridge: Harvard University Press, 1958.

Chikán, Attila (ed.) (1990), *Inventory Models*, Dordrecht, Kluwer Academics Publishers, Series B: Mathematical and Statistical Methods, vol. 16.

Chuchman, George (1982), 'A Model of the Evolution of Exchange Processes' Unpublished Ph. D. Thesis, Dept. of Economics, University of Western Ontario.

Clark, J. Maurice (1923), *Studies in the Economies of Overhead Costs*, Chicago: University of Chicago Press.

Clower, Robert W. (1955), 'Competition, Monopoly, and the Theory of Price', *Pakistan Economic Journal*, September, 219–26.

Clower, Robert W. (1959), 'Some Theory of an Ignorant Monopolist', *Economic Journal*, **69**, December, 705–16.

Clower, Robert W. (1965), 'The Keynesian Counter-Revolution: A Theoretical

Appraisal', in F. H. Hahn and F. P. R. Brechling (eds), *The Theory of Interest Rates*, London: Macmillan, 103–25.

Clower, Robert W. (1967), 'A Reconsideration of the Microfoundations of Monetary Theory', *Western Economic Journal*, **6** (1), December, 1–8.

Clower, Robert W. (1971), 'Theoretical Foundations of Monetary Policy', in G. Clayton, J. C. Gilbert and R. Sedgwick (eds), *Monetary Theory and Monetary Policy in the 1970's: Proceedings of the 1970 Sheffield Money Seminar*, London: Oxford University Press; as reprinted in Donald A. Walker (ed.), *Money and Markets*, Cambridge: Cambridge University Press, 1984, 107–19.

Clower, Robert W. (1977), 'The Anatomy of Monetary Theory', *American Economic Review*, **67** (1), February; as reprinted in Donald A. Walker (ed.), *Money and Markets*, Cambridge: Cambridge University Press, 1984, 231–41.

Clower, Robert W. (1994a), 'The Fingers of the Invisible Hand', *Brock Review*, **3** (1), 3–13.

Clower, Robert W. (1994b), 'The Effective Demand Fraud', *Eastern Economic Journal*, **20** (4), Fall, 377–85.

Clower, Robert W. (1995a), 'Axiomatics in Economics', *Southern Economic Journal*, **62** (2) October, 307–19.

Clower, Robert W. (1995b), 'On the Origin of Monetary Exchange', *Economic Inquiry*, **33**, October, 525–36.

Clower, Robert W. (1996), 'On Truth in Teaching Macroeconomics', in Daniel Vaz and Kumaraswamy Velupillai (eds), *Inflation, Institutions and Information. Essays in Honour of Axel Leijonhufvud*, London: Macmillan, 35–61.

Clower, Robert W. and Daniel Friedman (1986), 'Trade Specialists and Money in an Ongoing Exchange Economy', in Richard H. Day and Gunnar Eliasson (eds), *The Dynamics of Market Economies*, New York: North-Holland, 115–31.

Clower, Robert W. and Peter W. Howitt (1996), 'Taking Markets Seriously: Groundwork for a Post-Walrasian Macrofoundation', in David Colander (ed.), *Beyond Microfoundations. Post Walrasian Macroeconomics*, Cambridge: Cambridge University Press, 21–37.

Clower, Robert W. and Peter W. Howitt (1997a), 'Foundations of Economics', in Antoine d'Autume and Jean Cartelier (eds), *Is Economics Becoming a Hard Science?*, Cheltenham: Edward Elgar, 17–34.

Clower, Robert W. and Peter W. Howitt (1997b), 'Money, Markets and Coase' Economics', in Antoine d'Autume and Jean Cartelier (eds), *Is Economics Becoming a Hard Science?*, Cheltenham: Edward Elgar, 189–203.

Clower, Robert W. and Axel Leijonhufvud (1975), 'The Coordination of Economic Activities: A Keynesian Perspective', *American Economic Review*, **65** (2), May, 182–88.

Coase, Ronald H. (1937), 'The Nature of the Firm', *Economica*, **4** (n.s.); as reprinted in O. E. Williamson and S. Winter (eds), *The Nature of the Firm*, 1991, 18–33.

Coase, Ronald H. (1977), 'The Wealth of Nations', *Economic Inquiry*, **15** (3), July, 309–25.

Coase, Ronald H. (1988a), 'The Nature of the Firm: Origin, Meaning, Influence', *Journal of Law, Economics, and Organization*, **4**; as reprinted in O. E. Williamson and S. G. Winter (eds), *The Nature of the Firm*, 1991, 34–74.

Coase, Ronald H. (1988b), 'The Firm, the Market, and the Law', *The Firm, the Market, and the Law*, Chicago: The University of Chicago Press, 1–31.

Coase, Ronald H. (1992), 'The Institutional Structure of Production', *American Economic Review*, **82** (4), September, 713–19.

Colander, David (1992), 'The Lost Art of Economics', *Journal of Economic Perspectives*, **6** (3), Summer, 191–98.

Colander, David (1994), 'Is New Keynesian Economics New?', mimeo, forthcoming as 'Beyond New Keynesian Economics: Post Walrasian Economics', in Roy Rothheim (ed.), *Post Keynesian Perspectives on New Keynesian Economics*, Cheltenham: Edward Elgar, 1998.

Cournot, Augustin (1838), *Researches into the Mathematical Principles of the Theory of Wealth*, New York: Macmillan, 1927.

Daal, Jan van and Albert Jolink (1993), *The Equilibrium Economics of Léon Walras*, New York: Routledge.

Davis, Douglas D., Glenn W. Harrison and Arlington W. Williams (1993), 'Convergence to Nonstationary Competitive Equilibria. An Experimental Analysis', *Journal of Economic Behavior and Organization*, **22**, 305–26.

Dean, Joel (1976), *Statistical Cost Estimation*, Bloomington: Indiana University Press.

Debreu, Gerard (1959), *Theory of Value. An Axiomatic Analysis of Economic Equilibrium*, New Haven: Yale University Press, 1987.

Debreu, Gerard (1970), 'Economies with a Finite Set of Equilibria', *Econometrica*, **38**, 387–92.

Debreu, Gerard (1974), 'Excess Demand Functions', *Journal of Mathematical Economics*, **1**; as reprinted in *Mathematical Economics: Twenty Papers of Gerard Debreu*, Cambridge: Cambridge University Press, 1983, 203–09.

Debreu, Gerard (1976), 'Regular Differentiable Economies', *American Economic Review*, **66** (2), 280–87; reprinted as 'The Application to Economics of Differential Topology and Global Analysis: Regular Differentiable Economies', in *Mathematical Economics: Twenty Papers of Gerard Debreu*, Cambridge: Cambridge University Press, 1983, 232–41.

Debreu, Gerard (1982), 'Existence Of Competitive Equilibrium', in K. J. Arrow and M. D. Intriligator (eds), *Handbook of Mathematical Economics*, vol. 2, Amsterdam: North-Holland, 697–743.

Debreu, Gerard (1986a), 'Four Aspects of the Mathematical Theory of Economic Analysis', in Stanley Reiter (ed.), *Studies in Mathematical Economics*, **25**, The Mathematical Association of America, 405–22.

Debreu, Gerard (1986b), 'Theoretic Models: Mathematical Form and Economic Content', *Econometrica*, **54** (6), November, 1259–70.

Demsetz, Harold (1968), 'The Cost of Transacting', *Quarterly Journal of Economics*, **82** (1), February, 33–53.

Demsetz, Harold (1988), 'The Theory of the Firm Revisited', *The Organization of Economic Activity*, vol. 1, Basil Blackwell; as reprinted in O. E. Williamson and S. G. Winter (eds), *The Nature of the Firm*, 1991, 159–78.

Diamond, Peter A. (1971), 'A Model of Price Adjustment', *Journal of Economic Theory*, **3**, 153–68.

Diamond, Peter A. (1981), 'Mobility Costs, Frictional Unemployment and Efficiency', *Journal of Political Economy*, **89**, 798–812.

Diamond, Peter A. (1982a), 'Aggregate Demand Management in Search Equilibrium', *Journal of Political Economy*, **90**, 881–94.

Diamond, Peter A. (1982b), 'Wage Determination and Efficiency in Search Equilibrium', *Review of Economic Studies*, **49**, 217–27.

Diamond, Peter A. (1984a), 'Money in Search Equilibrium', *Econometrica*, **52** (1), January, 1–20.

Diamond, Peter A. (1984b), *A Search-Equilibrium Approach to the Micro Foundations of Macroeconomics*, Cambridge, Mass.: MIT Press.

Diamond, Peter A. (1987a), 'Multiple Equilibria in Models of Credit', *American Economic Review*, **77** (2), May, 82–86.

Diamond, Peter A. (1987b), 'Equilibrium without an Auctioneer', in Truman F. Bewley (ed.), *Advances in Economic Theory*, Fifth World Congress, Cambridge: Cambridge University Press, 363–78.

Diamond, Peter A. (1988), 'Credit in Search Equilibrium', in Meir Kohn and Sho-Chieh Tsiang (eds), *Finance Constraints, Expectations, and Macroeconomics*, Oxford: Clarendon Press, 36–53.

Diamond, Peter A. (1990), 'Pairwise Credit in Search Equilibrium', *The Quarterly Journal of Economics*, **105**, (2), May, 285–319.

Diamond, Peter A. and Drew Fudenberg (1989), 'Rational Expectations Business Cycles in Search Equilibrium', *Journal of Political Economy*, **97** (3), 606–19.

Diamond, Peter A. and E. Maskin (1979), 'An Equilibrium Analysis of Search and Breach of Contract. I. Steady States', *Bell Journal of Economics*, **10**, 282–316.

Diamond, Peter A. and E. Maskin (1981), 'An Equilibrium Analysis of Search and Breach of Contract. II. A Nonsteady State Example', *Journal of Economic Theory*, **25**, 165–96.

Dierker, Egbert (1982), 'Regular Economies', in K. J. Arrow and M. D. Intriligator (eds), *Handbook of Mathematical Economics*, vol. 2, Amsterdam: North-Holland, 795–830.

Drèze, J. H. (1975), 'Existence of an Exchange Equilibrium under Price Rigidities', *International Economic Review*, **16** (2), June, 301–20.

Eatwell, John, Murray Milgate and Peter Newman (eds) (1987), *The New Palgrave. A Dictionary of Economics*, London: Macmillan, 4 vol..

Edgeworth, F. Y. (1881), *Mathematical Psychics. An Essay on the Application of Mathematics to the Moral Sciences*, London: C. Kegan; reprint New York: Kelley, 1967.

Edgeworth, F. Y. (1889), '*The Mathematical Theory of Political Economy. Éléments d'Économie Politique Pure*. By Léon Walras', *Nature*, **40**, September 5, 434–36.

Edgeworth, F. Y. (1925), 'On the Determinateness of Economic Equilibrium', in *Papers Relating to Political Economy*, vol. 2, New York: Burt Franklin, 313–15.

Feiwel, George R. (1987), 'The Potentials and Limits of Economic Analysis: The Contributions of Kenneth J. Arrow', in George R. Feiwel (ed.), *Arrow and the Ascent of Modern Economic Theory*, London: Macmillan, 1–187.

Feldman, Allan M. (1973), 'Bilateral Trading Processes, Pairwise Optimality, and Pareto Optimality', *Review of Economic Studies*, **40**, October, 463–73.

Fisher, Franklin M. (1970), 'Quasi-Competitive Price Adjustment by Individual Firms: a Preliminary Paper', *Journal of Economic Theory*, **3**, 195–206.

Fisher, Franklin M. (1972), 'On Price Adjustment Without an Auctioneer', *The Review of Economic Studies*, **39** (1), no. 117, January, 1–15.

Fisher, Franklin M. (1973), 'Stability and Competitive Equilibrium in Two Models of Search and Individual Price Adjustment', *Journal of Economic Theory*, **6**, 446–70.

Fisher, Franklin M. (1979), 'Diagnosing Monopoly', *Southern Economic Journal*, **45**, (4), 7–33.

Fisher, Franklin M. (1983), *Disequilibrium Foundations of Equilibrium Economics*, Cambridge: Cambridge University Press.

Fisher, Franklin (1987), 'Adjustment Processes and Stability', in John Eatwell *et al.* (eds), *The New Palgrave*, vol. 1, London: Macmillan, 26–29.

Fisher, Franklin M. (1989), 'Games Economists Play: a Noncooperative View', *Rand Journal of Economics*, **20** (1), Spring, 113–37.

Fowles, John (1983), *The Tree*, New York: The Ecco Press.

Friedman, Daniel (1984), 'On the Efficiency of Double Auction Markets', *American Economic Review*, **74**, 60–72.

Friedman, Daniel (1989), 'Producers' Markets. A Model of Oligopoly with Sales Costs', *Journal of Economic Behavior and Organization*, **11**, 381–98.

Friedman, Daniel and Joseph Ostroy (1995), 'Competitivity in Auction Markets: An Experimental and Theoretical Investigation', *Economic Journal*, **105**, January, 21–53.

Fudenberg, D. and J. Tirole (1983), 'Sequential Bargaining with Incomplete Information', *Review of Economic Studies*, **50**, 221–47.

Fudenberg, D. and J. Tirole (1987), 'Understanding Rent Dissipation: On the Use of Game Theory in Industrial Organization', *American Economic Review*, **77**, 176–83.

Gale, Douglas (1963), 'A Note on Global Instability of Competitive Equilibrium', *Naval Research Logistics Quarterly*, **10**, 81–87.

Gale, Douglas (1986a), 'Bargaining and Competition Part I: Characterization', *Econometrica.*, **54**, (4), July, 785–806.

Gale, Douglas (1986b), 'Bargaining and Competition Part II: Existence', *Econometrica*, **54** (4), July, 807–18.

Gale, Douglas (1987), 'Limit Theorems for Markets with Sequential Bargaining', *Journal of Economic Theory*, **43** (1), October, 20–54.

Gale, Douglas (1992), 'A Walrasian Theory of Markets with Adverse Selection', *Review of Economic Studies*, **59** (2), April, 229–55.

Gale, Douglas (1996), 'Equilibria and Pareto Optima of Markets with Adverse Selection', *Economic Theory*, **7** (2), February, 207–235.

Gandolfo, Giancarlo (1987) 'Stability', in John Eatwell *et al.* (eds), *The New Palgrave*, vol. 4, London: Macmillan, 461–64.

Goodwin, R. M. (1951), 'Iteration, Automatic Computers, and Economic Dynamics', *Metronomica*, **3**, 1–7.

Gordon, Donald F. and Allan Hynes (1970), 'On the Theory of Price Dynamics', in E. S. Phelps *et al.* (eds), *Microeconomic Foundations of Employment and Inflation Theory*, New York: W. W. Norton, 369–93.

Gottfries, Nils (1986), 'A Permanent Demand Theory of Pricing', Seminar Paper No. 345, Institute for International Economic Studies, University of Stockholm.

Gottfries, Nils (1991), 'Customer Markets, Credit Market Imperfections and Real Price Rigidity', *Economica*, **58**, August, 317–23.

Gretsky, Neil and Joseph M. Ostroy (1985), 'Thick and Thin Market Nonatomic Exchange Economies', in C. D. Aliprantis, O. Burkinshaw and N. J. Rothman (eds), *Advances in Equilibrium Theory*, Berlin: Springer Verlag, 107–29.

Grossman, Herschel I. (1969), 'Theories of Markets with Recontracting', *Journal of Economic Theory*, **1**, 476–79.

Haavelmo, Trygve (1958), 'What Can Static Equilibrium Models Tell Us?', *Economic Inquiry*, **12** (1), March, 1974, 27–34.

Hackett, Steven C. (1992), 'A Comparative Analysis of Merchant and Broker Intermediation', *Journal of Economic Behavior and Organization*, **18** (3), 299–315.

Hackett, Steven C. (1993), 'Consignment Contracting', *Journal of Economic Behavior and Organization*, **20**, 247–53.

Hahn, F. H. (1965), 'On Some Problems of Proving the Existence of an Equilibrium in a Monetary Economy', in F. H. Hahn and F. P. R. Brechling (eds), *The Theory of Interest Rates*, London: Macmillan, 126–35.

Hahn, F. H. (1970), 'Some Adjustment Problems', *Econometrica*, **38** (1), January, 1–17.

Hahn, F. H. (1971), 'Equilibrium with Transaction Costs', *Econometrica*, **39** (3), May, 417–39.

Hahn, F. H. (1973a), *On the Notion of Equilibrium in Economics*, Cambridge: Cambridge University Press.

Hahn, F. H. (1973b), 'On Transaction Costs, Inessential Sequence Economies and Money', *Review of Economic Studies*, **40** (4), no. 124, October, 449–61.

Hahn, F. H. (1978), 'On Non-Walrasian Equilibria', *Review of Economic Studies*, **45** (1) no.139, February, 1–17.

Hahn, F. H. (1981), 'General Equilibrium Theory', in Daniel Bell and Irving Kristol (eds), *The Crisis in Economic Theory*, New York: Basic Books, 123–38.

Hahn, F. H. (1982), 'Stability', in K. J. Arrow and M. D. Intriligator (eds), *Handbook of Mathematical Economics*, vol. 2, Amsterdam: North-Holland, 745–93.

Hahn, F. H. (1987), 'Auctioneer', in John Eatwell *et al.* (eds), *The New Palgrave*, vol. 1, London: Macmillan, 136–38.

Hahn, F. H. (1989a), 'Introduction', in F. H. Hahn (ed.), *The Economics of Missing Markets, Information, and Games*, Oxford: Clarendon Press, 1–4.

Hahn, F. H. (1989b), 'Information Dynamics and Equilibrium', in F. H. Hahn (ed.), *The Economics of Missing Markets, Information, and Games*, Oxford: Clarendon Press, 106–26.

Hahn, F. H. (1994), 'An Intellectual Retrospect', Banca Nazionale del Lavoro Quarterly Review, **48** (190), September, 245–58.

Hahn, F. H. and Takashi Negishi (1962), 'A Theorem of Non-Tâtonnement Stability', *Econometrica*, **30** (3), July, 463–69.

Hayek, F. A. (1945), 'The Use of Knowledge in Society', *American Economic Review*, **35** (4), September, 519–30.

Hayek, F. A. (1948), 'The Meaning of Competition', in *Individualism and Economic Order*, Chicago: The University of Chicago Press, 92–106.

Heller, Walter P. and Ross M. Starr (1976), 'Equilibrium with Non-convex Transaction Costs: Monetary and Non-monetary Economies', *Review of Economic Studies*, **43**, June, 195–215.

Hey, John D. (1974), 'Price Adjustment in an Atomistic Market', *Journal of Economic Theory*, **9**, 483–99.

Heymann, D. and A. Leijonhufvud (1995), *High Inflation*, Oxford : Oxford University Press.

Hicks, John R. (1934), 'Léon Walras', *Econometrica*, **2**, October, 338–48.

Hicks, John R. (1935), 'Annual Survey of Economic Theory: The Theory of Monopoly', *Econometrica*, **3**, 1–20; as reprinted in G. J. Stigler and K. E. Boulding (eds), *Readings in Price Theory*, 1952, 361–83.

Hicks, John R. (1939), *Value and Capital. An Inquiry into some Fundamental Principles of Economic Theory*, 2nd edn, Oxford: Clarendon Press, 1946.

Hicks, John R. (1954), 'The Process of Imperfect Competition', *Oxford Economic Papers*, February, 41–54.

Hicks, John R. (1965), *Capital and Growth*, Oxford: Oxford University Press.

Hicks, John R. (1967), *Critical Essays in Monetary Theory*, Oxford: Clarendon Press.

Hicks, John R. (1969), *A Theory of Economic History*, Oxford: Clarendon Press.

Hicks, John R. (1974), *The Crisis in Keynesian Economics*, Oxford: Basil Blackwell.

Hicks, John R. (1976), 'Time in Economics', in *Money, Interest and Wages. Collected Essays on Economic Theory*, vol. 2, Cambridge, Mass.: Harvard University Press, 1982, 282–300.

Hicks, John R. (1983), 'A Discipline not a Science', in *Classics and Moderns. Collected Essays on Economic Theory*, vol. 3, Oxford: Basil Blackwell, 365–75.

Hicks, John R. (1988), 'Towards a more General Theory', in Meir Kohn and Sho-Chieh Tsiang (eds), *Finance Constraints, Expectations and Macroeconomics*, Oxford: Clarendon Press, 6–14.

Hicks, John R. (1989), *A Market Theory of Money*, Oxford: Clarendon Press.

Hicks, John R. and R. G. D. Allen (1934), 'A Reconsideration of the Theory of Value', *Economica*, (n.s.) **1**, Part I: (1), 52–76; Part II: (2), 196–219.

Hildenbrand, Werner (1974), *Core and Equilibria of a Large Economy*, Princeton University Press.

Hildenbrand, Werner (1983), 'Introduction', in Gerard Debreu, *Mathematical Economics: Twenty Papers of Gerard Debreu*, Cambridge: Cambridge University Press, 1–29.

Hill, Poly (1987), 'Market Places', in John Eatwell *et al.* (eds), *The New Palgrave*, vol. 3, London: Macmillan, 332–34.

Hirshleifer, Jack (1973), 'Exchange Theory: The Missing Chapter', *Western Economic Journal*, **11** (2), June, 129–46.

Hirshleifer, Jack (1980), *Price Theory and Applications*, 2nd edn, Englewood Cliffs: Prentice-Hall.

Hosios, Arthur J. (1990), 'On the Efficiency of Matching and Related Models of Search and Unemployment', *Review of Economic Studies*, **57**, 279–98.

Howitt, Peter W. (1973), 'Walras and Monetary Theory', *Western Economic Journal*, **11** (4), December, 487–99.

Howitt, Peter W. (1986), 'The Keynesian Recovery', *Canadian Journal of Economics*, **19** (4); as reprinted in *The Keynesian Recovery and Other Essays*, New York: Philip Allan, 1990, 70–85.

Howitt, Peter W. (1988), 'Business Cycles with Costly Search and Recruiting' *The Quarterly Journal of Economics*, **103** (1), 147–65.

Howitt, Peter W. (1990), 'Introduction: Prices and Coordination in Keynesian Economics', in *The Keynesian Recovery and Other Essays*, New York: Philip Allan, 1990, 1–23.

Howitt, Peter W. (1996), 'Cash in Advance, Microfoundations in Retreat', in Daniel Vaz and Kuraswamy Velupillai (eds), *Inflation, Institutions and Information*, London: Macmillan, 62–88.

Howitt, Peter W. (1997), Book Review of Frank Hahn and Robert Solow, *A Critical Essay on Modern Macroeconomic Theory*, London: MIT Press, 1995, *Journal of Economic Literature*, **35**, March, 132–34.

Howitt, Peter W. and R. Preston McAfee (1987), 'Costly Search and Recruiting', *International Economic Review*, **28** (1), February, 89–107.

Howitt, Peter W. and R. Preston McAfee (1988), 'Stability of Equilibria with Externalities', *The Quarterly Journal of Economics*, **103** (2), May, 261–77.

Hubbard, R. Glenn and Robert J. Weiner (1992), 'Long-Term Contracting and Multi-Price Systems', *Journal of Business*, **65** (2), April, 177–98.

Hurwicz, Leonid (1945), 'The Theory of Economic Behavior', *American Economic Review*, **35**; as reprinted in G. J. Stigler and K. Boulding (eds), *Readings in Price Theory*, Chicago: Richard D. Irwin, 1952, 505–26.

Hurwicz, Leonid (1960), 'Optimality and Informational Efficiency in Resource Allocation Processes', in K. J. Arrow, S. Karlin and P. Suppes (eds), *Mathematical Methods in the Social Sciences 1959*, Stanford: Stanford University Press; as reprinted in K. J. Arrow and L. Hurwicz (eds), *Studies in Resource Allocation Processes*, Cambridge: Cambridge University Press, 1977, 393–412.

Hurwicz, Leonid (1969), 'Centralization and Decentralization in Economic Systems. On the Concept and Possibility of Informational Decentralization', *American Economic Review*, **59** (2), May, 513–24.

Hurwicz, Leonid (1972), 'On Informationally Decentralized Systems', in C. B. McGuire and R. Radner (eds), *Decision and Organization*, Amsterdam: North-Holland; as reprinted in K. J. Arrow and L. Hurwicz (eds), *Studies in Resource Allocation Processes*, 1977, 425–59.

Hurwicz, Leonid (1973), ' The Design of Resource Allocation Mechanisms', *American Economic Review*, **58**, May; as reprinted in K. J. Arrow and L. Hurwicz (eds), *Studies in Resource Allocation Processes*, Cambridge: Cambridge University Press, 1977, 3–37.

Hurwicz, Leonid (1994), 'Economic Design, Adjustment Processes, Mechanisms, and Institutions', *Economic Design*, **1**, 1–14.

Ingrao, Bruna and Giorgio Israel (1990), The Invisible Hand, *Economic Equilibrium in the History of Science*, Cambridge, Mass.: MIT Press.

Irvine, F. Owen (1981), 'An Optimal Middleman Firm Price Adjustment Policy: The "Short-Run Inventory Based Pricing Policy" ', *Economic Inquiry*, **19**, April, 245–69.

Jaffé, William (ed.) (1954), *Elements of Pure Economics*, by Léon Walras, Philadelphia: Orion Editions.

Jaffé, William (1967), 'Walras' Theory of *Tâtonnement*: A Critique of Recent Interpretations', *The Journal of Political Economy*, **75** (1), February, 1–19.

Jaffé, William (1969), 'A. N. Isnard, Progenitor of the Walrasian General Equilibrium Model', *History of Political Economy*, **1** (1), Spring, 19–43.

Jaffé, William (1980), 'Walras's Economics as Others See It', *Journal of Economic Literature*, **58**, June, 528–49.

Jaffé, William (1981), 'Another Look at Léon Walras's Theory of *Tâtonnement*', *History of Political Economy*, **13** (2), 313–36.

Jones, Robert A. (1976), 'The Origin and Development of Media of Exchange', *Journal of Political Economy*, **84** (4), pt.1, August, 757–75.

Kaldor, Nicholas (1934), 'The Determinateness of Static Equilibrium', *Review of Economic Studies*, February; as reprinted in *Essays on Value and Distribution*, London: Gerald Duckworth, 1960, 13–33.

Kaldor, Nicholas (1935), 'Market Imperfection and Excess Capacity', *Economica*, **2**, February, 33–50.

Kaldor, Nicholas (1938), 'Professor Chamberlin on Monopolistic and Imperfect Competition', *Quarterly Journal of Economics*, May; as reprinted in *Essays on Value and Distribution*, London: Gerald Duckworth, 1960, 81–95.

Kalecki, Michael (1939), *Essays in the Theory of Economic Fluctuations*, London: Allen and Unwin.

Katzner, Donald (1991), 'In Defense of Formalization in Economics', *Methodus*, June, 17–24.

Kawasaki, S., J. McMillan and K. F. Zimmermann (1982), 'Disequilibrium Dynamics: An Empirical Study', *American Economic Review*, **72**, 992–1003.

Kirman, Alan P. (1989), 'The Intrinsic Limits of Modern Economic Theory: The Emperor Has No Clothes', *The Economic Journal*, **99**, Conference, 126–39.

Kirman, Alan P. (1992), 'Whom or What Does the Representative Individual Represent?', *Journal of Economoic Perspectives*, **6** (2), Spring, 117–36.

Kiyotaki, N. and R. Wright (1989), 'On Money as a Medium of Exchange', *Journal of Political Economy*, **97** (4), 927–54.

Kiyotaki, N. and R. Wright (1991), 'A Contribution to the Pure Theory of Money', *Journal of Economic Theory*, **53** (2), April, 215–35.

Kiyotaki, N. and R. Wright (1993), 'A Search-Theoretic Approach to Monetary Economics', *American Economic Review*, **83** (1), March, 63–77.

Klein, Benjamin, Robert G. Crawford and Armen A. Alchian (1978), 'Vertical Integration, Appropriable Rents, and the Competitive Contracting Process', *Journal of Law and Economics*, **21** (2), October, 297–326.

Klein, Lawrence R. (1947), *The Keynesian Revolution*, New York: Macmillan.

Klemperer, Paul and Margaret Meyer (1986), 'Price Competion vs. Quantity Competition: The Role of Uncertainty', *Rand Journal of Economics*, **17** (4) Winter, 618–38.

Kohn, Meir (1995) 'Economics as a Theory of Exchange', Discussion paper, mimeo.

Koizumi, Tetsunori (1991), 'On the Stability of a Competitive Economy without Recontracting', in Lars Jonung (ed.), *The Stockholm School of Economics Revisited*, Cambridge: Cambridge University Press, 164–92.

Koopmans, Tjalling C. (1951), 'Analysis of Production as an Efficient Combination of Activities', in T. C. Koopmans (ed.), *Activity Analysis of Production and Allocation*, Cowles Commission Monograph 13, New York, 33–97.

Koopmans, Tjalling C. (1957), *Three Essays on the State of Economic Science*, New York: McGraw Hill.

Kornai, Janos (1979), 'Resource-Constrained versus Demand-Constrained Systems', *Econometrica*, **47**, 801–20.

Kornai, Janos and B. Martos (eds) (1981), *Non-price Controls*, Amsterdam: North-Holland.

Kregel, Jan A. (1992), 'Walras' Auctioneer and Marshall's Well-informed Dealers: Time, Market Prices and Normal Supply Prices', *Quaderni di Storia dell'Economia Politica*, **10** (1), 531–51.

Kregel, Jan A. (1995), 'Neoclassical Price Theory, Institutions, and the Evolution of Securities Market Organization', *Economic Journal*, **105**, March, 459–70.

Kreps, David M. (1990), *Game Theory and Economic Modelling*, Oxford: Clarendon Press.

Kuenne, R. E. (1958), 'On the Existence and Role of Money in the Stationary System', *Economic Journal*, **25**, July, 1–10.

Lange, Oscar (1945), *Price Flexibility and Employment*, Cowles Commission for Research in Economics, Monograph no. 8, San Antonio, Texas: Principia Press of Trinity University.

Leijonhufvud, Axel (1974), 'The Varieties of Price Theory: What Microfoundations for Macrotheory?', Discussion Paper no. 44, January, Department of Economics. University of California, L.A.

Leijonhufvud, Axel (1993), 'Towards a Not-Too-Rational Macroeconomics', *Southern Economic Journal*, **60**, July, 1–13.

Leijonhufvud, Axel (1995), 'Adaptive Behavior, Market Processes and the Computable Approach', *Révue Economique*, **46** (6), September 1995, 1497–511.

Leijonhufvud, Axel, and Robert Clower (1973), 'Say's Principle, What it Means and Doesn't Mean', *Intermountain Economic Review*, Fall; as reprinted in A. Leijonhufvud, *Information and Coordination. Essays in Macroeconomic Theory*, Oxford: Oxford University Press, 1981, 79–101.

Lucas, Robert E. Jr. (1986), 'Adaptive Behavior and Economic Theory', *Journal of Finance*, **59** (4), pt. 2, S401–26.

Madden, Paul J. (1975), 'Efficient Sequences of Non-Monetary Exchange', *Review of Economic Studies*, **42** (4), no. 132, October, 581–96.

Manin, Yu I. (1977), *A Course in Mathematical Logic*, New York: Springer Verlag.

Mantel, R. (1974), 'On the Characterisation of Aggregate Excess Demand', *Journal of Economic Theory*, **7**, 348–53.

Marshall, Alfred (1890), *Principles of Economics*, 1st edn, London: Macmillan.

Marshall, Alfred (1920), *Principles of Economics*, 8th edn, London: Macmillan, 1938.

Marshall, Alfred (1949), *The Pure Theory of Foreign Trade. The Pure Theory of Domestic Values*, London: The London School of Economics and Political Science.

Martos, Béla (1990), *Economic Control Structures. A Non-Walrasian Approach*, New York: North Holland.

Mas-Colell, Andreu (1985), *The Theory of General Economic Equilibrium. A Differentiable Approach*, Cambridge: Cambridge University Press.

Mas-Colell, Andreu, Michael D. Whinston and Jerry R. Green (1995), *Microeconomic Theory*, Oxford: Oxford University Press.

McKenzie, Lionel W. (1954), 'On Equilibrium in Graham's Model of World Trade and Other Competitive Systems', *Econometrica*, **22** (2), April, 147–61.

McKenzie, Lionel W. (1981), 'The Classical Theorem on Existence of Competitive Equilibrium', *Econometrica*, 49 (4), July, 819–41.

McLennan, Andrew and Hugo Sonnenschein (1991), 'Sequential Bargaining as a Noncooperative Foundation for Walrasian Equilibrium', *Econometrica*, **59** (5), September, 1395–424.

Meyer, Donald J., John B. Van Huick, Raymond C. Battalio and Thomas R. Saving (1992), 'History's Role in Coordinating Decentralized Allocation Decisions', *Journal of Political Economy*, **100** (2), 292–316.

Mill, John Stuart (1848), *Principles of Political Economy*, London: Longmans, Green and Co., 1915.

Mirman, Leonard J., Larry Samuelson and Amparo Urbano (1993), 'Monopoly Experimentation', *International Economic Review*, **34** (3), August, 549–81.

Morgenstern, Oskar (1941), 'Professor Hicks on Value and Capital', *Journal of Political Economy*, **49** (3), June, 361–93.

Morishima, Michio (1977), *Walras' Economics: A Pure Theory of Capital and Money*, Cambridge: Cambridge University Press.

Mortensen, Dale T. (1982a), 'The Matching Process as a Noncooperative Bargaining Game', in John J. McCall (ed.), *The Economics of Information and Uncertainty*, Chicago: The University of Chicago Press, 233–58.

Mortensen, Dale T. (1982b), 'Property Rights and Efficiency in Mating, Racing, and Related Games', *American Economic Review*, **72** (5), December, 968–79.

Mortensen, Dale T. (1990) 'The Persistence and Indeterminacy of Unemployment in Search Equilibrium', in Seppo Honkapohja (ed.), *The State of Macroeconomics, Proceedings of a Symposium: 'Whither Macroeconomics?'* Oxford: Basil Blackwell, 129–52.

Nash, John F. (1950), 'Equilibrium Points in *N*-Person Games', *Proc. Nat. Academy of Sciences*, USA, **36**, 48–49.

Negishi, Takashi (1961), 'Monopolistic Competition and General Equilibrium', *Review of Economic Studies*, **28**, June, 196–201.

Negishi, Takashi (1962), 'The Stability of a Competitive Economy: A Survey Article', *Econometrica*, **30** (4), October, 635–69.

Negishi, Takashi (1987), 'Monopolistic Competition and General Equilibrium', in John Eatwell *et al.* (eds), *The New Palgrave*, vol. 3, London: Macmillan, 535–38.

Neumann, J. von and O. Morgenstern (1947), *Theory of Games and Economic Behavior*, 2nd edn, Princeton: Princeton University Press.

Niehans, J. (1969), 'Money in a Static Theory of Optimal Payment Arrangements', *Journal of Money, Credit and Banking*, **1** (4), November, 706–26.

Niehans, J. (1971), 'Money and Barter in General Equilibrium with Transaction Costs', *American Economic Review*, **61** (5), 773–78.

Niehans, J. (1987), 'Transaction Costs', in John Eatwell *et al.* (eds), *Money. The New Palgrave*, London: Macmillan, 320–27.

Oh, Seonghwan (1989), 'A Theory of Generally Acceptable Medium of Exchange and Barter', *Journal of Monetary Economics*, **23**, January, 101–19.

Okun, Arthur M. (1981), *Prices and Quantities. A Macroeconomic Analysis*, Washington D.C.: The Brookings Institution.

Osborne, M. F. M. (1965), 'The Dynamics of Stock Trading', *Econometrica*, **33** (1), January, 88–113.

Osborne, M. F. M. (1977), *The Stock Market and Finance from a Physicist's Viewpoint*, Temple Hills, Md: Osborne.

Ostroy, Joseph M. (1973), 'The Informational Efficiency of Monetary Exchange', *American Economic Review*, **63** (4), September, 597–610.

Ostroy, Joseph M. and Ross M. Starr (1974), 'Money and the Decentralization of Exchange', *Econometrica*, **42** (6), November, 1093–113.

Ostroy, Joseph M. and Ross M. Starr (1990), 'The Transactions Role of Money', in B. M. Friedman and F. H. Hahn (eds), *Handbook of Monetary Economics*, vol. 1, Amsterdam: Elsevier Science Publishers, 3–62; formerly published as Working Paper No. 505, 1988 Department of Economics, University of California, Los Angeles.

Ostroy, Joseph M. and William R. Zame (1994), 'Nonatomic Economies and the Boundaries of Perfect Competition', *Econometrica*, **62** (3), May, 593–633.

Pareto, Vilfredo (1909/1927), *Manual of Political Economy*, New York: Kelley, 1971.

Pareto, Vilfredo (1911), 'Mathematical Economics' in *International Economic Papers*, 5, 1955, 58–102; translated from *Encyclopédie des Sciences Mathématiques*, I (iv, 4), Paris: Teubner, Gauthier, Villars.

Patinkin, Don (1956), *Money, Interest, and Prices*, Evanston: Row.

Patinkin, Don (1965), *Money, Interest, and Prices*, 2nd edn, New York: Harper and Row.

Patinkin, Don (1989), 'Introduction', *Money, Interest, and Prices*, Abridged edn, Cambridge: MIT Press, xv–lxv.

Phelps, Edmund S. and Sidney G. Winter Jr. (1970), 'Optimal Price Policy under Atomistic Competition', in E. S. Phelps *et al.* (eds), *Microeconomic Foundations of Employment and Inflation Theory*, New York: W. W. Norton, 309–37.

Pissarides, Christopher A. (1984), 'Search Intensity, Job Advertising, and Efficiency', *Journal of Labor Economics*, **2**, 123–43.

Punzo, Lionello (1991), 'Comment' on Grandmont's Chapter, in *Value and Capital: Fifty Years Later*, Proceedings of a Conference held by the International Economic Association at Bologna, Italy. New York: New York University Press, 31–37.

Rader, T. (1968), 'Pairwise Optimality, Multilateral Optimality, and Efficiency with and without Externalities', in J. P. Quirk and A. M. Zarley (eds), *Papers in Quantitative Economics*, University of Kansas.

Radner, Roy (1968), 'Competitive Equilibrium under Uncertainty', *Econometrica*, **36**, January, 31–58.

Radner, Roy (1972), 'Existence of Equilibrium of Plans, Prices and Price Expectations in a Sequence Market', *Econometrica*, **40** (2), March, 289–303.

Reiss, Peter C. and Ingrid M. Werner (1994), 'Transaction Costs in Dealer Markets: Evidence from the London Stock Exchange', NBER Working Paper No. 4727, May, reprinted in Andrew W. Lo (1996) (ed.), *The Industrial Organization and Regulation of Securities Industry*, National Bureau of Economic Research Conference Report, Chicago: University of Chicago Press, Chapter 5.

Roberts, Donald J. and Andrew Postlewaite (1976), 'The Incentives for Price-Taking Behavior in Large Exchange Economies', *Econometrica*, **44** (1), January, 115–27.

Robinson, Joan (1933), *The Economics of Imperfect Competition*, London: Macmillan.

Robinson, Joan (1977), 'What are the Questions?', in *What are the Questions and other Essays. Further Contributions to Modern Economics*, Armonk, New York: M. E. Sharp, 1980.

Roth, Alvin E. and Marilda Sotomayor (1990), *Two-sided Matching. A Study in Game-theoretic Modeling and Analysis*, Cambridge: Cambridge University Press.

Rothschild, Michael (1973), 'Models of Market Organization with Imperfect Information: A Survey', *Journal of Political Economy*, **81**, 1283–308.

Rothschild, Michael (1974), 'A Two-Armed Bandit Theory of Market Pricing', *Journal of Economic Theory*, **9**, 185–202.

Rubinstein, Ariel (1982), 'Perfect Equilibrium in a Bargaining Model', *Econometrica*, **50** (1), January, 97–109.

Rubinstein, Ariel (1987), 'A Sequential Strategic Theory of Bargaining', in Truman B. Bewley (ed.), *Advances in Economic Theory*, Fifth World Congress, Cambridge: Cambridge University Press, 197–224.

Rubinstein, Ariel (1995), 'John Nash: The Master of Economic Modeling' *Scandinavian Journal of Economics*, **97** (1), 9–13.

Rubinstein, Ariel and Asher Wolinski (1985), 'Equilibrium in a Market with Sequential Bargaining', *Econometrica*, **53** (5), September, 1133–50.

Rubinstein, Ariel and Asher Wolinski (1987), 'Middlemen', *Quarterly Journal of Economics*, **102**, August, 581–93.

Rubinstein, Ariel and Asher Wolinski (1995), 'Decentralized Trading, Strategic Behavior and the Walrasian Outcome', *Review of Economic Studies*, **57** (1), January, 63–78.

Saari, Donald G. (1985a), 'Iterative Price Mechanisms', *Econometrica*, **53** (5), September, 1117–31.

Saari, Donald G. (1985b), 'The Representation Problem and Efficiency of the Price Mechanism', *Journal of Mathematical Economics*, **14** (2), 135–67.

Saari, Donald G. (1992), 'The Aggregated Excess Demand Function and Other Aggregation Procedures', *Economic Theory*, **2** (3), July, 359–88.

Saari, Donald G. and C. Simon (1978), 'Effective Price Mechanisms', *Econometrica*, **46** (5), 1097–125.

Saari, Donald G. and S. R. Williams (1986), 'On the Local Convergence of Economic Mechanisms', *Journal of Economic Theory*, **40** (1), October, 152–67.

Samuelson, Paul A. (1941), 'The Stability of Equilibrium: Comparative Statics and Dynamics', *Econometrica*, **9** (2), April, 97–120.

Samuelson, Paul A. (1947), *Foundations of Economic Analysis*, Enlarged Edition. Cambridge, Mass.: Harvard University Press, 1983.

Scarf, Herbert E. (1960), 'Some Examples of Global Instability of the Competitive Equilibrium', *International Economic Review*, **1** (3), September, 157–72.

Scarf, Herbert E. (1973), *The Computation of Economic Equilibria*, With the collaboration of Terje Hansen. Cowles Foundation Monograph no. 24, New Haven: Yale University Press.

Scarf, Herbert E. (1982), 'The Computation of Equilibrium Prices: An Exposition', in K. J. Arrow and M. D. Intriligator (eds), *Handbook of Mathematical Economics*, vol. 2, Amsterdam: North-Holland, 1007–61.

Schultz, Henry (1935), 'Interrelations of Demand, Price and Income', *Journal of Political Economy*, **43** (4), August, 433–81.

Schumpeter, J. A. (1954), *History of Economic Analysis*, New York: Oxford University Press.

Shafer, Wayne and Hugo Sonnenschein (1982), 'Market Demand and Excess Demand Functions', in K. J. Arrow and M. D. Intriligator (eds), *Handbook of Mathematical Economics*, vol. 2, Amsterdam: North-Holland, 671–93.

Shoven, John B. and John Whalley (1992), *Applying General Equilibrium*, Cambridge: Cambridge University Press.

Simon, Herbert A. (1986), 'Rationality in Psychology and Economics', *Journal of Business*, **59** (4), pt. 2, S209–24.

Slutsky, Eugen E. (1915), 'On the Theory of the Budget of the Consumer', *Giornali degli Economisti*, as reprinted in G. J. Stigler and K. Boulding (eds), *Readings in Price Theory*, 1952, 27–52.

Smale, Steve (1976a), 'A Convergent Process of Price Adjustment and Global Newton Methods', *Journal of Mathematical Economics*, **3**, 107–20.

Smale, Steve (1976b), 'Exchange Processes with Price Adjustment', *Journal of Mathematical Economics*, **3** (3), December, 211–26.

Smale, Steve (1976c), 'Dynamics in General Equilibrium Theory', *American Economic Review*, **66** (2), May, 288–94.

Smale, Steve (1981), 'Global Analysis and Economics', in K. J. Arrow and M. D. Intriligator (eds), *Handbook of Mathematical Economics*, Amsterdam: North-Holland, vol. 1, 331–70.

Smith, Adam (1776), *An Inquiry into the Nature and the Causes of the Wealth of Nations*, Oxford: Clarendon Press, ed. by R. H. Campbell and A. S. Skinner, 1976.

Sonnenschein, Hugo (1972), 'Market Excess Demand Functions', *Econometrica*, **40**, 549–63.

Sonnenschein, Hugo (1973), 'Do Walras Identity and Continuity Characterise the Class of Community Excess Demand Functions?', *Journal of Economic Theory*, **6**, 345–54.

Starr, Ross M. (1971), 'Notes on Microeconomic Monetary Theory', Chapter 1 of Ph. D. Dissertation, Stanford University.

Starr, Ross M. (1972), 'The Structure of Exchange in Barter and Monetary Economies', *Quarterly Journal of Economics*, **86**, May, 290–302.

Starr, Ross M. (1976), 'Decentralized Nonmonetary Trade', *Econometrica*, **44** (5), September, 1087–89.

Starr, Ross M. (1997), *General Equilibrium Theory. An Introduction*, Cambridge: Cambridge University Press.

Starr, Ross M. and Maxwell B. Stinchcombe (1993), 'Exchange in a Network of Trading Posts', in G. Chichilnisky (ed.), *Markets, Information and Uncertainty. Essays in Honor of Kenneth Arrow*, Cambridge: Cambridge University Press.

Starr, Ross M. and Maxwell B. Stinchcombe (1997), 'Monetary Equilibrium with Pairwise Trade and Transaction Costs', mimeo.

Stern, Louis and Adel El-Ansary (1982), *Marketing Channels*, Prentice-Hall.

Stigler, George J. (1949), 'Monopolistic Competition in Retrospect', *Five Lectures on Economic Problems*, London School of Economics; as reprinted in *The Organization of Industry*, Chicago: Irwin, 1968, 309–21.

Stigler, George J. (1954), 'The Early History of Empirical Studies of Consumer Behavior', *Journal of Political Economy*, **42**, April; as reprinted in *Essays in the History of Economics*, Chicago: The University of Chicago Press, 1965, 198–233.

Stigler, George J. (1957), 'Perfect Competition, Historically Contemplated', *Journal of Political Economy*, **65**, February; as reprinted in *Essays in the History of Economics*, Chicago: The University of Chicago Press, 1965, 234–67.

Stigler, George J. (1961), 'The Economics of Information', *Journal of Political Economy*, **69** (3), June, 213–25.

Stigler, George J. and K. Boulding (eds) (1952), *Readings in Price Theory*, Chicago: Irwin.

Telser, Lester G. (1967), 'The Supply of Speculative Services in Wheat, Corn, and Soybeans', *Food Research Institute Studies*, **7**, Supplement, 131–76.

Telser, Lester G. and Harlow N. Higinbotham (1977), 'Organized Futures Markets: Costs and Benefits', *Journal of Political Economy*, **85** (5), 969–1000.

Thore, S. and F. Billström (1954), 'Dynamic Models Involving a Price Strategy. Models or a Production Monopoly', *Report of the 16th European Meeting of Econometric Society*, Uppsala, 2-4 August.

Thore, S., F. Billström and O. Johansson (1954), 'Models Involving Monopolistic Strategies for Price and Supply', (Report 2), *Report of the 16th European Meeting of the Econometric Society*, Uppsala, 2-4 August.

Thornton, Henry (1802), *An Enquiry into the Nature and Effects of the Paper Credit of Great Britain*, with an Introduction by F. A. v. Hayek, London: Frank Kass and Co., 1962.

Tobin, James (1980), 'Are New Classical Models Plausible Enough to Guide Policy?', *Journal of Money, Credit, and Banking*, **12** (4), November, 788–99.

Townsend, Robert M. (1978), 'Intermediation with Costly Bilateral Exchange', *Review of Economic Studies*, **45** (3), no. 141, October, 417–25.

Townsend, Robert M. (1987), 'Arrow-Debreu Programs as Microfoundations of Macroeconomics', in Truman F. Bewley (ed.), *Advances in Economic Theory*, Fifth World Congress, Cambridge: Cambridge University Press, 379–428.

Tricou, Fabrice (1994), 'Le Marché Marshallien Revisité. L'Equilibration Concurrentielle en Ultra-courte Période', *Economies et Sociétés*, Série Théorie de la Régulation, **8**, December, 25–59.

Triffin, Robert (1940), *Monopolistic Competition and General Equilibrium Theory*, Cambridge, Mass.: Harvard University Press.

Uzawa, Hirofumi (1958), 'Iterative Methods for Concave Programming', in Kenneth J. Arrow, L. Hurwicz and H. Uzawa (eds), *Studies in Linear and Non-Linear Programming*, Stanford: Stanford University Press, 154–65.

Uzawa, Hirofumi (1960), 'Walras' Tâtonnement in the Theory of Exchange', *Review of Economic Studies*, **27**, June, 182–94.

Uzawa, Hirofumi (1962a), 'Walras's Existence Theorem and Brower's Fixed-Point Theorem', *Economic Studies Quarterly*, 13, 59–62; as reprinted in *Preference, Production and Capital. Selected Papers of Hirofumi Uzawa*, Cambridge: Cambridge University Press, 1988, 175–78.

Uzawa, Hirofumi (1962b), 'On the Stability of Edgeworth's Barter Process', *International Economic Review*, **3** (2), May, 218–32.

Veendorp, E. C. H. (1969), 'A Theorem on Nontâtonnement Stability: A Comment', *Econometrica*, **37**, 142–43.

Veendorp, E. C. H. (1970a), 'General Equilibrium Theory for a Barter Economy', *Western Economic Journal*, **8** (1), March, 1–23.

Veendorp, E. C. H. (1970b), 'Instability, the Hicks Conditions, and the Choice of the Numéraire', *International Economic Review*, **11** (3) October, 497–505.

Velupillai, K. (1991), 'Formalization, Rigor, Proof, Existence and Axiomatics: Some Subversive Thoughts', Department of Economics, Politics and Public Administration, Aalborg University.

Vickers, John (1995), 'Concepts of Competition', *Oxford Economic Papers*, **47**, 1–23.

Walker, Donald A. (1971), 'The Determinateness of Equilibrium in Isolated Competitive Markets', *Rivista Internazionale di Scienze Economiche e Commerciali*, **18** (12), 1158–79.

Walker, Donald A. (1972), 'Competitive Tâtonnement Exchange Markets', *Kyklos*, **25** (2), 345–63.

Walker, Donald A. (1987a), 'Walras's Theory of Tatonnement', *Journal of Political Economy*, **95** (4), 758–74.

Walker, Donald A. (1987b), 'Léon Walras', in Eatwell *et al.*(eds), *The New Palgrave*, vol. 4, London: Macmillan, 852–63.

Walker, Donald A. (1987c), 'Edgeworth versus Walras on the Theory of Tatonnement', *Eastern Economic Journal*, **13** (2), April–June, 155–65.

Walker, Donald A. (1988), 'Iteration in Walras's Theory of Tatonnement', *De Economist*, **136** (3), 299–316.

Walker, Donald A. (1990a), 'Institutions and Participants in Walras's Model of Oral Pledges Model', *Révue Economique*, **41** (4), July, 651–68.

Walker, Donald A. (1990b), 'Disequilibrium and Equilibrium in Walras's Model of Oral Pledges Model', *Révue Economique*, **41** (6), November, 961–78.

Walker, Donald A. (1990c), 'The Structure of Walras's Barter Model of Written Pledges Markets', *Révue d'Economie Politique*, **100** (5), 619–42.

Walker, Donald A. (1993), 'Walras's Models of the Barter of Stocks of Commodities', *European Economic Review*, **37**, 1425–46.

Walker, Donald A. (1994a), 'The Structure of Walras's Consumer Commodities Model in the Mature Phase of his Thought', *Révue Economique*, **45** (2), March, 239–56.

Walker, Donald A. (1994b), 'The Adjustment Process in Walras's Consumer Commodities Model in the Mature Phase of his Thought', *Révue Economique*, **45** (6), 1357–75.

Walker, Donald A. (1996), *Walras's Market Models*, Cambridge: Cambridge University Press.

Walker, Donald A. (1997a), *Advances in General Equilibrium Theory*, Cheltenham: Edward Elgar.

Walker, Donald A. (1997b), 'The Relation between the Nineteenth Century Bourse and Léon Walras's Model of an Organized Market', Conference paper, Meetings of the History of Economics Society, Charleston, South Carolina.

Walras, Léon (1885) 'Un Economiste Inconnu, Hermann-Henri Gossen', *Journal des Economistes*, **30**, as quoted in Pascal Bridel, *Money and General Equilibrium Theory*, Cheltenham: Edward Elgar, 1997.

Walras, Léon (1889), *Eléments d'Economie Politique Pure, ou Théorie de la Richesse Sociale*, 2nd edn, Lausanne: F. Rouge; Paris: Guillaumin; Leipzig: Dunkler & Humblot.

Walras, Léon (1895), 'Enclosure to Vilfredo Pareto', January 9. Reprinted in William Jaffé, *Correspondence of Léon Walras and Related Papers*, vol. 2, Amsterdam: North-Holland, 1965, 623–32.

Walras, Léon (1900), *Eléments d'Economie Politique Pure, ou Théorie de la Richesse Sociale*, 4th edn, Lausanne: F. Rouge; Paris: F. Pichon.

Walras, Léon (1926), *Eléments d'Economie Politique Pure, ou Théorie de la Richesse Sociale*, Definitive ed., Paris: Economica, 1988.

Weintraub, E. Roy (1985), *General Equilibrium Analysis. Studies in Appraisal*, Ann Arbor: The University of Michigan Press, 1993.

Weintraub, E. Roy (1991), *Stabilizing Dynamics. Constructing Economic Knowledge*, New York: Cambridge University Press.

Whitaker, John K. (1987), '*The Limits of Organization* Revisited', in George R. Feiwel, *Arrow and the Foundations of the Theory of Economic Policy*, London: Macmillan, 565–83.

Wicksteed, P. H. (1933), *The Commonsense of Political Economy*, (1st edn 1910), London: Routledge.

Wiles, P. J. D. (1961), *Price, Cost, and Output*, New York: Frederick A. Praeger, 1963.

Williamson, Oliver E. (1987), 'Kenneth Arrow and the New Institutional Economics', in George R. Feiwel (ed.), *Arrow and the Foundations of the Theory of Economic Policy*, London: Macmillan, 584–99.

Williamson, Oliver E (1991) 'Introduction', in Oliver E. Williamson and Sidney G. Winter (eds), *The Nature of the Firm. Origins, Evolution and Development*, New York: Oxford University Press, 3–17.

Williamson, Oliver E. and Sidney G. Winter (eds) (1991), *The Nature of the Firm. Origins, Evolution and Development*, New York: Oxford University Press.

Wilson, Robert (1987a), 'On Equilibria of Bid–Ask Markets', in George R. Feiwel (ed.), *Arrow and the Ascent of Economic Theory: Essays in Honor of Kenneth J. Arrow*, London: Macmillan, 375–414.

Wilson, Robert (1987b), 'Game-theoretic Analysis of Trading Processes', in Truman F. Bewley (ed.), *Advances in Economic Theory*, Fifth World Congress, Cambridge: Cambridge University Press, 33–70.

Wilson, Robert (1992), 'Strategic Analysis of Auctions', in R. J. Aumann and S. Hart (eds), *Handbook of Game Theory*, vol. 1, Amsterdam: Elsevier Science Publishers, 227–79.

Winter, Sidney G. (1975), 'Optimization and Evolution in the Theory of the Firm', in Richard H. Day and Theodore Groves (eds), *Adaptive Economic Models*, New York: Academic Press, 179–95.

Winter, Sidney G. (1991), 'On Coase, Competence, and the Corporation', in O. E. Williamson and S. G. Winter (eds), *The Nature of the Firm*, 1991, 179–95.

Working, Holbrook (1967), 'Tests of a Theory Concerning Floor Trading on Commodity Exchanges', *Food Research Institute Studies*, **7**, Supplement, 5–48.

Young, Warren (1991), 'The Early Reactions to *Value and Capital*: Critics, Critiques and Correspondence in Comparative Perspective', *Review of Political Economy*, **3** (3), 289–308.

Name index

Subject index

adaptive learning 98, 100–101
adjustment processes vs equilibrium
    states 1, 46–7
administered prices *see* pricing
adverse selection 6, 8, 13, 128
advertising *see* selling costs
aggregation, problem of 8–9, 69, 78, 122
    see also representative agent
anonimity in exchange 65, 75, 101, 150,
    158
arbitrage 30, 76, 123
    in trading posts exchange 16–17,
        19–20, 30, 109
    see also no-arbitrage assumption
Arrow–Debreu models 5, 9, 25–31, 37,
    39, 46–7, 51–2, 60, 67, 126–7, 130
    absence of decentralized trading in
        11, 29, 32, 35, 39, 62, 72–3, 75,
        101–2, 128, 152
    as logic of choice 5, 9, 54, 108, 126
    consistency with mathematical
        conditions 4, 9, 25–7, 35, 127
    incomplete markets and 60–62 *see*
        also missing markets
    not satisfying decentralization
        criteria 11, 29, 52, 62, 69, 72, 82,
        118, 152
    out-of-equilibrium trading in 28, 39,
        76
    role of the auctioneer in 25, 27–9,
        35, 44, 72–3, 119
    transaction costs and 61–2
    see also general equilibrium models
auctioneer
    as central agent in Arrow–Debreu
        models 25, 27, 29–31, 35, 44–5,
        52, 62, 151

as enforcer of budget constraint 117,
    138
as enforcer of transactions, in Hahn
    Process 76
as organizer of centralized transac-
    tions/logistics 73, 124, 175
computation ability of 79
determination of equilibrium prices
    by 72–3, 77, 79, 104, 124,
    151–2, 167
dispensed with, in Edgeworth
    Process 76
functions of 28–9, 67, 142
in 'theory of price adjustment' 111
information allegedly disseminated
    by 69, 72–3, 79, 82
informational requirements of
    68–70, 73, 77, 79, 82, 113
introduction of, in the literature 31
one in each market 76 *see also*
    'specialized broker'
see also Arrow–Debreu models
auctions *see* markets, specific forms and
    notions
axiomatic approach 4–5, 14, 26, 106

bargaining
    axiomatic vs strategic 123
    bilateral, and decentralized exchange
        69–71, 103
    in brokered markets 64–5
    in decentralized markets 66, 71–2
    in double auctions 143–4, 174
    in general equilibrium analysis 8, 27,
        35, 39, 53, 71–2, 105–6, 123,
        128
    in Marshall 35, 38, 45